UNDERSTANDING MARINE BIOLOGY

UNDERSTANDING MARINE BIOLOGY

By
Dr. Veena
Dept. of Zoology
M.M.H. College
Ghaziabad (U.P.)
(India)

DPH
DISCOVERY PUBLISHING HOUSE PVT. LTD.
NEW DELHI-110 002

Published by:
Namit Wasan

DISCOVERY PUBLISHING HOUSE PVT. LTD.
4383/4B, Ansari Road, Darya Ganj
New Delhi-110 002 (India)
Phone : +91-11-23279245; 23253475; 43596065
E-mail : discoverybooksindia@gmail.com
discoverypublishinghouse@gmail.com
namitwasan9@gmail.com
web : www.discoverypublishinggroup.com

***First Edition:* 2010**

***Reprinted:* 2012**

ISBN: 978-81-8356-542-4

Understanding Marine Biology

Preface

The present title "Understanding Marine Biology" has been written for those students interested in careers in diverse fields of biological sciences. It provides a structured approach to learning by covering all the important topics in a uniform, systematic format. The book has been comprehensively designed incorporating recent advances in this fast moving field. It also provides accessible information on molecular biology in compact form for undergraduate students in biology and related life sciences. It is intelligible to the educated layman, though it deals with some complex ideas. It is an adequate text for all the requirements of students in this area. In addition, busy lecturers who require a quick reference compendium will find it useful, particularly for tutional planning. Simple, yet hopefully clear figures and tables are provided throughout the book.

The over-riding goal of this book, and indeed of the whole *Understanding series,* is to present the essential information concering molecular biology in a compact, readily accessible form which leads itself to student learning and revision. The convergence of various approaches has generated a rich panorama of detail, the significance of which we are still attempting to unraval. The present text has been written as an introduction to this rapidly growing field.

To make the work more comprehensive and informative, the author has consulted many authoritative books, research journals, abstracts, monographs etc., so there can be no claim to originality except in the manner of treatment.

The author expresses his thanks to his friends and colleagues whose continue inspirations have initiated him to bring out this book.

The author expresses his gratitude to Mr. Wasan and staff of M/s Discovery Publishing House Pvt. Ltd. for their whole hearted cooperation in the publication of this book.

In the mean time, the author will remain sincerely responsible for any shortcomings of the book and be grateful to the readers for their suggestions and constructive criticism for the continuous betterment of the book. He takes this opportunity to appeal to the readers to send their suggestions straightaway to his Publisher.

Author

Contents

Chapter 1 **1—50**

INTRODUCTION

Environmental Conditions, Tides, Temperature, Wave Action, Salinity, Other Factors, Adaptations of Intertidal Organisms, Resistance to Water Loss, Maintenance of Heat Balance, Mechanical Stress, Respiration, Feeding, Salinity Stress, Reproduction, Rocky Shores, Zonation, Causes of Zonation, Small Scale Distribution Patterns, Interactions Among Factors: A Summary, Horizontal Distribution Patterns, Succession, Age Structure, Tidepools, Sandy Shores, Environmental Conditions, Adaptations of Organisms, Types of Organisms, Feeding Biology, Zonation and Community Organization, Muddy Shores, Physical Factors, Adaptations of Organisms, Types of Organisms, Feeding Biology and Trophic Structure, Zonation, Intertidal Fishes

Chapter 2 **51—74**

THE ORIGIN OF OCEANS

Chapter 3 **75—88**

THE ATMOSPHERE OF THE OCEAN

Chapter 4 **89—123**

DEEP SEA ENVIRONMENT

The Deep-sea Floor, Oceanic Waters: The Pelagic Environment, Water, Salt and Heat Balance, Density, Water Masses and Circulation, Patterns of Circulation Near the Surface, Light in The Ocean, Life Zones and Life Forms

Chapter 5 **124—144**

THE NATURE OF OCEANIC LIFE

Chapter 6 145—157

ACTIVE ANIMALS OF THE DEEP-SEA FLOOR

Chapter 7 158—177

OCEANIC PLANTS

Plants Groups, General Features of Distribution, The Euphotic Zone, Patterns of Primary Productivity, Animal Life in the Deep Seal

Chapter 8 178—187

THE SEA SHORE ENVIRONMENT

Tides, Desiccation, Temperature, Substratum, Wave Action, Salinity, Light

Chapter 9 188—194

THE SEA SHORE AND THE SEA

Phytoplankton, Zooplankton, Food Chains and Webs, Organic Cycle, Plankton Cycle, Fertility of the Sea, Dispersal of Shore Animals

Chaper 10 195—217

ROCKY SHORES

Physical factors influencing rocky shore zonation, Tidal Heights, Temperature, Desiccation, Exposure, Algae: Primary Producers, Green, Brown, Red, Molluscs, Echinoderms, Secondary Consumers, Molluscs, Decapod Crustaceans, Universal Patterns of Zonation, Rock Pools

Chapter 11 218—235

PLANTS OF ROCKY SHORES

Reproduction, Brown Seaweeds and Zonation, Shallow Pools, Red Seaweeds, Blue-Green Algae, Litchens, Flowering Plants of Rocky Coasts

Chapter 12 236—252

ANIMALS OF ROCKY SHORESD

Chapter 13 253—265

LIFE ON SANDY SHORES

Zonation

Chapter 14 **266—277**

LIFE ON MUDDY SHORES

Constant Salinity, Variable Salinity, Salt-Marshes and Their Vegetation

INDEX **278—301**

1

INTRODUCTION

Although it constitutes by far the smallest area of all in the world's oceans, existing as an extremely narrow fringe a few meters in extent between high and low water, the intertidal zone is perhaps the best known and studied of all areas of the sea because it is the most accessible to humans.

Here, and only here, can direct observations be made of *aquatic* organisms during the period of low tide, without special equipment. The *intertidal* zone has been of interest and use to humans since prehistoric time.

Despite its extremely restricted area, the intertidal has within the greatest variations in environmental factors of any marine area, and these can occur within centimeters of each other. *Coupled* with this is a tremendous diversity of life, which is greater than that found in the more *extensive* subtidal areas.

It should be emphasized that this area is truly an extension of the marine environment and his inhabited almost exclusively by *marine* organisms. Although this area is terrestrial as much as half the time, the *terrestrial* fauna and *flora* have not invaded it to any extent, except at the *uppermost* fringes.

The richness, the diversity of environmental factors, and the case of access act together to attract to this area an inordinate amount of scientific attention. More knowledge is thus available for this small area and its organisms, and their interactions are better known than in any other area.

Thanks to such interest and knowledge, this area has produced more unifying concepts with respect to the organization of marine communities than any other.

ENVIRONMENTAL CONDITIONS

In part, the tremendous array of environmental factors and ranges found in the intertidal is due to the fact that this zone is exposed to the air for a certain amount of time during the year and most *physical factors* show greater range in air than in water.

Tides

The periodic, predictable rise and fall of the level of the sea over a given time interval is called a *tide.* Certainly, this is the most important environmental factor influencing life in the intertidal zone. Without the presence of the tide or some other means of inducing a *periodic* rise and fall in the water level, this zone would not exist as it is, and many of the other factors would cease to be of *influence.*

This is because the great range observed in many of the physical factors in the intertidal is a result of alternating exposure to air and to water. If there were no tide, these great *fluctuations* would not occur. With very few exceptions, most shore area of the world *experience tides.*

The only major seas that virtually lack tidal action are the Mediterranean and the Baltic. In these areas, the water level on the shore line *fluctuates* primarily due to the effects of wind action pushing water. This does not mean, however, that all seashores experience the same tidal range, or even the same type of tide.

The reasons for the occurrence of different tides and different ranges are complex, having to do with the interaction of the tide-generating forces, the sun and moon, the rotation of the earth, the *geomorphology* of the ocean basins, and the natural uscillations of the various ocean basins.

Most of the explanation is beyond the scope of this text, but a simplified explanation will be given here. Tides occur due to the interaction between the gravitational attraction of the sun and the moon on the earth and the *centrifugal* force generated by the rotating earth and moon system.

As a result of these forces, the water in the ocean basins is pulled into bulges. Gravitational attraction of one body for another is a function of the mass of each body and their distance apart. In the case of the sun and the moon, the *gravitational generating* force of the moon on the earth is about twice that of sun, even though the sun is many times more massive than the moon.

This is due to the great distance of the sun from the earth relative to the moon. The earth and moon form an orbiting system that revolves around their common center of mass. Because of the large size of the earth relative to the moon, this point is located inside the earth. The revolution of the earth-moon, system creates a *centrifugal* force (acting outward) which is balanced overall by the gravitational force acting between the two bodies.

However, gravitational force is much stronger than centrifugal force on the side of the earth facing the moon than on the side opposite. As a result, the side facing the moon has the water pulled into a bulge (=*high tide*). On the opposite side of the earth, the gravitational force of the moon will be the least, and the stronger centrifugal force will pull water into a bulge away from earth (another high tide). Thus, we have the two high tides.

These then circle the earth following the position of the moon as the earth revolves on its axis once every 24 hours. Low tides are about halfway between the high tides. The system as described above would give two high tides and two low tides of equal magnitude each day. As we know, however, tides are not equal, nor are there always four tides per day.

How do these discrepancies arise? In part; this is due to the *fact* that the earth is not vertical with respect to its plane of orbit around the sun. It actually is inclined 23J° from the vertical. As a result, during the earth's *rotation* on its axis, a given point on the earth's surface is subjected to different tidal heights. It should also be noted from that, at the highest *latitudes* (*polar seas*), only a single high tide would occur.

Further changes in the height of the tides result from changes in the moon relative to the earth as the moon moves in its orbit around the earth. Since the orbit of the moon is not circular but elliptical, there are times when the moon is close to the earth (*perigee*) and others when it is further away (*apogee*). Tides are greater at perigee and *diminished* at apogee.

The effect of the sun is seen in spring and neap tides. *Spring* tides are tides that snow the greatest range (both high and low) and result when the moon and sun are directly aligned so these two forces are combined. Neap tides, on the other hand, are tides *snowing* minimum range and result when sun and moon are at right *angles* to each other and thus counteract each other. Differences both in number of high and low tides per day and in height in various parts of the world are due to peculiarities of the various ocean *basins* in which the tides occur.

The well-known extremely high tides of the Bay of Fundy or Cook Inlet in *Alaska* are the result of the basic tide forces acting in the geometry of the basin. Tides that are *expressed* as a single low and high per day are called *diurnal tides*. Tides that nave two highs and lows per lunar day are termed *semidiurnal tides.*

Where there is a mixture of diurnal and semidiurnal we nave what are called *mixed tides.* The heights of the highs and low vary from day to day as the positions of the tun and moon relative to each other change, each being *alternately* fully aligned and 90° out of alignment every 14 days.

Perhaps the most significant effect of the tide with respect to intertidal organism and communities is that it subjects them to periodic exposure to the air, with its considerably wider range of physical parameters. It is this exposure to aerial conditions that necessitates most of the adaptations required by *intertidal* organisms in order to inhabit this zone.

Physical factors, the extremes of which are reduced for organisms inhabiting water, become limiting or lethal when the insulating water is removed. Tides in combination with time can, however, nave two significant direct effects on the presence and organization of intertidal communities.

The first effect results from the time that a given area of the intertidal is exposed to the air relative to the time that it is submerged in water. It is the duration of *exposure* to air that is most important, because that is when the marine organisms will be subjected to the greatest temperature ranges and the possibility of desiccation (=water loss).

The longer the duration of exposure, the greater the chance for encountering a lethal temperature of *desiccating* beyond tolerable limits. Since most of these animals also must wait until covered with water to feed, the longer the duration, the less *opportunity* to feed and thus obtain *sufficient* energy.

Animals and plants of the tidal zone vary in their ability to tolerate immersion in air and this differential is part of the reason for the different pattern of *distribution* of organisms observed on many *rocky shores*.

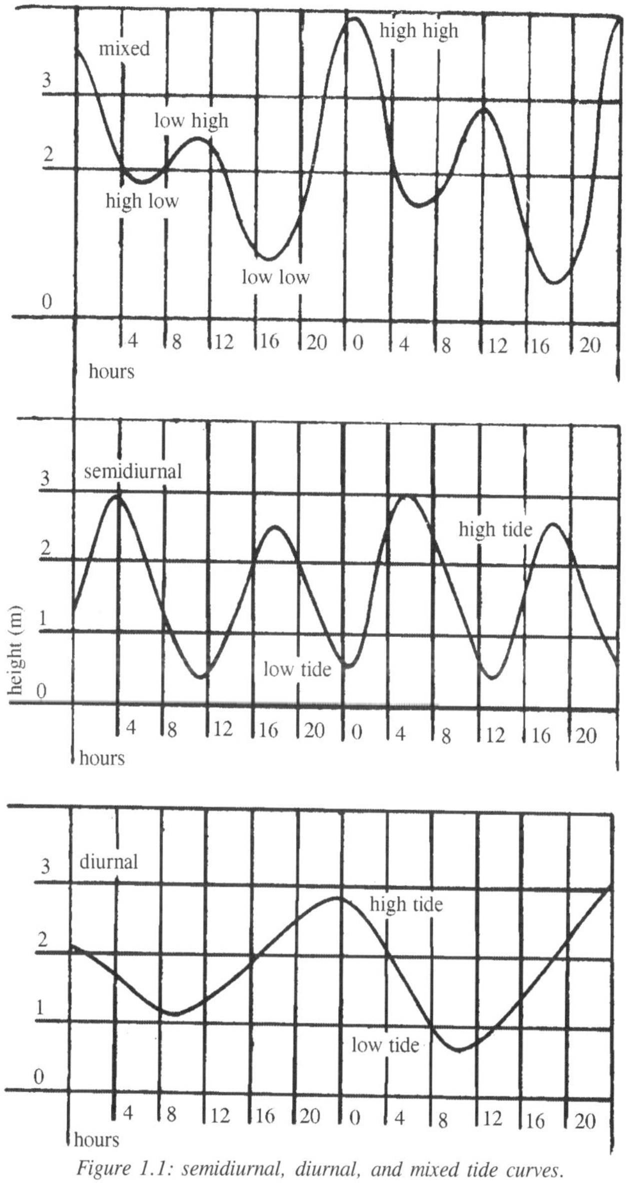

Figure 1.1: semidiurnal, diurnal, and mixed tide curves.

In certain areas of the world there are two high and two low tides per day, and where the two highs or two lows are not equal (areas with *mix tides),* it can be shown that the duration of immersion is not smooth going from low to high tide levels and that there are break points where the duration changes greatly in a short distance. What this means is that an organism living just a few inches above one of these points would be subjected to a greatly increased immersion relative to one just a few inches below.

The existence of these *critical tide levels* was early suggested as the reason for the sharp changes in fauna and flora distribution observed on rocky shores since they were thought to *delineate* an important break point.

The second effect is the result of the time of day during which the intertidal is exposed so the air. As before, the potentially lethal ranges for *physical parameters* are *encountered* by *marine organisms* only when exposed to air and in any daily cycle, these vary greatly at different times of the day.

If, for example, the low tides in the tropics occurred only during the hours of darkness. the intertidal fauna and flora would be exposed to much lower temperatures and less *desiccation* than if exposed during midday. Hence, we might expect a greater diversity of organisms in the intertidal of a tropical area where the tides regularly occurred during night or early morning or evening than in an area where they occurred during midday.

In the cold temperate zones, the reverse would be true, because in winter, the lowest temperatures would occur in early morning or at night and may act to *freeze* the animals, whereas at *midday*, temperatures would be high enough not to do so.

A final effect of the tide is that, because of its *predictability*, it tends to induce certain rhythms in the activities of shore organisms. These rhythms may be with respect to time of spawning such as that seen in the grunion, a fish of the Pacific coast of the United States that spawns on the beach only on certain nights of the highest *spring tides*, or with respect to feeding or other activity.

Most intertidal organisms are *quiescent* when the tide is out and resume normal activity, such as feeding, only when the tide is in.

Temperature

Because of its *inherent* physical *characteristics*, water, particularly large bodies of water such as the oceans, shows a minimum range of change in temperature. Furthermore, this range rarely exceeds the lethal limits for the organisms. *Intertidal* areas are, however, regularly subjected to aerial termperatures for varying periods and these temperatures have a much wider range, on both a daily and a seasonal basis.

The range may often exceed the *lethal limits* of the marine organisms. Should low tide occur when the air temperature is at a minimum (cold temperate, polar) or a maximum (tropics), the lethal limits may be exceeded and the organisms will die.

Even if death does not occur immediately, the organisms may be so weakened by the extreme temperatures that they cannot resume normal activities and will suffer mortality from secondary causes. Temperature also has an indirect effect. Marine organisms are subject to death by desiccation. *Desiccation* may be hastened by increased temperatures.

Wave Action

It is in the intertidal zone that wave action exerts the most influence on organisms and communities of any area in the sea. This influence is *manifested* directly and indirectly. Wave action affects shore life directly in two major ways.

In the first place, it has a mechanical effect, which acts to smash and tear away objects with which it makes contact. One can appreciate this action by noting the many pictures and stories of destruction wrought upon man-made structures due to storm waves of varying types. The action is similar in the intertidal zone, and hence, any creature that inhabit this zone must be adapted to this persistent force in some way.

On shores that are made up of loose sand or gravel, the wave action is even more profound in that it moves the entire substrate around, influencing the actual shape of the zone. Wave exposure may thus prove to be limiting for certain organisms that are unable to *sustain* the force, and necessary to others that cannot exist other than in heavy wave areas.

Secondly, wave action acts to extend the limits of the intertidal zone. It does this by throwing water higher on the shore than would normally occur as a result of the tide alone. This continual splashing allows the marine organisms to live higher in wave-swept areas than in calm areas within the same tidal range.

Wave action has some other, perhaps minor, effects also. It acts to mix *atmospheric* gases into the water, thus increasing the oxygen content so *wave-washed* areas never lack for oxygen. Because of the constant interaction with the atmosphere and the formation of bubbles plue the stirring up of the substrate, *wave-swept* areas may have decreased *penetration* of light. This is, however, of little *ecological* significance.

Salinity

Salinity changes may occur in the intertidal in two situations that may affect the organisms. In the first place, the intertidal may be exposed at low tide and *subsequently* flooded by heavy rains or runoff from heavy rains. This means they will be subjected to greatly reduced *salinities*.

In certain cases, this reduction in salinity may exceed the limits and the organisms may die, as most intertidal organisms show a limited tolerance to decreased salinity. The second situation has to do with tidepools, those areas that retain sea water at low tide.

These may either be flooded with fresh water runoff from heavy rains, thus reducing salinity, or they may show increased salinity when exposed to heavy *evaporation* during the day.

Other Factors

Different *substrates-rock*, sand, mud have very different faunas and community structure in the intertidal, but these are taken up separately in this chapter. Oxygen seems not to be a factor exerting a limiting effect except in certain special cases and pH and nutrients are also unimportant to organisms and *community structure*.

ADAPTATIONS OF INTERTIDAL ORGANISMS

Since the intertidal organisms are primarily marine in origin, the adaptations that we observe have to do primarily with avoiding or minimizing the stresses imposed by the daily exposure to the terrestrial *environment*. The major stress from the marine environment is wave action.

Resistance to Water Loss

As soon as marine organisms are removed from the water into air, they begin to lose water. If they are to survive in the intertidal, this loss must somehow be minimized and/or the organisms must have body systems that will *tolerate* considerable losses during the hours of exposure to the air. The simplest mechanism for avoiding water loss is seen in mobile animals such as crabs.

These animals simply move from the exposed surface areas of the intertidal into very moist cracks, crevices, or burrows, where water loss is reduced or absent. *Alternatively*, they may seek refuge under the moist covering of algae. In other words, these animals avoid the adverse *environmental* condition of the shore by actively selecting suitable *microhabitats*.

A similar situation occurs in some species of anemones such as *Anthopleura xanthogrammica* of the Pacific coast of North America. It is soft bodied, with no way of perventing water loss. However, it normally, is found only among barnacles or in crevices where water loss is reduced. Physiological adaptation is not needed.

Another simple mechanism is that seen in several of the high intertidal algae genera such as *Porphyra, Fucus,* and *Enteromorpha.* These plants cannot move and have no mechanism to avoid water loss. They simply are adapted to withstand a severe loss of water from their tissues. *Specimens* of these genera can be found that are dry and brittle after a long exposure at low tide, yet will quickly take up water and resume normal body processes when the tide returns.

Kanwisher found that they can tolerate as much as a 60-90 per cent loss of water and still recover. A similar tolerance to great water loss is see in some intertidal sedentary animals. Boyle (1969), for example, reports chitons can tolerate a 75 per cent water loss and limpets, according to Davis (1909), from 30-70 per cent, depending on the species.

Many species of *intertidal animals*, in contrast to the above, have mechanisms for prevention of water loss. These mechanisms may be structural, behavioral, or both. Barnacles of many species are *predominant* members of the *intertidal zone* all over the world. These animals are sessile and avoid water loss by closing up within their shells at low tide.

Here, the presence of an impermeable shell cuts down the evaporative water loss. Limpets of the genera *Patella, Acmaea,* and *Collisella* are also dominant animals of the rocky intertidal. Certain species of these limpets have a "*home scar*" into which their shells exactly fit. At low tide, they return to these "*homes*" and by fitting into these grooves, greatly reduce water loss.

Other limpets that have no scar simply clamp down tightly against the rock so no tissue is exposed, only shell. Other gastropods such as the periwinkles *(Littorina)* have opercula which completely seal off the aperture to their shells. At low tide, they may pull into the shell, closing the aperture with the operculum and thus reduce water loss.

Certain bivalves, such as *Mytilus edulis,* are able to survive in the intertidal because of their ability to close their valves tightly to prevent water loss. Still other organisms, such as the anemone *Actinia* and the hydroid *Clara squamata,* produce *mucus* that prevents water loss. Many inhabitants of sand or mud simply burrow into the substrate to prevent desiccation.

Maintenance of Heat Balance

Intertidal organisms are also exposed to *extremes* of heat and cold and show behavioral and structural adaptations to maintain their internal heat balance. Though deaths by *freezing* have been recorded for intertidal organisms, extreme low temperatures seem to be less of a problem to shore organisms than high temperatures. This may be due to the fact that organisms are often living much closer to their upper lethal temperature than to their lower lethal one.

Hence, most *mechanisms* for heat balance concern the avoidance of too high temperatures. This may be accomplished by (1) reducing heat gain from the environment and (2) increasing the heat loss from the body of the animal. Heat gain from the environment is reduced in several ways.

One way is to have a relatively large body size when compared to similar species, either lower in the intertidal or in the subtidal. Large body size means less surface area relative to volume and hence, less area to gain heat. At the same time, a larger body takes longer to heat' up than a smaller one.

It has been recorded for gastropod mollusks such as *Littorina littorea* and *Olivella biplicata* that the large individuals occur higher in the tidal zone and the smaller ones lower. Yet another mechanism to reduce beat gain is to reduce the area of body tissue in contact with the substrate.

This is, however, difficult to achieve for most intertidal animals, since they need the extra purchase provided by a large area of tissue in contact with the substrate to avoid being swept off by waves. Yet, there are some shore animals that do have such a small area of attachment or none at all.

These occur where wave action is not severe, and, in those animals that lose attachment, the ability to reattach as the tide comes in is well developed. Heat loss can be *attributed* to a number of causes. One mechanism, found in hard-shelled organisms such as mollusks, is greater elaboration of ridges and other sculpturing on the hell.

These act as radiator fins and facilitate beat loss. Examples of such sculptured mollusks are best found in the tropics and include *Tectarius muricata* and *Nodolittorina tuberculata*. Enhancement of heat loss occurs when the organism is light in color. (Dark organisms gain heat by absorption.) Many *tropical* and *subtropical snails* of the high intertidal such as *Nerita peleronta* (*Caribbean*) and *Littorina unifasciata* (New Zealand) are much lighter in color than their lower level relatives, presumably then, facilitating heat loss.

Finally and most importantly, heat loss can occur through evaporation of water. Unfortunately, again, intertidal organisms must face the problem of *desiccation* and can ill afford to cool themselves through evaporation or else chance a lethal desiccation.

Many intertidal organisms show a strategy of adaptation that allows them some cooling by evaporating water and, at the same time, avoiding excessive desiccation. To facilitate this balance, many intertidal animals have an extra water supply from which cooling may take place.

This extra water is held in the mantle cavity of *barnacles* and *limpets*, and it is above the amount the animal needs to survive desiccation. Secondly, most high intertidal animals can withstand a *remarkable* amount of desiccation and finally, many animals have the ability to reduce the rate of water loss from the tissues when necessary.

Mechanical Stress

As noted previously, wave action reaches a zenith in the intertidal zone. As a result, it is necessary for any organism that lives intertidally to adapt in order to resist the *smashing* and *tearing* effects of waves. Waves action has different effects on rocky shores as opposed to sandy shores and requires different adaptations, which are discussed subsequently.

However, some generalities may be noted here. In order to maintain position in the face of wave action, several adaptations have been developed by intertidal organisms One such adaptation, observed in *barnacles*, *oysters*, and *serpulid polychaete worms*, is simply to become fixed to the substrate.

Similarly, the majority of algae in the intertidal are fused via a holdfast to the bottom. Still other organisms develop attachments that are strong but not permanent, thus giving limited movement. Such attachments are the *byssal threads* of *Mytilus,* which anchor the animals securely but still can be broken and remade to allow limited slow movement.

The dominant intertidal mollusks such as the various limpets and chitons, resists wave action through a strong, enlarged foot which clamps them to the substrate.

Motile organisms such as crabs have no structural mechanism to resist being swept away and survive only because they seek shelter from the waves in crevices or under rocks.

Most intertidal *mollusks* arc adapted to wave skock by possessing thicker shells than their subtidal relatives and lack delicate sculpturing which is easily broken in the waves.

Respiration

Since the animals inhabiting the intertidal are marine, they have respiratory surfaces adapted to extract O_2 from water. Usually, these are thin-walled extensions from the body surface. These *respiratory* organs are thus very susceptible to *desiccation* in air and do not function unless *immersed* in water. Such organs would be a distinct *disadvantage* in the intertidal.

Among intertidal animals, there is a tendency to enclose the respiratory surfaces in a protective cavity to prevent them from drying. This is seen particularly in various mollusks where the gills are in mantle cavity, which itself is protected by the shell. A similar situation prevails in barnacles where the mantle tissue acts as a respiratory organ.

Because animals with protected respiratory organs must also conserve water at low tide, they often close up (operculum) or clamp down (chitons, limpetes) such that gaseous exchange is reduced. Thus, to conserve O_2 and water, most animals are quiescent during low tide.

Feeding

All intertidal animals must expose the fleshy parts of their bodies to feed. This means exposing those parts most susceptible todesiccation. As a result virtually all intertidal animals are active only during the time the tide is in and they are covered with water. This is true whether the animals are *grazers*, *filter feeders*, *detritus feeders*, or *predators*.

Salinity Stress

As noted above, the intertidal zone may be subjected to flooding by fresh water, which would create an osmotic stress on the intertidal organisms adapted to be *submerged* only in sea water. This is particularly true since most intertidal organisms do not show adaptations to tolerate salinity changes, certainly net like estuarine organisms do.

Most have no mechanism to control the salt content of their body fluids and hence, are *osmoconformers*. The only adaptations observed are the same as those for preventing desiccation, such as closing up valves or shells in barcles and mollusks. Perhaps this is why there are records of catastrophic mortality of intertidal organisms following heavy rain or runoff.

Apparently, however, such events are so rare or *unpredictable* that special mechanisms have not evolved.

Reproduction

Because so many of the intertidal organisms are sedentary or sessile, they must rely upon eggs and/or larvae that are free floating in the plankton for dispersal. Hence, we see a high incidence of planktonic larvae among intertidal organisms. These larvae are of many types.

A second reproductive adaptation attributable to the intertidal position is that most organisms have a breeding cycle that is closely synchronised with the occurrence of certain tides, such as spring tides. An example is *Mytilus edulis,* in which gonads mature during periods of spring tides and spawning occurs on subsequent neap tides. In *Littorina neritoides,* the egg are spawned at time of spring tides.

Rocky Shores

Of all the intertidal shores, those composed of hard material, the rocky shores, are the most densely inhabited by macroorganisms and have the greatest diversity of animal and plant species. They stand in strinking contrast to the almost barren appearance of sand and mud shores.

It is these *densely populated*, *topographically diverse*, and species rich rocky areas that have fascinated marine biologists and ecologists for many years. In recent years, these areas have been subject of several classic studies that have enhanced our understanding of how these associations of species interact with each other to maintain or change the community.

Zonation

On of the most *striking feature* of any rocky shore anywhere in the world, when seen at low tide is the prominent *horizontal* banding or *zonation* of the organisms. Each zone or band is set off from those adjacent by differences in color, morphology of the major organism, or some combination of color and *morphology*.

These horizontal bands or zones succeed each other vertically as one progresses up from the level of the lowest low tides to true terrestrial conditions. This zonation observed on intertidal rocky shores is similar to the zonation pattern that one observes with increasing elevation on a mountain, where the different horizontal zones of *trees* and *shrubs* succeed each other vertically until, if one progresses far enough, permanent snow cover is reached.

The major difference between these two areas is the scale, mountain zones being perhaps *kilometers* in width as opposed to intertidal zones extending a few meters vertically.

Rocky intertidal zones vary in vertical extent, depending upon the slope of the rocky surface, the tidal range, and the exposure to wave action. Where there is a gradual slope to the rock, individual zones may be broad, whereas under similar tidal and exposure conditions on a vertical face, the same zone would be narrow.

In the same manner, exposed areas tend to have broader zones than protected shores, and shores with greater tidal range have broader vertical zones. Of course, these striking bands may be interrupted or altered in various places along a rocky shore wherever the rock substrate itself shows changes in slope, composition, or irregularities that change its exposure or position relative to the prevailing water movement.

The fact that these prominent zones can be observed on nearly all rocky shores throughout the world under many different tidal regimes led the team of Stephenson and Stephenson (1949) to propose, after some 30 years of study, a "universal" scheme of zonation for rocky shores.

This "universal" scheme was really a framework using common terms that would allow comparison of diverse. It is characterized by establishing the zones on the basis of distributional limits of the certain common groups of organisms and not on the basis of tides. It thus reflects the knowledge of the Stephensons, and other intertidal ecologists, that distribution patterns of the organisms and zones vary not only with tides, but with slopes and exposure.

Thus, under similar tidal conditions, there could be different band widths due to different exposures or slopes of rocks. It was this universal scheme that established a standard format for describing shore zonation, replacing a bewildering host of schemes and names established by earlier biologists.

The Stephenson scheme has three main divisions of the intertidal area. The uppermost is termed the *supralittoral fringe*. Its lower limit is the upper limit of barnacles, and it extends to the upper limit of snails of the genus *Littorina* (periwinkles). The dominant organisms are the littorine snails and black encrusting lichens (verrucaria type).

Part of this zone is reached by extreme high water of spring tides, but must of its water comes from wave splash. Above this zone is the terrestrial supralittoral zone.

The middle part of the intertidal is termed the *midlittoral* zone and is the broadest in extent. Its upper limit is coincident with the upper limit of barnacles, while its lower limit is that point where large kelps reach their uppermost distribution. This zone is often subdivided and

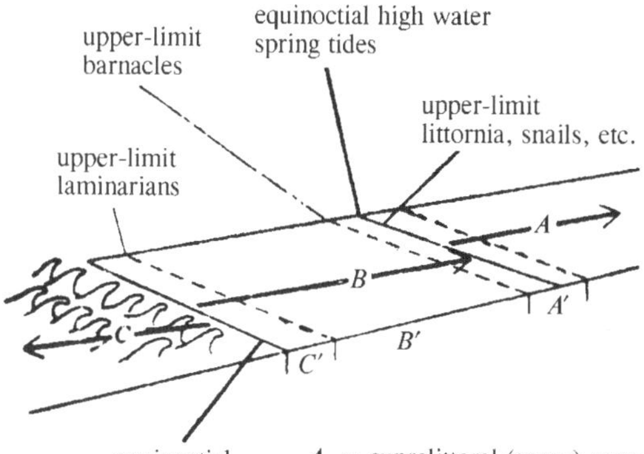

Figure 1.2: The Stephenson "Universal" scheme of zonation for rocky shores.

contains a host of different organisms. Perhaps the only universally present dominant group are the barnacles.

The lowermost zone of the scheme is the *infralittoral fringe,* which extends from the lowest low tide up to the upper limit of the large kelps. This is an extremely rich zone composed of organisms that can tolerate only limited exposure to air. It is really an intertidal extension of the *infralittoral zone* or what we know as the sublittoral area.

Although the above scheme does set forth a means for describing zonation on rocky shores, it does not offer an explanation as to why the zonation occurs. It is this explanation of zonal patterns that intrigues current marine biologists.

Causes of Zonation

Whereas it is fairly easy to recognize and measure the extent of the zones on a rocky shore, it is more difficult to came up with suitable explanations as to why organisms are distributed into these zones. Two sets of factors can be considered to explain the phenomenon : physical and biological. We shall take each up in turn.

Physical Factors

The most obvious explanation for the occurrence of the zones is that they are a result of the tidal action on the shore and therefore reflect the different tolerances of the organisms to increasing exposure to the air and the resultant desiccation and temperature extremes.

One difficulty with this explanation is that the rise and fall of a tide tends to follow a smooth curve with no obvious sharp breaks, which would correspond to the often sharp boundaries observed in the intertidal zones.

If, however, one observes a whole series of such tidal curves, such a series of breaks does become apparent, gives a typical tidal curve for a mixed tide area on the California coast gives the maximum time of continuous submergence for various tide levels. As can be seen from the graph, there are certain points on this curve that reflect sharp increases in exposure to air.

This can also be deduced which represents a single typical lunar tide cycle. Consider an organism at point X on the graph. At this point, the tide will cover the organism at least once every six hours. If, however, the organism moves up only a few inches, the tide will not cover it for 12 hours.

Thus, there is a great change in exposure time with a very short vertical movement. Points exhibiting sharp increases in exposure time over short distances have been termed *critical tide levels* by Doty (1946) and were offered as one of the early explanations for the zonation patterns described above.

In this explanation, it is important to remember that it is not the tide per se that causes the limit, but rather the fact that, at these critical points, the organisms are subjected to greatly increased time in the air and hence to greater temperature fluctuations and desiccation.

The critical tide hypothesis has been tested in various places by several scientists since its original promulgation by Doty in 1946. In general, it is difficult to find good correlations, particularly at the lower tide levels.

This lack of good correlations, can be partly attributed to the varying topography of the various shores and to the variation in exposure. Thus, a species may well be able to exist above the critical tide level if the rocky shore is exposed to persistent violent wave action, which would throw water up higher and thus decrease desiccation.

Similarly, eaves, overhangs, and crevices remain moist when exposed areas are dried out, thus allowing persistence of organisms above the level predicted by the citical tides. The effects of these topography and exposure differences suggest, however, that the real upper limits are set by certain physical factors, namely desiccation and temperature.

Since the intertidal organisms are marine, desiccation is a serious problem. Several natural observations as well as field experiments have suggested that desiccation can set the upper limits to organisms and zones. In the North Temperate Zone, for example, rocks which have a north-facing slope often have the same organism occurring higher than do adjacent south-facing slopes.

Since such rocks experience no difference in wave exposure or tide only reason for the height difference is that north faces dry out more slowly than south faces. Similarly, field experiments by Frank (1965) and others in which water was slowly dripped down slopes have resulted in the organisms extending higher up.

In other experiments organisms were transplanted above their normal positions. Notable in this respect are barnacles which, of course, cannot move. When transplanted by Foster (1971) above their normal tidal height, they died, with younger ones dying more quickly than older ones. Again, desiccation can be suspected.

Along with desiccation and often acting in concert with it, temperature is the other major physical limiting factor. As noted previously, aerial temperatures have ranges that may exceed the lethal limits and hence, intertidal organisms may die from either freezing or "cooking".

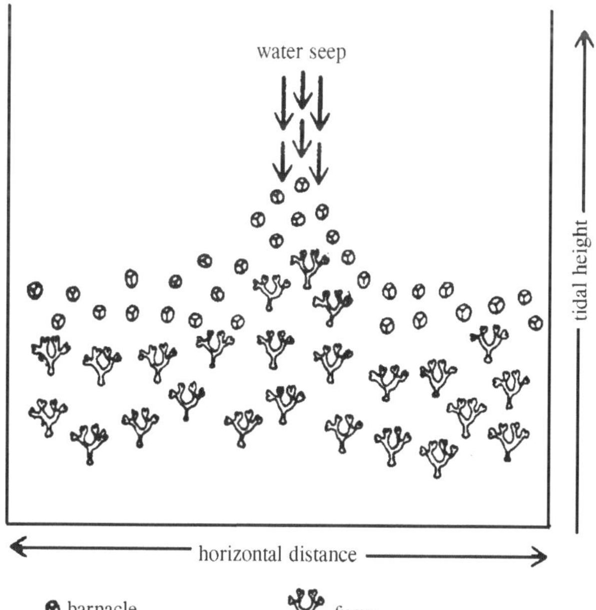

Figure 1.3: Zonation change in the presence of a water seep.

Upper limits to zones may therefore be partly attributable to the tolerable temperature limits of the intertidal organism. In addition, high temperature promotes desiccation, and the synergistic effect of these factors may be even more devastating than each acting alone.

Finally, sunlight itself may act adversely to limit organisms on the shore. Sunlight includes wavelengths in the ultraviolet region that are deleterious to living tissue. Water quickly absorbs these wavelengths and so serves to protect most marine animals. However, intertidals animals have direct exposure to such rays at low tide.

The higher an organism is in the intertidal, the greater the exposure to these rays. At the present time, there is little information concerning whether such UV radiation is active in controlling distribution of organisms, but the possibility remains. Light also has been suggested as a regulator of the distribution of intertidal algae.

This has to do primarily with the spectral quality of the light. As noted different wavelengths of light are absorbed differentially by water. In the case of intertidal algae, those that need light of longer wavelength (reds) and that are absorbed most quickly by water would tend to be found higher in the intertidal so that when submerged (when they actually photosynthesize), they would not be too deep for the penetration of red light (about 2 m).

Since the main intertidal algae belong to three different groups, reds, browns, and greens, each of which has a slightly different absorption spectrum, it might be thought that they would be arranged along a depth gradient. In such a gradient, the green algae would be expected to be the highest, since they absorb mainly red light ; the brown next; and the red algae, which absorb mainly the deep, penetrating green light, deepest.

This, however, has not been found to be the case, the intertidal algae are a mixture of all types at most levels . This is likely due to the interaction of other factors and the physiology of the algae, and it points out again the fallacy of attempting to explain patterns of species distribution with only single factors when a multitude are acting at all times.

We can summarize the above by stating that it appears that physical factors are strong determinants of the upper limits of the distribution of intertidal organisms.

Biological Factors

Although the early work in the intertidal focused on the importance of physical factors in setting the zonal patterns, more recent work has begun to clearly establish the great importance of various biological factors in setting various observed distribution patterns.

In general, these biological factors are more complex, often subtle, and closely linked to other factors, which is probably why we have only recently begun to understand how they act.

The major biological factors are *competition, predation,* and *grazing* (=herbivory). We shall take them up in order. Competition for a certain resource does not occur if the resource is so plentiful that adequate supplies of it are available for all species or individuals. In the rocky intertidal zone, only one resource is commonly in limited supply and that is space.

This is perhaps the most restricted area in the marine environment in terms of physical dimensions; at the same time, it is densely populated, at least in the temperate cone. As a result, there is an intense competition for space. This has resulted in observed zonal patterns.

On the intertidal shores of Scotland, there is a distinct zonation of barnacles with the *small Chthamalus stellatus* living in the highest zone and the larger Balanus *balanoides* occupying the major portion of the mid-intertidal. Studies done by Connell (1961) showed that *Chthamalus* larvae settled out throughout the zones occupied by both barnacles, but survived to adulthood only in upper zones.

The reason for the disappearance in the mid littoral region was due to competition from *Balanus balanoides*, which either overgrew, uplifted, or crushed the young *Cathamalus.*

Balanus was prevented from completely eliminating *Chthamalus* because it did not have the tolerance to drying and high temperatures that prevailed at the higher tidal levels and hence did not survive there, whereas *Chthamalus* could survive there. Here, then, is a case where the zonation is at least partially a function of biological competition.

A more complex example concerning competition is that among the mussel *Mytilus californianus* and several species of barnacles on the Pacific coast of North America. In this case, studies by Dayton (1971) have shown that *M. californianus* is the dominant space competitor on open coast shores.

Given enough time and freedom from predators, the *M. californianus* eventually overgrow and outcompete all other macroorganisms and take over the substrates throughout most of the midintertidal. *Mytilus californianus* takeover is, however, slow. Wherever open space occurs, it may be rapidly colonized by other organisms, including three species of barnacles, *Balanus glandula*, *B. cariosus,* and *Pollicipes polymerus*

These, in turn, displace any rapidly growing algal species. The barnacles persist only until the mussels enter. The mussels outcompete and destroy the barnacles by setttling on top of them and smothering them.

Since nothing appears to be large enough to settle and smother the *M. californianus,* they remain in control of the intertidal space. Given this competitive edge, it would appear that eventually, the rocky Pacific coast of North America would be a monotonus band of *M. californianus.* It is also curious that *M. californianus* forms dense clumps or bands only in the intertidal, though it is perfectly capable of living subtidally.

Since it is a premier space competitor, why this abrupt lower limits? The reasons for this have to do with other biological factors which act to prevent such resource monopolization and may be grouped under the term *predation.*

Intertidal algae, particularly those on temperate shores, also often show abrupt limits to their upper and lower distribution. Earlier, these limits were ascribed to critical tide levels, but it has also been suggested that this could be due to competition for space and/or access to light.

Unfortunately, very little information is available concerning actual or potential competition among algal species to test these hypotheses. In two experimental studies none on the Pacific coast of North America, evidence was found for competition.

The first study by Dayton (1975) was directed at the larger kelps, and he found that the dominant kelps, *Hedophyllum sessile, Laminaria setchelli,* and *Lessionopsis Ititoralis* all outgrew and outcompeted certain smaller species in the lower intertidal. These smaller species were generally fast-growing species, which quickly colonized open areas. As noted they are *opportunistic* or *fugitive* species.

In turn, among the three dominants, *Hedophyllum* was outcompeted by the other two such that they came to dominate the areas. The second study was actually done in the subtidal, where Vadas (1968) found that the giant kelp *Nerencystis* outcompteted and overgrew the brown alga *Agarum.*

On the New England coast, similar studies by Lubchenko (1978) directed at tidepool algae indicated that *Enteramorpha intestinal is* was a dominant space competitor as opposed to *Chondrus crispus;* in the absence of grazers, *E. intestimalis* would quickly outcompete *Chondrus* and take over the space.

These few studies suggest that competition among algal species may be more widespread than originally assumed and may be a fertile ground for future ecological work.

The role of predators in determining the distribution of organisms in the intertidal, and hence, the zonal patterns, is best documented for the Pacific coast of North America and is discussed here as an example of how complex biological interactions serve to give the prevailing observed distributions.

The dominant abundant intertidal animals on the Pacific coast other than the space-dominating *Mytilus californianus* are the barnacles *Balanus cariosus* and *Balanus glandula.* These latter two species occur abundantly in the intertidal region, despite the fact that they are competitively inferior to *M. californianus,* because a predatory starfish.

Pisaster ochraceus, preys upon *M. californianus,* thus preventing it from completely overgrowing the barnacles *Pisaster ochraceus is* a voracious predator of muscles, consuming them at a rate that effectively prevents them from occupying all the space.

At the same time, *Balanus glandula is* found primarily as a band of adults in the high intertidal, while *Balanus cariosus* occurs as cattered, large individuals of clumps in the mid intertidal. This pattern, as Connell (1970) has shown, is also due to predation. *Balanus glandula,* like *Chthamalus* in England, is capable of living throughout the intertidal zone and indeed settles throughout.

The same is true for *B. cariosus.* That both show a restricted distribution is due to predation by three species of predatory gastropods of the genus *Thais : T. lamellosa, T. emarginata,* and *T. canaliculata.* The abundance and motility of these predators is such that they are capable of completely consuming all the young *B. glandula* settling out in the mid-intertidal in 12-15 months. *Balanus glandula* survives only in a narrow band at the top of the intertidal, where the *Thais* species are prevented from entering because of excessive desiccation.

In the case of *B. cariosus,* however, the situation is somewhat different. There is no high level refuge for this barnacle, but, as with *B glandula,* the youg are consumed by the *Thais.* The refuse for *B. cariosus* is that once it reaches 2 years of age, it is too large for *Thais* to attack. The only problem, as yet unresolved, though it may have to do with periodic events like big freezes at low tide, is how it manages to survive the *Thais* for two years.

As a result, the pattern of distribution for *B. cariosus is* random clumps of large, older barnacles. It is not known for certain what regulates *Thais* populations, but they are preyed upon by large *Pisaster* and are also vulnerable to periodic events such as freezing during winter low tides. Such periodic events may reduce the population by such a significant amount that the *Balanus cariosus* could successfully establish themselves in an area. This may explain the differences among various shores with respect to the abundance of this barnacle.

Pisaster ochraceus can consume *Thais* and barnacles of any size and is the primary predator of small and medium-sized *Mytlius*. It is the top predator in the system. Because of its ability to influence the structure of the entire community in the intertidal—through its ability to consume *Mytilus* and therefore prevent monopolization of the space-it has been called by Paine (1966) a *keystone species.*

The reasons that refuges from predator occur in the upper intertidal is that both *Pisaster* and *Thais* can feed only when the tide is in, and they require a long period to successfully attack their prey. The short period of immersion of the upper intertidal does not allow sufficient time for them to make successful forays into that area.

In subtidal areas, unlimited time is available; hence the starfish have sfficient time to attack and consume any prey item. It is probably for that reason that *Mytilus,* for example, do not extend into the subtidal areas, even though they can certainly live there; hence, the reason for the sharp lower boundaries to the zonation of this species.

Lubchenco and Menge (1978) have also demonstrated that predation is important in setting zonal patterns in the intertidal of the North Atlantic Ocean. In the low intertidal of New England, the competitive dominant species is *Mytilus edulis. Mytilus edulis is* able to outcompete and eliminate the barnacle *Balanus balanoides* and the alga *Chondrus crispus.*

It is prevented from doing this by the starfish *Asterias forbesi* and *Asterias rulgaris* and the *snail Thais lapilius,* all of which prey upon *M. edulis*. In the areas where these predators are absent namely the most exposed, wave-beaten was, *M. edulis* eliminates *Balanus* and *Chondrus*. Thus, the exposed wave-beaten areas exhibit a zonal pattern where the low intertidal is *a M. edulis* band, while in protected areas, a diverse lower zone exists with *Mytilus, Balanus,* and *Chondrus* present

The role of *grazers* or herbivores in regulation· upper and lower limits of algal species is less well studied documented, but evidence suggests this process may also be considerable importance. The dominant groups of intertidal grazers are the various limpets, sea urchins, and littorine snails.

In the tidepools and on the shores of New England studied by Lubchenco (1978), one of the dominant is *Chondrus crispus*. In the tidepools, but not on the exposed intertidal, it is out competed by the

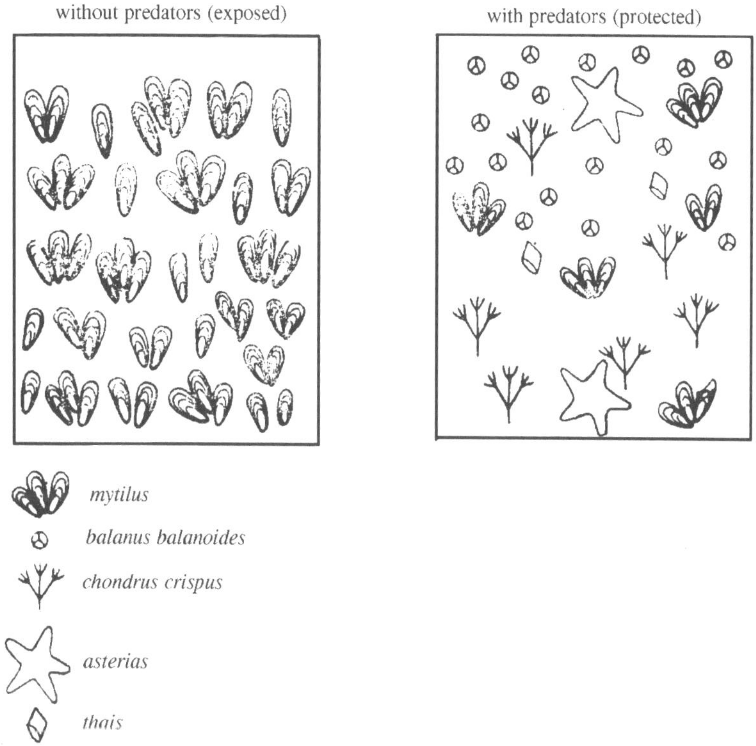

Figure 1.4: Composition of the low intertidal in the North Atlantic Ocean with and without mussel predators.

green alga *Enteromorpha intestinalis,* but it is able to persist in those pools that have a high population of the grazer *Littorina littorea,* because the latter preferentially consume *E. intestinalis.*

Similarly, in England, when Jones (1948) removed all the limpets *(Patellavulgata)* from an intertidal strips, strip was densely settled by the algae and appeared in marked contrast to the surrounding barer areas. Since the only alteration was the removal of the main grazers, this suggests their great importance in determining at least the abundance of algal species.

In this same study, after a few years, the limpets again returned (via settlement) and the algae were consumed until the area appeared like the rest of the shore. In somewhat similar studies on the Pacific coast of North America, dimination of limpets *(Acmaea, Collisella)* from intertidal areas has resulted in heavy algal growth where none, or little, had been before.

Sea urchins are large grazers and often occur on shores in dense aggregations. Removal experiments with sea urchins in both the Atlantic Ocean (England) by Jones and Kain (1967) and the Pacific Ocean (Washington coast) by Dayton (1975) have had similar results. In both cases, removal resulted in dense growth of algae where there had been sparse or no growth before.

In all of these cases, the small, rapidly growing opportunistic algal species were the first to settle, and later, they were replaced by the dominant, larger algae. What is important here is that the algae that settle in these areas often differ from those in the immediately surrounding areas.

This suggests that the urchins prefer to eat certain species, leaving others, and thus effectively alter the appearance of those areas of the intertidal that they occupy. In spite of this evidence as to their ability to remove certain algae and determine the composition of the zones, there is as yet, no direct evidence that they set the limits to the distribution of any species.

Small Scale Distribution Patterns

Although the major large-scale patterns of organism distribution in the rocky intertidal, the zonation, can be explained through some combination of exposure, desiccation, temperature, competition, predation, or grazing acting separately or together, these vertical bands are never perfect.

Often smallscale local variations occur that act to alter the bands and affects the immediate local distribution of certain organisms. Such small-scale or *local distribution* patterns can result from either biological or physical factors. Perhaps the easiest of these local distribution patterns to explain are those that result from physical factors, primarily the variation in the nature, slope, and exposure of the rock surface.

Existence of a different rock type in a local area as compared to the surrounding shore almost always means the presence of different organisms, or at least different abundances. An outcrop of sandstone among an otherwise granite rock shore usually means a different complement of organisms. Similarly, slopes facing south and those facing north often have different organisms, or the densities and/or levels to which the organisms are found differ.

This reflects the different amount of desiccation and harmful effects of direct exposure to the sun's rays (=insolation). On the Pacific coast of North America, for example, two limpet species. *Collisella (Acmaea) digitalis* and *Collisella (Acmaea) scabra* inhabit the high intertidal zone, but, as Haven (1971) has shown. their local distribution within the zone reflects their reaction to the small-scale changes in the substrate. *Collisella scabra* is found primarily on horizontal surfaces where it has a home "scar" or depression in which it remains during periods of low tide.

Collisella digitalis has no scar and is found on the cooler, moist shaded vertical slopes. *Collisella scabra* is able to survive on the drier horizontal rocks because of its depression or scar, in which the fit is tight enough to prevent desiccation at low tide. *Collisella digitalis,* on the other hand, without the increased desiccation protection of the scar, must live where desiccation is not a intense (i.e.. north-facing slopes and crevices).

Similarly, certain species do not prefer to settle on vertical faces or overhangs. These area are then settled by other species unable to compete on the flat surfaces. Much small-scale patchiness probably results from the destructive effects of wave action and wave-borne objects, such as logs, that may be hurled against the shore, smashing into small areas and clearing them of organisms.

Such battering was studied by Dayton (1971) in the state of Washington, and it was found that any point on an open shore had a 5-30 per cent chance of being hit by a log within a three-year period. An additional effect of wave action is that it produces aggregations of mobile species, such as snails and crabs, in crevices or other protected areas.

Heavy wave action from storms, even if unaccompanied by battering of objects, also is responsible for removal of organisms from the intertidal. Thus, Menge (1976) found in the exposed intertidal in New England that winter storms could clear as much as 90 per cent of the intertidal, whereas during summer and fall, less than 10 per cent of the same space was free of organisms.

The premier space competitors, *Mytilus edulis* in New England, or *M. californianus* on the Pacific coast of North America, both tend to form large clumps that grow out from the substrate. As a result, as the clumps get larger, fewer mussels are attached directly to the substrate through their byssal threads and more are attached to each other.

This creates an unstable situation in which the battering waves are more likely to tear off a clump, and hence, older, larger clumps become more vulnerable. Creation of such open spaces in any zone usually results is in quick colonization by a series *of opportunistic* or *fugitive* species. These species quickly settle an open area, mature, and reproduce before the slower growing dominant species retake the open space and force them out through competition. The most common of these opportunists are the smaller filamentous green and red algae and smaller animals such as hydroids.

These initial species are then replaced successively by competitively better species until the competitives dominant in the area takes over. In any one zone, then, there may be many of these patches, which, depending on the time since their initial clearance, will be in differing stages of *succession* towards the dominant community characterizing the zone.

This accounts for the differences one observes in different patches in the same zone in the same area. Small scale distribution anomalies may also be the result of biological interactions of various types. Some of these are *passive,* such as the fact that many species of animals must inhabit moist arrears in order to survive the exposure of air and hence shelter under the fronds of various intertidal algae.

The patchiness of these forms follows the distribution of the algae, but it is not due to any direct action of the algae. Removal of the algal canopy also results in the disappearance of the sheltering organisms.

Other biological effects are more direct and lead to definite distribution patterns, which can be observed. Thus, for example, the intertidal anemone *Anthopleura elegantissima* of the Pacific coast of North America tends to occur in large clumps, uniformly separated from each other.

Each clump has resulted from the continued asexual division of the original anemone, such that each clump consists of genetically identical individuals, a *clone.* Francis (1973) discovered that the sharp boundaries that exist between adjacent clones are the result of active fighting between the outer individuals of each clones.

In these fights, special tentacles called acrorhagi are employed and are able to inflict massive tissue damage to other anemones. The result of such clonal "border wars" is the separation of clones by anemone-free strips, which are just the width that prevent two anemones from reaching each other.

Thus, clumps of anemones are always separated from other such clumps. Yet another example of biological interaction that produces spacing is the phenomenon of *territoriality.* Territoriality is defined as an individual or group of individuals actively keeping other members of the same or different species out of an area.

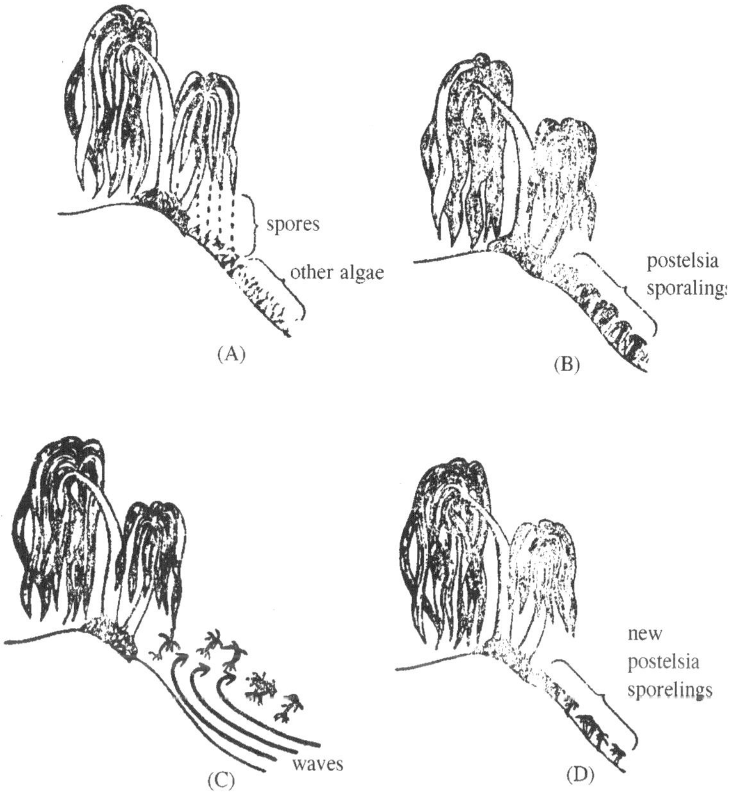

Figure 1.5: Mechanism of perpetuation of Postelsia patch on a rocky shore.

This phenomenon is well known among various birds and mammals, but it also occurs among certain invertebrate organisms. On the north Pacific coast of America, the largest limpet in the intertidal is *Lottic gigantea.* Stimson (1970) has shown that individuals of this species create a territory in the intertidal, which they actively defend against other *Lottia* and other limpets.

Should other limpets invade this territory, the resident *Lottia* pushes the interloper out. In this way, each *Lottia* keeps a small patch of rock free of potential competition and ensure that all algae growing on the site will be consumed by itself.

Another type of interaction producing small patches is that observed by Dayton (1973) in the alga *Postelsia palmaeformis,* which occurs in isolated clumps in the most wave-swept portions of the Pacific coast. This alga creates its own patch by sacrificing a portion of its offspring.

Young *Postelsia* plants always settle close to the parent plants.

Usually, this means settling on various barnacles, algae, or *Mytilus*. As they grow in the wave-swept area, they eventually produce so much surface of resistance to the wave battering that the young are pulled free at the same time, removing the barnacle, alga, or *Mytilus* to which they were attached.

This creates a new open area, which is then invaded by a second wave of *Postelsia* sporelings, which this time attach directly to the rock surface and grow up into adults. Thus, the space around *a Postelsia* maintained, and competitive dominants do not force *Postelsio* patch is out.

Predation and grazing can also create small patches or patchy distribution. Predation is the reason for the occurrence of *Balanus cariosus* in small clumps in the intertidal; grazing by sea urchins may result in tidepools free of algae, while others without urchins have an abundant growth.

On the New England coast, as noted above, tidepools without *Littorina litrorea* are dominated by *E. intestinalis* whereas those with the snail have *Chondrus crispus*. A final biological factor contributing to the patchiness, both large- and small-scale, is the preference for settlement shown by various intertidal invertebrate larvae.

Most intertidal invertebrates have a larval stage that is free swimming or floating, which serves to allow dispersal of the otherwise sessile or sedentary adult. Over the years, a great number of studies have been done on various invertebrate larvae.

Interactions Among Factors : A Summary

We have seen how various physical and biological factors each act to cause the large-scale vertical distribution patterns of algae and invertebrates that we call vertical zonation on rocky shores. We have also seen how some of these same factors, plus others, act to introduce small-scale distribution anomalies into this pattern.

In general, different factors tend to operate in different areas and at different levels on the shore. The high intertidal tends to have the distribution pattern of its characteristic species set by physical factors, whereas biological factors become more important in setting limits in the low intertidal.

It is important to realize that these factors do not act in isolation and the final distribution pattern observed, either on a small or large scale, is often the result of the interaction among two or more factors.

In the case of *Chthamalus stellatus* and *Balanus glandula,* without a refuge in the highest intertidal (physical factor), both would be eliminated from the intertidal, the former by competition and the latter by predation (biological factor).

Similarly, persistence of *B. cariosus* in the mid-intertidal of the Pacific coast depends upon the predation of *Master ochraceus* for, without this predator to remove *Mytilus* and *Thais, B. cariosus* would be outcompeted by *Mytillus or* completely consumed by *Thais.*

On the coast of Scotland, where *Balanus balanoides* and *Chthamalus stellatus* occur, the competition between the two barnacle species is ameliorated by the activity of the predator *Thais lapilus,* which consumes *Balanus.* When several factors begin to act simultaneously, the picture becomes even more complicated and we can begin to appreciate the real complexities that act to give the observed patterns.

One the best examples is the aforementioned patterns worked out for the New England intertidal by Lubchenco and Menge (1978) and summarized here. In the low intertidal of New England, the dominant space competitor is *Mytilus edulis,* which can outcompete other space occupiers such as *Balanus balanoides* and the alga *Chondrus crispus.*

On open, exposed rocky headlands, no predators exist for *M. edulis* and hence, it outcompetes the barnacles and alga to dominate the low intertidal. In protected areas, three predators occur : *Thais lapillus, Asterias forbesi* and *A. vulgaris*, all of which prey upon *M. edulis,* with the result that *Chondrus* is able to persist because *M edulis* never becomes abundant enough to monopolize the space.

The only major herbivore in this system, *Littorina litrorea,* prefers to graze on ephemeral algae that compete with *Chondrus.* Thus, the presence of the herbivore reduces competition by other algae on *Chondrus,* allowing it to persist and dominate protected areas.

In this same system, the high intertidal is dominated by *B. balanoides.* Its lower limits are apparently set in exposed areas by competition with the lower-living *M. edulis* and in protected areas by predation by *T. lapillus.* The mid-intertidal in this system has a distribution pattern in exposed areas that is determined primarily by competition between *B. balanoides* and *M. edulis,* but modified by wave action.

Thus, winter storms clear much open space, which is first settled by *B. balanoides* in the spring. The barnacles are, in turn, outcompeted by the *M. edulis,* which settle in the summer so that by the onset of winter again, the area is dominated by *M. edulis.*

In protected areas, predators become abundant and heavy predation by *Tha's* prevents either the barnacle or the mussel from monopolizing the space.

Thus, in this relatively simple system, the final structure of the intertidal and its changes depends upon the interaction of wave action, predation, grazing, and several levels of competition. As we learn more about the intertidal in other parts of the world, it can be anticipated that more such examples will come to light.

Horizontal Distribution Patterns

As we noted in the preceding section, the appearance of the various vertical bands or zones changes as one moves from areas of high wave exposure to protected and quiet water. This is true not only for the New England example, but for other areas as well. Partly, this is due to the action of water restricting certain species in or out of wave-swept areas.

In other words, some species of algae or invertebrates simply cannot tolerate the wave action and are absent from wave-swept areas. Usually, these are species with delicate structure or with poor means of holding on to the substrate.

In a similar fashion, certain species cannot tolerate quiet water areas. This may be due to their inability to complete, to lack of enough or proper food, or to the presence of predators that are not present in wave-swept areas.

Thus, we have seen that *Mytilus edulis* outcompetes *Balanus balanoides* and *Chondrus crispus* in exposed areas of New England because no predators can tolerate the wave action ; in protected areas, predators reduce competition allowing the barnacle and algae to exist and thus altering the appearance of the zones.

Succession

Succession, as defined is an ecological concept referring to the orderly progression of communities or *seres,* in which one community or association of species occupies a site and somehow modifies its conditions before the next one can take over.

This replacement of one association by another continues until reaching the last or *climax* community, which persists indefinitely under a given climatic regime. Thus, in any one area, when open space appears, there is an orderly, predictable sequence of communities that develops on that site, which will be culminated by a known climax community.

A fundamental requirement of this concept is that certain species must be present before others in order to modify the environment for subsequent ones. Does such a prodictable sequence occur in the rocky intertidal?

Current thinking has it that succession, as defined above, does not occur in the rocky intertidal. When areas are cleared in the rocky intertidal, there is often a sequence of species that occurs, but in other instances, there is not.

The discrepancy appears to be with the size and location of the cleared area. If the area is small and near the dominant association for that part of the intertidal, it is quickly overgrown by the dominant. If, however, the area is large, there may well be a sequence of species occupying it before the dominant species again reoccupy the area.

Usually, these initial species are those that we have termed opportunistic or fugitive, and they are gradually replaced by the better competitors. In this sequence, usually the first settlers on cleared area are colonial diatams or fastgrowing small algal species.

These are followed by barnacles and tube worms, which are followed by the dominant large algae and/or mussels. The reason for the sequence is not, however, that the earlier species must be present or modify the substrate, but simply that their larvae are more quickly produced and dispersed and hence, arrive first. *Mutilus,* for example, is perfectly capable of settling on newly cleared areas.

Age Structure

As we noted terrestrial communities or associations consist of a matrix of long-lived plant species, which allow us to characterize terrestrial communities on the basis of the dominant plant species. In the marine environment, specially the intertidal, the long-lived species tend to , be various invertebrate animals, whereas the plants and the various algal species tend to be more short lived.

We, in turn, tend to name zones in the intertidal on the basis of animals—*Mylitus* zone, barnacle zone, and so forth. Even though the potential longevity is great for various marine invertebrates, it is well to consider under what conditions such longevity is achieved and what the age structure of the animals actually is.

A noted previously on the Pacific coast of North America, the high intertidal has a band of *Balanus glandula*; below that, any of these species found are usually less than 2 years old.

If the age structure of the large barnacles in the band is analyzed, it is generally found to consist primarily of a single age class. Why?

Because the physical conditions are so harsh in this area that most years, the juvenile barnacles simply do not survive. As a consequence, the barnacles there result from a single good year in which conditions allowed survival through the vulnerable juvenile stage.

Once adult, the barnacles can survive succeeding harsh years. The reason that all of the lower level *B. glandula* are less than 2 years old is that in two years, *Thais* completely consumes all mid-tide barnacles. Similarly, *B. cariosus* populations in the mid-intertidal consist primarily of animals less than 2 years old.

However, there are a few that may be large and many years old. Again, the majority are less than 2 years old, because that is the time period during which *Thais* consume them. The few large, old individuals are those that somehow avoided predation until they were 2 years old and thus invulnerable to *Thais*.

Unless consumed *by Pisaster,* these individuals may live for many years. Thus, under very stringent environmental conditions or under optimal conditions low in the intertidal, the age structure of the dominant organisms is mainly of single-year classes.

Predators also seem to consist mainly of older individuals. Examples are *Pisaster ochraceus* and *Thais lamellosa*. Herbivores such as *Lottia gigantea* and the turban snail *Tegula funebralis also* have populations dominated by older individuals. Why this should be the case is not known at the present time.

Tidepools

A characteristic feature of many rocky shores is the presence of tidepools of various sizes, depths, and locations. Certain conditions affecting life of tidepools differ markedly from the surrounding intertidal and hence, necessitate a separate discussion here.

Tidepools can, of course, occur at any level in the intertidal; however, low-level pools often are little different from the surrounding sea and are essentially extensions of the sublittoral. They will not be considered here.

Only in midlittoral and infralittoral pools do we observe the conditions that characterize these areas. Our remarks here will be restricted to those pools that undergo a complete interchange with the ocean water during the tidal cycle.

At first glance, tidepools would appear to be more or less ideal places for aquatic organisms seeking to escape the harshness of the intertidal during its exposure to air. In reality, however, escape from certain physical factors such as desiccation may mean exposure to others that operate more severely in tidepools.

Tidepools, of course, vary a great deal in size and, hence, volume of water which they contain. Since water is a great moderator of harsh physical conditions, the larger the pool and the greater the water volume, the less the fluctuations in physical factors.

Three major physical factors are subject to variation in tidepools. The first is temperature. Whereas the ocean itself is a vast reservoir that heats and cools very slowly and usually within very narrow limits, the same is not true of tidepools.

These relatively small bodies of water are subject to considerably more rapid changes. Shallow tidepools exposed to the sun on warm days may quickly reach lethal or near lethal temperatures. Similarly tidepools in cold temperate or subpolar regions may have temperatures in the freezing range in winter.

An additional problem is this: The pool may either heat up or cool down over a several-hour period while exposed to the air, but when the tide returns, it will be flooded at some point with ocean water at quite a different temperature; this will suddenly change the temperature of the whole pool.

Thus, any organism inhabiting such pools must be adapted to considerable sudden fluctuation. The second factor to vary in pools is salinity. During exposure at low tide, tidepools may heat up. When that happens, evaporation occurs and the salinity increases. Under hot tropical conditions, the salinity increase can be dramatic enough in some instances to reach the point of precipitating out salt.

The opposite situation is the case when heavy rains occur at low tide and flood pools with fresh water, dramatically lowering the salinity. Again. tidepool animals and plants may have to be adapted to wider ranges in salinity than typical marine or intertidal organisms.

As before, when the tide returns, the pool will be flooded with sea water at some point and again, there will be a sudden, abrupt return to normal conditions. The final physical factor undergoing change in pools is oxygen concentration. Since the amount of oxygen that can be held in sea water is a function of temperature, it follows that those pools that heat up during exposure to the air will lose oxygen.

Under normal conditions, this may not be serious enough to produce oxygen stress, but if the pool is crowded with organisms, it may well produce a stress situation.

For example, a pool filled with algae that was exposed at night would produce a situation in which the lack of photosynthesis coupled with high respiration could reduce the oxygen level significantly. Oxygen has been recorded as falling to 18 per cent of saturation in topical tidepools.

Tidepools are thus areas of refuge from desiccation for intertidal organisms, but, in turn, these organisms suffer from rapid changes in temperature, salinity, and occasionally oxygen, thus restricting the fauna and flora to those organisms that are able to tolerate such ranges.

SANDY SHORES

Intertidal sand beaches are common throughout the world and are certainly better known than rocky shores to most humans, because they are the substrate of choice for various recreational activities. At the same time, they present a very marked change from the previously described rocky shores because, in contrast to the crowded life on the latter, sand beaches appear devoid of macroscopic life.

They are not, of course, but the environmental factors acting on these shores create conditions where virtually all organisms bury themselves in the substrate. In this section, we shall explore the action of physical factors on sand beaches and see bow these factors act to impose certain adaptations upon the larger organisms found, in this area. The very specialized conditions and organisms existing in the tiny spaces between the sand grains are the subject of the next chapter.

Environmental Conditions

As with rocky intertidal shores, sand beaches are subject to a similar array of physical factors, but the relative importance of these factors in structuring the community and their effect on the substrate differ. Perhaps the most important physical factor governing life on sand beaches is *wave action* and its attendant effect on *particle size.*

Anyone who has visited marine beaches is aware of the fact that the particle size of the sand can differ among beaches and also among seasons on the same beach. Particularly in the temperate zone, the profile of the beach also changes between winter and summer.

The particle size of sand on a beach is a function of wave action on that beach. Where wave action is light, the particles are fine, but where wave action is heavy and strong, the particles are coarse, forming deposits called gravel or shingle rather than sand.

The importance of the particle size to organism distribution and abundance rests with its effect on *water retention* and its suitability for burrowing. Fine sand, through its capillary action, tends to hold much

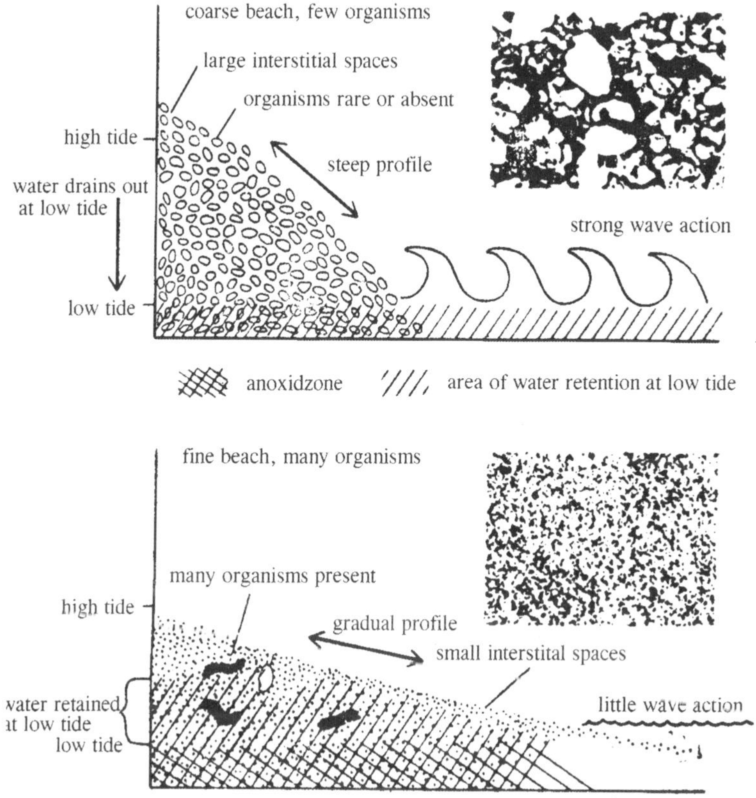

Figure 1.6: Comparison of the physical conditions between fine-grained and coarse-grained beaches.

water above the tide level in its interstices after the tide has retreated. Coarse sand and graval, on the other hand, allow water to drain away quickly as the tide retreats.

Since the organisms inhabiting the intertidal are aquatic, they are well protected against desiccation in a fine sand beach but subject to desiccation in a coarse gravel beach. This make the latter less hospitable. Fine sand is also more amenable to burrowing than coarse gravel.

A second important physical factor in sand beaches, which was not of concern in rocky shores, is also the product of wave action. That is wave-induced *substrate movement*. The particles on sand or gravel beaches are not large enough to be stable when waves strike the shore.

As a result, with each passing wave, the substrate particles are picked up, churned in the water, and redeposited. Particles are thus

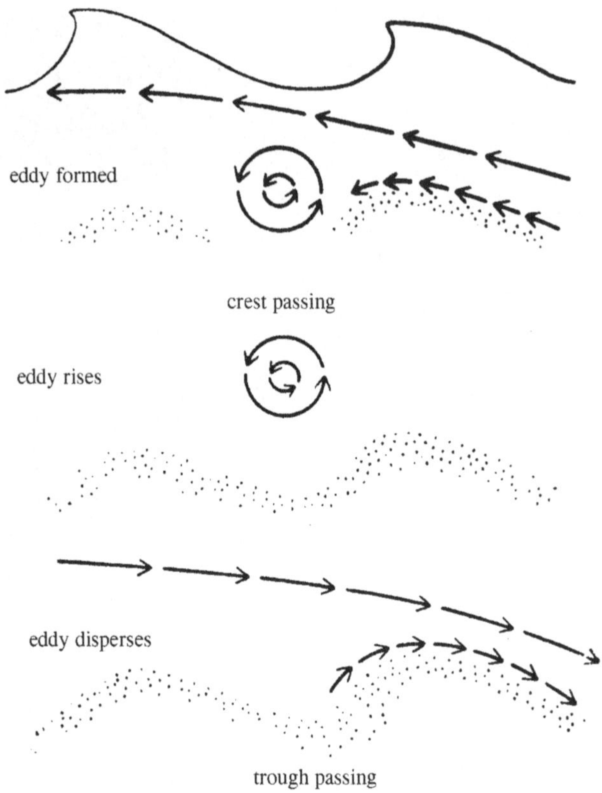

Figure 1.7: Transport of sand particles by wave act ion.

being continually moved and soted. The reason that fine sand beaches occur only where wave action is light and coarse ones where it is heavy is that, in heavy wave action, the smaller particles remain in suspension so long that they are carried away from the beach, leaving only those heavy enough (=coarse) to settle immediately.

Light wave action also means that a smaller depth of particles is affected by the passage of a wave, whereas heavy wave action disturbs the substrate to a greater depth.

Many beaches show a gradation of particle sizes from fine near low water to coarser at the high tide mark. This reflects the distribution of wave energy on the beach, being greater near the high tide mark, where waves break more often, and lesser with increasing depth in the tidal zone.

Since the substrate itself, at least the surface layers, is in constant motion and be picked up and held for greater or lesser amounts of time in suspension, depending upon the strength of the waves ; it follows that any change in wave intensity on a given beach will mean a change not only in grain size, but also in the profile or shape of the beach.

This comes about when gentle wave action is replaced by heavier waves, which dig deeper into the beach, pick up more and heavier grains, and hold them in suspension longer, so they are deposited some distance away, usually, offshore.

This changed profile is a common seasonal occurrence on many temperate zone beaches, where a gentle slope of fine sand occurs during the summer months and is replaced by a steep, coarse beach during winter storms. Significant for organisms is the fact that the depth of substrate that may be physically moved can be several feet.

Because of this condition of ceaseless movement of the surface layers of the sediment, few large organisms have the capability of permanently occupying the surface of sand or gravel beaches. This is the reason for the barren appearance of such beaches.

In contrast so rocky shore, sand beaches usually have a rather smooth, uniform profile and thus lack the great topographic diversity of rocky shores. There are, for example, no crevices, no slopes facing different directions and offering different moisture conditions, nor are there overhangs or tidepools.

As a result, the environmental factors such as temperature, desiccation, wave action, and insolation act uniformly at each tidal level on the beach. Wave action is the dominant environmental factor acting on the sand beaches, creating the special conditions that make it difficult, or impossible, for many organism to inhabit this area.

At the same time, sand beaches offer some positive advantages to marine organisms with respect to other physical factors. Sand is an excellent buffer against large temperature and salinity changes. Measurements of temperature with depth on sand beaches at low tide have demonstrated that, below the first few centimeters, the temperature is very nearly that of the surrounding sea water.

The amelioration of temperature is partly due to the insulating properties of sand itself and partly due to the water held in the interstices of the deeper layers. In a similar manner, salinity changes are also minimal below 10 or 15 cm on beaches, even if the upper layers have fresh water flowing over or falling on them.

Again, this is due to the fact that the water held in the interstices is salt water, which has a higher density than fresh water. As a result, the fresh water remains perched on the surface. Sand is further a barrier to any harmful effects of exposure to direct sunlight (insolation) for any organism living in the sand, simply becausethe sand is opeque to light and reflects or absorbs it in the surface layers.

Desiccation is not a problem as long as the beach sand is fine enough to hold water by capillary action during periods of low tide. Thus, any organism burrowing into the sand will be constantly moist. A final physical factor acting on beaches is *oxygen content.*

Oxygen is never limiting in the water bathing the beach because the turbulence of wave action ensures constant saturation. Where it might become limiting is in the substrate itself. The water held in the beach and responsible for ameliorating the changes in temperature and salinity also contains oxygen, which is available for use by the organisms.

This supply, however, is used up by respiration of the organisms and must be replenished. This replenishment comes through interchange of the water with the sea above, and is dependent on the fineness of the sediments.

Fine sediments have a slow rate of exchange and coarse sediments a rapid exchange. Thus, in fine-grained beaches, water interchange is slow and may result in reduced oxygen supplies.

Adaptations of Organisms

The dominant environmental factor acting on sand beaches is wave action, which creates the unstable, constantly moving substrate. In order to inhabit this area, organisms must first be adapted to tolerate these features.

There are two routes that may be taken by organisms in adapting. The first is to burrow deeply enough into the substrate such that the organism is deeper than the depth of sediment affected by the passing wave. This strategy is employed by many large clams such as *Tivela stultorum,* the Pismo clam.

Such animals are usually also aided by developing a very heavy shell, which helps in keeping the animal down in the substrate. The only difficulty with this type of adaptation is that a very severe storm may generate waves large enough to pull these animals out and throw them on the beach. This is the reason for the catastrophic destruction that occasionally occurs in these forms.

The second route of adaptations is the ability to burrow in very quicky as soon as the pissing wave has removed the animal from the substrate. This appears to be more common mechanism and is employed by many annelid worms, small clams, and crustaceans. A good example of this type of adaptation can be found in the various sand crabs of the family Hippidae found in many beaches around the world. These animals have a short body with limbs highly modified to dig quickly into wet sand.

As soon as they are pulled out of the substrate by a passing wave, they reburrow before the water motion can carry them off. Small clams of the genus *Donax* also do the same thing, and razor clams of the genus *Siliqua* are extraordinarily fast at reburrowing.

Other adaptations are correlated with the above. For example, most burrowing mollusks tend to have very smooth shells that reduce the resistance to burrowing into the sand. Similarly, shore echinoderms such as sand dollars have much reduced spines to allow them to burrow into the sand.

A special adaptation observed by Chia (1973) in small sand dollars *(Dendraster excentricus)* is that they tend to accumulate iron compounds in a special area of their digestive tracts, which serve as a "weight belt" to keep them down in the presence of wave action.

A final set of adaptations has to do with the problem of preventing clogging of respiratory surfaces by the resuspended sand. In order to prevent this from occurring, the intake siphons of sandy beach clams are often fitted with various screens, which prevent entrance of sand but allow passage of water.

Similarly, in the sand crabs, the antennae held together form a tube to the surface through which water enters the branchial chamber. These are densely clothed clothed with closely spaced hairs designed to prevent entrance of sand.

Types of Organisms

The most noticeable group that is absent from sand beaches is the large plants. No macroscopic plants occur on open sand beaches, presumably because there is no way for them to attach and maintain themselves in the wave. action.

Small benthic diatoms, however, may be present on the sand grains. The second major group of organisms conspicuous by its absence is the sessile animals such as barnacles and mussels, so dominant on rocky shores. Again, there is no place for them to attach.

The sand beach is dominated by representative from three invertebrate classes: polychaete worms bivalve mollusks, and crustaceans. Various combinations of species from these three groups dominate sand beaches throughout the world.

Feeding Biology

The absence of large multicellular plants means that there is very little primary productivity. Although diatoms are present, the opaqueness of the sand ensures that even the diatom population is restricted to the very surface layers.

As a result, there are no macroscopic herbivores on a sand beach. Since there is virtually no primary productivity, the animals living on the beach must depend for food upon either the phytoplankton carried in sea water above the beach, the organic debris brought in by the waves, or consuming the other beach animals.

There are relatively few true carnivores among beach animals, because to be such would require active movement across the substrate in search of prey. This is probably not feasible in the face of the heavy wave action.

As a result, most of the organisms in a beach are either suspension or detritus feeders. Suspension feeding animals are those that filter particles out of the water column. These particles may be plankton organisms or, particularly on the sand beach, they may be various organic particles resuspended from the bottom by the passing waves.

The dominant group of suspension feeders on sand beaches are the bivalve mollusks such as razor clams *(Siliqua, Ensis),* surf clams *(Tivela, Spisula)* and coquinas *(Donax).* Sand beaches tend to have lesser amounts of organic detritus than muddy shores, but enough debris from various sources finds its way to the beach to be a reliable source of food for certain organisms.

Since this detrital material is often carried up and down the beach suspended in the wave wash rather than being deposited on the bottom, the mechanisms employed by detritus feeders on the beach are aften different from those employed by detritus feeders on muddy shores. The sand crabs of the family Hippidae, such as *Emerita analoga* and *Blepharipoda occidentalis* of the Pacific coast of America, employ a unique mechanism to trap debris in the wave wash.

MacGinitie and MacGinitie (1949) observed that *Emerita* orient so that their heads point shoreward. They remain completely buried as the incoming wave passes over them shoreward. After passage, as the water begins to run down the beach, they stick out their very large second antennae.

These are highly clothed in hairs forming a net that, when spread into the backwash, intercepts all particles within a certain size range. The particles are then wiped off by the mouth and ingested. As the tide rises and falls, the position of the wave wash front also moves. These crabs take advantage of this to maximize their feeding time by being moved up and down the beach with the tide. Movement is effected by surfacing as a wave rolls in and being carried up some distance by the wave and then quickly reburrowing.

In a similar manner, as the tide recedes, they emerge and roll down the beach before reburrowing and commencing feeding. A similar method of feeding is employed by the gastropod mollusk *Olivella columellaris* on the coast of Central America. In this case, a mucus net is produced by the animal and held across the wave backwash.

This net acts like a filter and captures small particles. Since the animal feeds by consuming the entire net with particles, it must produce a new net at frequent intervals. Most sand beaches also include one or more polychaetes, which burrow through the sand ingesting the sand digesting out the organic particles.

Much like earthworms on land, however, they are rarely abundant on open sand beaches because the amount of organic material is less than in mud shores. Sand dollars, one of the echinoderms common on sandy beaches, are generally deposit or detritus feeding animals.

These animals generally burrow through the sand. As they do so, the finer organic particles, but not the sand grains, tall down between the short spines, are trapped in mucus, and carried to the mouth. Some species, such as the Pacific coast *Dendraster excentricus*, according to Timko (1976), have even modified this basic feeding process to remove suspended particles by projecting part of the body up into the water column.

Carnivores are rare but the few found usually are polychaete worms or gastropod mollusks. The polychaetes, such as species of the genera *Nephtys* and *Glycera,* actively burrow through the sand and small prey items with their reversible proboscis.

The carnivorous gastropods are represented most commonly by burrowing snails of the family Naticidae (moon snails). These animals burrow slowly just below the surface layers of the sand in search of bivalve mollusks, which they consume by boring holes through the shell and eating out the contents.

A number of transient predators also occur. At low tide, various shorebirds actively feed on beach organisms, and at high tide, fishes invade the area.

Zonation and Community Organization

Since there are no organisms visible on the surface of the intertidal sand beaches, these areas do not display the surface zonation patterns so obvious on rocky shores. Furthermore, since the various physical factors such as desiccation and temperature that act to limit organisms on rocky shores are of far less importance to organisms living in the sand, it might be suspected that zonation of organisms would be reduced or absent.

In fact, there is a zonation of sandy shore organisms, but it is neither as clearly defined nor as well understood as that for rocky shores. The lack of clear zonation patterns is due partly to the habit of some dominant organisms moving up and down the beach for feeding and partly to the dearth of studies on the determinants of distribution patterns in this area.

Certainly one of the major contributors to the lack of understanding is the inability of researchers to set up field experiments is this area to determine the results of excluding certain organisms. Wave action precludes such work.

From the few data that are available, it is possible to establish a three-zone division of most sandy beaches that follows quite closely the universal scheme of Stephenson's mentioned earlier.

The highest parts of the sandy beach, corresponding to the supralittoral fringe, are usually inhabited by talitrid amphipod crustaceans (beach hoppers) in the temperate zone and by the fast-moving ghost

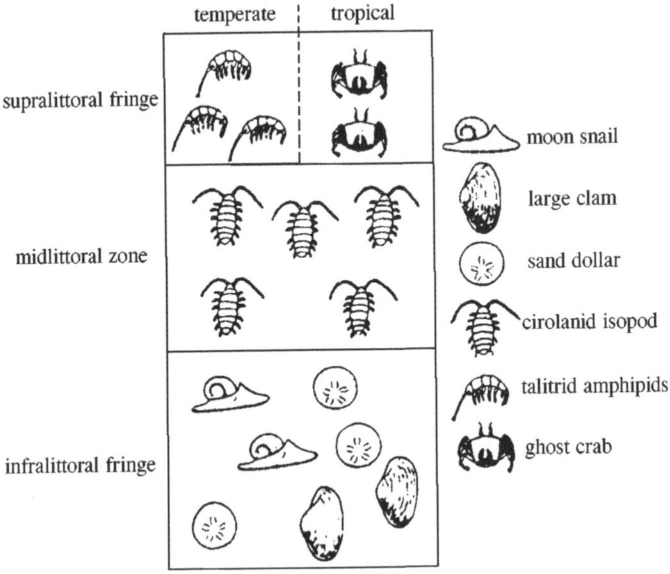

Figure 1.8: Generalized zonation patterns for sandy beaches.

crabs *(Oxypode)* in the tropics. Both groups excavate burrows and are scavengers. The broad mid-littoral area, which corresponds to the area inhabited by barnacles and mussels on rocky shores, is much more variable.

One group found here is isopods of the family Cirolanidae. Also coming into this zone when it is the area of wave swash are the various sand crabs and those other animals that feed in a similar way (see previous section). The lowest zone, or infralittoral fringe, is inhabited by the greatest number *of* species, including the large surf clams *(Tivela, Spisula),* sand dollars *(Dendraster),* various polychaete worms, a host of crustaceans, and the larger carnivorous snails *(Natlca, Polinices).*

In direct contrast to rocky shores, where experimental work has demonstrated the importance of physical factors, competition, and predation in determining the observed zonation patterns, the explanations for the establishment of the pattern in sandy beaches have not been subjected to rigorous experimental analysis.

As a result, we know little of the factors or their interactions that establish the sandy beach distribution patterns. The extremely crowded conditions for organisms observed on rocky shores are not found on sand beaches. Indeed, the fauna is very sparse and certainly not occupying all available space.

This immediately suggests that competition for space is not a major contributor to the observed distribution pattern. Competition for food also appears negligible, since the sparse populations and abundant plankton make competition unlikely. Similarly, there are relatively few indigenous invertebrate predators, and it seems unlikely that they are responsible for any major distributional pattern.

The effect, however, of large vertebrate predators such as birds and fishes remains to be investigated. This leaves the physical factors as probable major contributors to the patterns observed.

MUDDY SHORES

Whereas sharp boundaries exist between rocky shore and sandy shore, such that they are easily defined and recognizable, a similar situation does not prevail when trying to differentiate between sandy and muddy shores.

Indeed, it is not possible to draw sharp boundaries between the two, because as shores become more protected from wave action, they tend to become finer grained and accumulate more organic matter and thus become more "muddy".

Sand and mud shores are therefore the opposite ends of a continuum, the sand beaches having larger grain sizes and the muddy areas the finest grain sizes.

Since sharp boundaries do not exist and one grades into the other along a gradient of increasing protection from wave action, the fauna and flora also show a change from organisms typical of open sand beaches to those typical of muddy shores along the same gradient.

This section will discuss the features characteristic of typical muddy shores; that is, those at the opposite end of the continuum from the open sand beaches. It should be borne in mind, however, that various transitional communities exist that will show mixtures of organisms from both extremes.

Since muddy shores are also composed of sediments, similar factors will apply here as did with sandy shores and will not be repeated. Muddy substrates are also characteristic of estuaries and salt marshes. Indeed, most of the muddy shores of the world are associated with estuaries and similar embayments.

Hence, many of the types of organisms and adaptations are similar between the two areas. To avoid the problem of overlap in discussing these two areas, this section will treat the infaunal organisms of mud flats, their adaptations, feeding biology, and trophic structure.

These considerations will, of course, apply to the estuarine infauna. The role of other organisms, productivity and ecological relationships are taken up.

Physical Factors

The major contrast with open sand beaches is that muddy shores cannot develop in the presence of significant *wave action*. Therefore, muddy shores are restricted to intertidal areas completely protected from open ocean wave activity.

Muddy shores are best developed where there is a sources of finegrained sediment particles Muddy shores are located in various partially enclosed bays, lagoons, harbors, and especially estuaries.

Since these areas are developed where water movement is minimal, the slope of mud shores tends to be much flatter than that observed for sand beaches. This is why these areas are often referred to as "mud flats."

The very fine particle size coupled with the very flat angle of response of these sediments means that water in the sediments does not drain away and is held within the substrate. This long retention time for water, coupled with a very poor interchange of the interstitial water with the sea water above and a high internal bacterial population, usually results in complete depletion of the oxygen in the sediments below the first few centimeters of the surface.

Anaerobic conditions thus prevail within the sediment and this is one of the most important characteristics of the muddy shore. Muddy shores tend to accumulate organic material, which means that there is an abundant potential food supply for the, resident organisms; but the abundant small organic particles "*raining*" down on the mud flat also have the potential to clog respiratory surfaces.

Adaptations of Organisms

As we noted for sandy shores, the surface of muddy shores is also often rather barren, as few animals inhabit the surface of the mud flat. Most organisms inhabiting these areas show an adaptation to burrowing into and through the soft substrate or else inhabit permanent tubes in the substrate.

In contrast to sand beaches, however, the presence of the organisms in the mud flat is advertised on the surface by the presence of various holes of differing sizes and shapes. Thus, one of the primary adaptations of organisms in mud flats is the ability to burrow into the substrate or to form permanent tubes. A second major adaptation concerns the anaerobic conditions that prevail in the substrate.

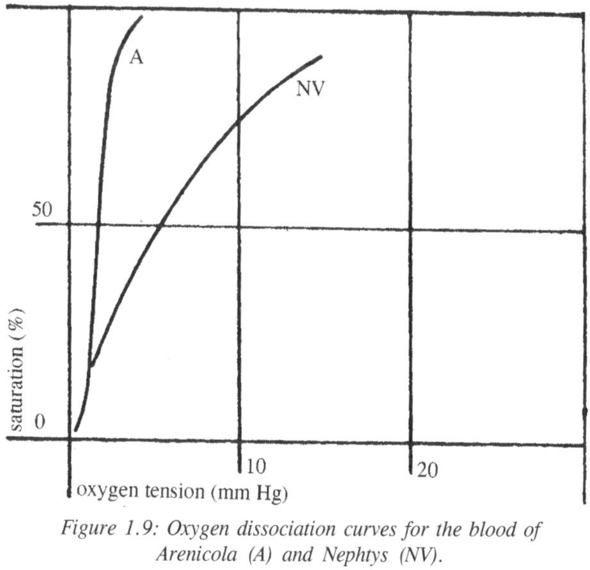

Figure 1.9: Oxygen dissociation curves for the blood of Arenicola (A) and Nephtys (NV).

If organisms are to survive while burrowed into the substrate, they must either be adapted to live under anaerobic conditions or else must have some way of bringing the overlying surface water with its oxygen supply down to them. Since most multicellular organisms cannot survive in the absence of oxygen, the latter is the more common adaptation.

It is to obtain this oxygen-rich surface water and food that the various burrows, holes, and tubes appear on the surface of the mud flat. Although most mud flat organisms are intolerant of completely anaerobic conditions, many have adaptations that permit them to exist at lower oxygen tensions than similar forms that live on open sand beaches.

The most common adaptation to low oxygen supply is the development of carriers (e.g., hemoglobin) that will continue to pick up oxygen at concentrations well below that of similar pigments in other organisms.

Since wave action is essentially absent on these mud flats, there is no necessity for development of either rapid burrowing or heavy bodies to maintain positions, as is the case for sandy shores.

Types of Organisms

In contrast to sand beaches, muddy shores often develop a substantial growth of various plants. On the bare mud flats. the most abundant plants are diatoms, which live in the surface layers of mud and often give a brownish color to the surface of the mud at low tide. Other plants include large macroalgae such as species of *Gracilaria* (*red algae*), *Ulva* and *Enteromorpha* (*green algae*).

These large algae often undergo seasonal cycles of abundance, becoming common in the warmer months and virtually disappearing in colder months. Other areas, particularly the lowest tidal levels, may be covered with a growth of various sea grasses such as the genus *Zostera*.

As a result of the occurrence of these various primary producers, there is substantial primary productivity in the mud flats. Mud flats contain large numbers of bacteria, which feed on the abundant organic matter. Bacteria are the only abundant organisms found in the anaerobic layers of the mud shore and constitute a significant biomass.

Among the dominant bacteria inhabiting this area are a number capable of utilizing the potential energy of the various reduced chemical compounds abundant here. These *chemosynthetic* or *sulfur bacteria* obtain energy through the oxidation of a number of reduced sulfur compounds, such as various sulfides (for example H_2S).

These organisms are thus primary producers of organic matter analogous to green plants. They produce organic matter using energy obtained from the oxidation of the reduced sulfur compounds, whereas plants produce organic matter using energy obtained from sunlight

Since these autotrophic bacteria are located in the anaerobic layer of the mud, mud flats are unique among marine environments in that they have two separate layers in which primary productivity occurs: the surface, where diatoms, algae, and marine grasses carry on photosynthesis, and a deep layer, where bacteria conduct chemosynthesis.

The dominant macrofaunal groups on muddy shores are the same as those encountered on sand beaches ; namely, various polychaete worms, bivalve mollusks, and small and large crustaceans, but of quite different sorts.

Feeding Biology and Trophic Structure

Because of the greater amount of organic matter present in and on muddy shores and because of increased productivity due to both bacteria and plants, there is vastly more food available on muddy shores than on sand beaches. This permits more large organisms to live on mud shore and, indeed, mud flats may be very densely populated. The dominant feeding types on mud flats are deposit feeders and suspension feeders, a situation similar to that on sand beaches.

Deposit feeders are particularly abundant due to the large amount of organic material and the large populations of bacteria in the sediments. Deposit feeding polychaetes are represented by genera such as *Arenicola* and *Capitella.* Both feed by burrowing through the substrate, ingesting it and digesting out the organic matter (or bacteria), and passing out the undigested material through the anus.

Arnenicola spp., however, from a U-shaped burrow in which one arm of the U is a permanently open shaft to the surface, while the other arm is filled with sediment that the worm ingests. The worm consumes sediment from the filled shaft, passes it through its gut, and then moves up in the open burrow to defecate at the surface, leaving characteristic mounds.

Capitellids, on the other band, form no permanent tubes, but move like aquatic earthworms through the surface layers of the substrate, ingesting it. Deposit feeding bivalves are also common in these areas. Temperate zone mud flats often have large numbers of small tellinid clams of the genus *Macoma* or *Scrobicularia.*

These bivalves have siphons that are separated. Each clam lies buried in the substrate with its siphons extended to the surface. There, the intake siphon is moved over the surface like a vacuum cleaner, ingesting organic particles and bringing them down to the clam for digestion. Suspension feeders include various other species of clams, some crustaceans, and numbers of polychaetes.

Suspension feeding mechanisms are not different from those observed in other areas. There is, however, some question as to how exclusively these forms are feeding on suspended plankton. The fine sediment particles are easily stirred up on mud flats and remain resuspended in the water. Hence, suspension feeders may possibly take in amounts of these particles in addition to various plankton organisms.

Perhaps most of the suspension feeders on mud flats also partially take in resuspended sediments and hence, are actually feeding on both deposited and suspended material. In general, deposit feeders are more common in fine-grained shores and suspension feeders become more abundant in coarser sediments, where there is little organic matter.

The major carnivores on mud shores are often the fishes, which feed when the tide is in, and the birds, feeding when the tide is out. Indigenous mud flat predators include a few polychaete worms such as *Glycera* spp., moon snails *(Polinices, Natica),* and crabs.

Despite the relative abundance of plant material on muddy shores, there are very few herbivores, and most plant material finds its way into the food chains only after it has been broken down into small pieces to enter the deposit feeding food web.

Thus, the tropic structure of a mud flat is often built up from two bases : a detritus-bacteria base and one based on plants. The detritus base web is derived from plants and other organic sources and includes the bacteria that live upon the detrital particles.

Detrital particles can thus either be taken in directly by the large macrofaunal invertebrates or else be consumed by bacteria. An additional bacterial component at the base of this tropic pyramid is the sulfur bacteria.

Bacteria are consumed commonly by various nematode worms, which thus occupy a position similar to that of herbivores in other areas. Bacteria are also consumed by deposit feeders as they ingest the organic particles upon which the bacteria are found.

Nematodes and deposit feeders are, in turn, consumed by various carnivores, including predatory invertebrates (moon snails, *(Glycera)* as well as birds and fishes.

A second food web is based primarily on the microscopic diatoms as the autotrophic base. The diatoms are consumed by several different polychaetes, mollusks, and crustaceans. These, in turn, are consumed

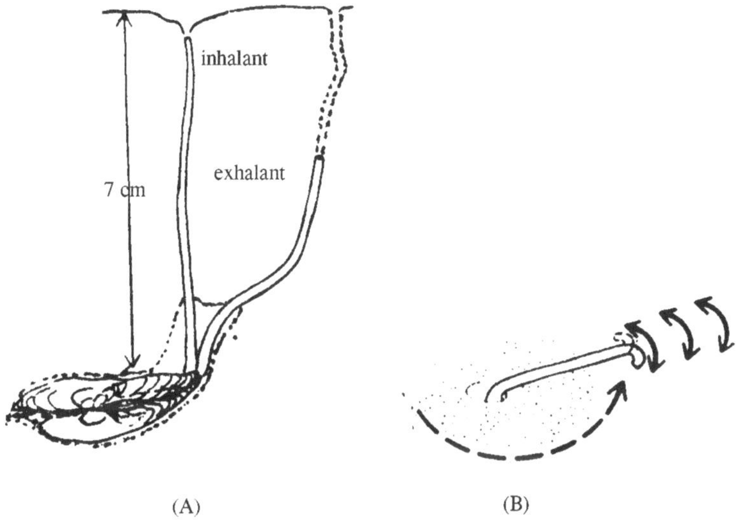

Figure 1.10: (A) Macoma nasuta in the substrate.
(B) Macoma nasuta feeding with its incurrent siphon

by the large predatory birds and fishes.

Zonation

Little information exists regarding the zonation of mud flats. The very gentle slope of these areas means that the intertidal is often very extensive, more so than rocky or sandy shores. The upqer area, the supralittoral fringe, is often inhabited by various species of crabs, many *of* which burrow into the substrate.

The very extensive midlittoral area is the home of most of the common species of clams and polychaetes. There is no sharp boundary with the infralittoral fringe, and similar organisms are ecountered. The role of physical factors and biological factors in structuring these communities has been little studied.

Some studies have demonstrated a separation among the species by depth in the substrate implying a "niche" separation. Experimental removal of a species or increased densities usually has resulted in corresponding changes in density of other species, which suggests some sort of biological interaction.

However, this is not well worked out at this time, and hence, we are not able to discuss how this interaction may produce the pattern we have observed. Since this area is often similar to the substrate found in shallow water subtidal soft bottoms, and estuarine areas, it is likely that a similar set of factors is acting.

INTERTIDAL FISHES

Whereas a Cleat deal of research has been concentrated on the ecology of invertebrates and plants of the intertidal zone on all three types of shores, there are very few accounts of the fishes of these areas or of the role they may play in community organization as grazers or predators.

Since fishes are often present in considerable numbers in the intertidal and since it is known that they have a significant effect on other communities such as coral reefs, it is reasonable to assume that future research may elucidate their role here as well.

2

THE ORIGIN OF OCEANS

The earth is uniquely favored among the planets: it has rain, rivers and seas. The large planets (Jupiter, Saturn, Uranus and Neptune) have only a small solid core, presumably overlain by gases liquefied by pressure; they are also surrounded by enormous atmospheres. The inner planets are more like the earth.

Mercury, however, has practically no atmosphere and the side of the planet facing the sun is hot enough to melt lead. Venus has a thick atmosphere containing little water and a surface that, according to recent measurements, may be even hotter than the surface of Mercury.

Mars and the moon appear to show us their primeval surfaces, affected only by craters formed by the impact of meteorites, and perhaps by volcanoes. Only on the earth has the repetition of erosion and sedimentation"—the colossal hour glass of rock destruction and rock formation"—run its course cycle after cycle and produced the diverse surface that we see.

The mountains are raised and then worn away by falling and running water, the debris is carried onto the lowlands and then out to the ocean. Geologically speaking, the process is rapid. The great plateau of Africa is reduced by a foot in a few thousand years, and in a few million years it will be near sea level, like the Precambrian rocks of Canada and Finland.

All trace of the original surface of the earth has been removed, but as far back as one can see there is evidence in rounded, water-worm pebbles for the existence of running water and therefore, presumably, of an ocean and of dry land. The obvious things that no one comments on are often the most remarkable, one of them is the constancy of the total volume of water though the ages.

The level of the sea, of course, has varied from time to time. During the ice ages, when much water was locked up in ice sheets on the continents, the level of the sea was lower than it is at present, and the continental shelves of Europe and North America were laid bare. Often the sea has advanced over the coastal plains, but never has it covered all the land or even most of it.

The mechanism of this equilibrium is unknown, it might have been expected that water would be expelled gradually from the interior of the earth and that the seas would grow steadily larger, or that water would be dissociated into hydrogen and oxygen in the upper atmosphere and that the hydrogen would escape, leading to a gradual drying up of the seas.

These things either do not happen or they balance each other. The mystery is deepened by the almost complete loss of neon from the earth, in the sun and the stars neon is only a little rarer than oxygen. The neon was presumably lost when the earth was built up from dust and solid grains because neon normally does not form compounds, but if that is so, why was the water not lost too ?

Water has a molecular weight of 18, which is less than the atomic weight of neon, and thus should escape more easily. It looks as if the water must have been tied up in compounds, perhaps hydrated silicates, until the earth had formed and the neon had escaped.

Water must then have been released as a liquid sometime during the first billion years of the earth's history, for which we have no geological record. The planet Mercury and the moon would have been too small to retain water after it was released.

Mars seems to have been able to retain a trace, not enough to make oceans but enough to be detectable by spectroscopy. These speculations about the early history of the earth are open to many doubts. The evidence is almost non-existent, and all one can say it, "It might have been that..."

The great increase in understanding of the present state and recent history of the ocean basins that we have gained in the past 20 years is something quite different. For the first time the geology of the oceans has been studied with energy and resources commensurate with the tremendous task.

It turns out that the main processes of geology can be understood only when the oceans have been studied, no amount of effort on land could have told us what we now know. The study of marine geology has unlocked the history of the oceans, and it seems likely to make intelligible the history of the continents as well.

We are in the middle of a rejuvenating process in geology comparable to the one that physics experienced in the 1890's and to the one that is now in progress in molecular biology. The critical step was the realization that the oceans are quite different from the continents. The mountains of the oceans are nothing like the Alps or the Rockies, which are largely built from folded sediments.

There is a world-encircling mountain range—the mid-ocean ridge-on the sea bottom, but it is built entirely of igneous rocks, of basalts that have emerged from the interior of the earth. Although the undersea mountains have a converting of sediments in many places, they are not made of sediments, they are not folded and they have not been compressed.

A cracklike valley runs along the crest of the . mid-ocean ridge for most of its length, and it is here that new ocean floor is being formed today. From a study of the numerous earth quakes along this crack it is clear that the two sides are moving apart and that the crack would continually widen if it were not being filled with matcrial from bclow.

As the rocks on the two sides move away and new rock solidifies in the crack, the events are recorded by a kind of geological tape recorder : the newly solidified rock is magnetized in the direction of the earth's magnetic field.

For at least the past 10,000 years, and possibly for as long as 700,000 years, the north magnetic pole has been close to its present location, so that the magnetic field is to the north and downward in the Northern Hemisphere, and to the north and upward in the Southern Hemisphere.

As the cracking and the spreading of of the ocean floor go on, a strip of magnetized rock is produced. Then one day, or rather in the course of several thousand years, the earth's field reverses, the next effusion of lava is magnetized in the reverse direction and a strip of reversely magnetized rocks is built up between the two split halves of the earlier strip.

The reversals succeed one another at widely varying intervals, sometimes the change comes after 50,000 years, often there is no change for a million years and occasionally, as during the Permian period, there is no reversal for 20 million years. The sequence of reversals and the progress of spreading is recorded in all the oceans by the magnetization of the rocks of the ocean floor.

The message can be read by a magnetometer towed behind a ship. We now have enough examples of these magnetic messages to leave no doubt about what is happening.

It is a truly remarkable fact that the results of magnetic surveys in the South Pacific can be explained—indeed predicted—from the sequence of reversals of the disrection of the earth's magnetic field known from magnetic and age measurements, made quite independently on lavas in California, Africa and elsewhere.

The only adjustable factor in the calculation is the rate of spreading. Such worldwide theoretical ideas and such detailed agreement between calculation and theory are rare in geology, where theories are usually qualitative, local and of little predictive value.

The speed of spreading on each side of a mid-ocean ridge varies from less than a centimeter per year to as much as eight centimeters.

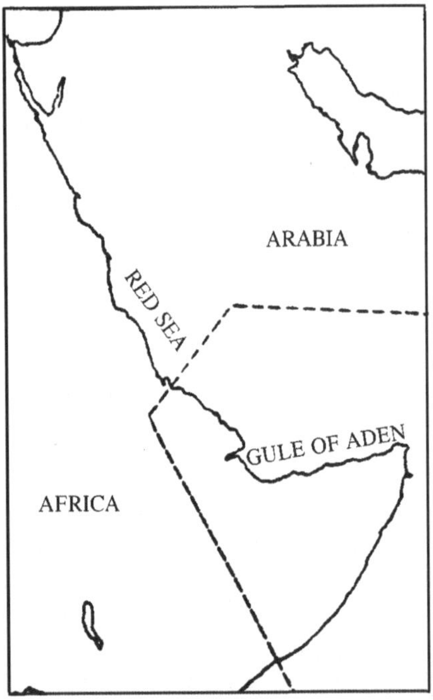

Figure 2.1: Rupture of Middle East is being caused by the Rec sea and the Gulf of Aden.

The fastest rate is the one from the East Pacific Rise and the slowest rates are those from the Mid-Atlantic Ridge and from the Carlsberg Ridge of the northwest Indian Ocean.

The rate of production of new terrestrial crust at the central valley of a ridge is the sum of the rates of spreading on the two sides. Since the rates on the two sides are commonly almost equal, this sum is twice the rate on each side and may be as much as 16 centimeters (six inches) per year.

Such rates are, geologically speaking, fast. At 16 centimeters per year the entire floor of the Pacific Ocean, which is about 15,000 kilometers (10,000 miles) wide, could be produced in 100 million years. When the mid-ocean ridges are examined in more detail, they are found not to be continuous but to be cut into sections by "*fracture zones*".

A study of the earthquakes on these fracture zones shows that the separate pieces of ridge crest on the two sides of a fracture zone are not moving apart, as might seem likely on first consideration.

The two pieces of ridge remain fixed with respect to each other

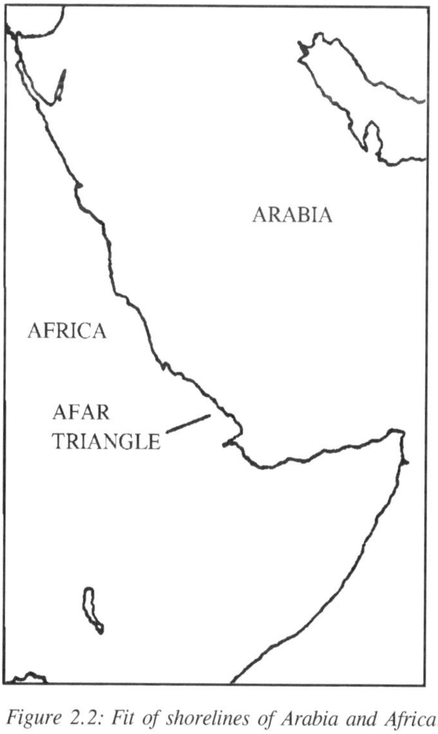

Figure 2.2: Fit of shorelines of Arabia and Africa.

while on each side a plate of the crust moves away as a rigid body, such a fracture is called a transform fault. The earthquakes occur only on the piece of the fracture zone between the two ridge crests, there is no relative motion along the parts outside this section.

If two rigid plates on a sphere are spreading out on each side of a ridge that is crossed by fracture zones, the relative motion of the two plates must be a rotation around some point, termed the pole of spreading. The "axis of spreading," around which the rotation takes place, passes through this pole and the center of the earth.

The existence of a pole of spreading and an axis of spreading is geometrically, necessary, as was shown by Leonhard Euler in the 18th century. If the only motion on the fracture zones is the sliding of the two plates past each other, then the fracture zones must lie alone circles of latitude with respect to the pole of spreading, and the rates of spreading at any point on the ridge must be proportional to the perpendicular distance from the point to the axis of spreading.

All of this is well verified for the spreading that is going on today. The rates of spreading can be obtained from the magnetic patterns and the dates of the reversals. The poles of spreading can be found from the directions of the fracture zones and checked by the direction of earthquake motions. It turns out that the ridge axes and the magnetic pattern are usually almost at right angles to the fracture zones.

This is not a geometrical necessity, but when it does happen it means that the lines of the ridge axes and of the magnetic pattern must, if they are extrapolated, go through the pole of spreading. If the ridge consists of a number of offset section at right angles to the fracture zones, the axes of these sections will converge on the pole of spreading. It is one of the surprises of the work at

sea that this rather simple geometry embraces so large a part of the facts. It seems that marine geology is truly simpler than continental geology and that this is not merely an illusion based on our lesser knowledge of the oceans.

The regularity of the magnetic pattern suggests that the ocean floor can move as a rigid piate over areas several thousand kilometers across. The thickness of the rigid moving plate is quite uncertain, but a value between 70 and 100 kilometers seems likely.

If this is. so, the greater part of the plate will be made of the same material as the upper part of the earth's mantle—probably of peridotite, a rock largely composed of olivine, a silicate of magnesium and iron, $(Mg, Fe)_2 SO_4$. The basaltic rocks; of the oceanic crust will form the upper five kilometer or so of the plate, with a veneer of sediments on top.

What happens at the boundary of an ocean and a continent ? Sometimes, as in the South Atlantic, nothing happens, there are no earthquakes, on distortion, nothing to indicate relative motion between the sea floor and the bordering continent.

The continent can then be regarded as part of the same plate as the adjacent ocean floor, the rocks of the continental crust evidently ride on top of the plate and move with it. In other places there is another kind of cost, what Eduard Suess called "*a Pacific coast.*" Such a coast is typified by the Pacific coast of South America.

Here the oceanic plate dives under the continent and goes down at an angle of about 45 degrees. On the upper surface of this sloping plate there are numerous earthquakes—quite shallow ones near the coast and others as deep as 700 kilometers inland, under the continent.

The evidence for the sinking plate has been beautifully confirmed by the discovery that seismic waves from shallow earthquakes and explosions, occurring near the place where the plate starts its dive, travel faster down the plate than they do in other directors. This is expected because the plate is relatively cold, whereas the upper mantle, into which the plate is sinking, is made of similar material but is hot.

Little is known of the detailed behavior of the plate, further study is vital for an understanding of the phenomena along the edges of continents. Near the point where the plate turns down there is an ocean deep, whose mode of formation is not precisely understood, but if a plate goes down, it is not difficult to imagine ways in which it could leave a depression in the sea floor.

It is probable that, as the plate goes down, soma of the sediment on its surface is scraped off and piled up in a jumbled mass on the landward side of the ocean deep. This sediment may later be incorporated in the mountain range that usually appears on the edge of the continent. The mountain range bordering the continent commonly has a row of volcanoes, as in the Andes.

The lavas from the volcanoes are frequently composed of andesites, which are different from the lavas of the mid ocean ridges in that they contain more silica. It may reasonably be supposed that they are formed by the partial malting of the descending plate at a depth of about 150 kilometers.

The first material to melt will contain more silica than the remaining material, it is also possible that the melted material is contaminated by granite as it rises to the surface through the continental rocks.

In many places the sinking plate goes down under a chain of islands and not under the continent itself. This happens in the Aleutians, to the south of Indonesia, off the islands of the Tonga group, in the Caribbean and in many other places.

The volcanoes are then on the islands and the deep earthquakes occur under the almost enclosed sea behind the chain or arc of islands, as they do in the Sea of Japan, the Sea of Okhotsk and the Java Sea. The destruction of oceanic crust explains one of the great paradoxes of geology.

There have always been oceans, but the present oceans contain no sediment more than 150 million years old and very little sediment older than 80 million years. The explanation is that the older sediments have been carried away with the plates and are either piled up at the edge of a continent or are carried down with a sinking plate and lost in mantle.

The picture is simple: the greater part of the earth's surface is divided into six plates. These plates move as rigid bodies, new material for them being produced from the upper mantle by lava emerging from the crack along the crest of a mid-ocean ridge. Plates are destroyed at the oceanic trenches by plunging into the mantle, where utimately they are mixed again with the material whence they came.

The scheme is not yet established in all its details Perhaps the greatest uncertainty is in the section of the ridge running south of South Africa, it is not clear how much of this is truly a ridge and a source of new crust and how much is a series of transform faults with only tangential motion.

It is also uncertain whether the American and Eurasian plates meet in Alaska or in Siberia. It appears certain, however, that they do not meet along the Baring Strait. A close look at the system of ridges, fracture zones, trenches and earthquakes reveals many other features of great interest, which can only be mentioned here. The Red Sea and the Gulf of Aden appear to be embryo oceans.

Their floors are truly oceanic, with no continental rocks, along their axes one can find offset lengths of crack joined by fracture zones, and magnetic surveys show the worldwide magnetic pattern but only the most recent parts of it. These seas are being formed by the movement of Africa and Arabia away from each other.

A detailed study of the geology, the topography and the present motion suggests that the separation started 20 million years ago in the

halfway between Africa and India), then the motion is continuing today. This motion may be the cause of the earthquakes of the Himalayas, and it may also be connected with the formation of the mountains and of the deep sediment-filled trough to the south of them.

The exact place where the joint occurs is far from clear and needs study by those with a detailed geological knowledge of northern India. It seems unlikely that all the continents were collected in a single *block* for 4,000 million years and then broke apart and started their wanderings during the past 100 million years.

It is more likely that the processes we see today have always been in action and that all through geologic time there have been moving plates carrying continents. We must expect continents to have split *many* times and formed new oceans and sometimes to have collided and been welded together.

We are only at the beginning of the study of pre-Tertiary events ; anything that can be said is speculation and is to be taken only as an indication of where to look.

It is virtually certain that the Atlantic did not exist 150 million years ago. Long before that, in the Lower Paleozoic, 650 to 400 million years ago, there was an older ocean in which the sediments now in the Caledonian-Hercynian. Appalachian mountains of Europe and North America were laid down.

Perhaps this ocean was closed long before the present Atlantic opened and separated the Appalachian Mountains of eastern North America from their continuation in northwestern Europe.

The Urals, if they are not unique among mountain ranges, are at least exceptional in being situated in the middle of a continent. There is some paleomagnetic evidence that Siberia is a mosaic of fragments that were not originally consiguous; perhaps the Urals were once near the borders of an ocean that divided Siberia from western Russia.

Similarly, it is desirable to ask where the ocean was when Rockies were being formed. A large part of California is moving rapidly northward, and the entire continent has overrun an ocean ridge ; clearly the early Tertiary geography must have been very different from that of the present.

Such questions are for the future and require that the ideas of moving plates be applied by those with a detailed knowledge of the various areas. A history of the oceans does not necessarily require an account of the mechanism behind the observed phenomena. Indeed, no very satisfactory account can be given.

The traditional view, put forward by Arthur Holmes and Felix A. Vening-Meinesz, supposes that the upper mantle behaves as a liquid when it is subjected to small forces for long periods and that differences in temperature under oceans and continents are sufficient to produce convection cells in the mantle-with rising currents under the mid-ocean ridges and sinking ones under the continents.

These hypothetical cells would carry the plates along as on a conveyor belt and would provide the forces needed to produce the split along the ridge. This view may be correct ; it has the advantage that the currents are driven by temperature differences that themselves depend on the position of the continents.

Such a back-coupling can produce complicated and varying motions. On the other hand, the theory is implausible in that convection does not normally happen along lines. It certainly does not happen along lines broken by frequent offsets, as the ridge is.

Also it is difficult to see how the theory applies to the plate between the Mid-Atlantic Ridge and the ridge in the Indian Ocean. This plate is growing on both sides, and since there is no intermediate trench the two ridges must be moving apart. It would be odd if the rising convection currents kept exact pace with them.

An alternative theory is that the sinking part of the plate, which is denser than the hotter sorroundmantle. pulls the rest of the plate after it. Again it is difficult to see how this applies to the ridge in the South Atlantic, where neither the African nor the American plate has a sinking part.

Another possibility is that the sinking plate cools the neighboring mantle and produces convection currents that move the plates. This last theory is attractive because it gives some hope of explaining the almost enclosed seas, such as the Sea of Japan.

These seas a typical oceanic floor except that the floor is overlain by several kilometers of sediment. Their floors have probably been sinking for long periods. It seems possible that a sinking current of cooled mantle material on the upper side of the plate might be the cause of such deep basins.

The enclosed seas are an important feature of the earth's surface and urgently require explanation; in addition to the seas that are developing at present behind island arcs there are a number of older ones of possibly similar origin, such as the Gulf of Mexico, the Black Sea and perhaps the North Sea.

The ideas set out in this attempt at a history of the ocean have developed in the past 10 years. What we have is a sketch of the outlines of a history; a mass of detail needs to be filled in and many major features are quite uncertain. Nonetheless, there is a stage in the development of a theory when it is most attractive to study and easiest to explain, that is while it is, still simple and successful and before too many details and difficulties have been uncovered.

This is the interesting stage at which plate theory now stands. Oceanic geology is in the midst of a revolution. All the data gathered over the past 30 years-the soundings of the deep ocean, the samples and photographs of the bottom, the measurements of heat flow and magnetism-are being reinterpreted according to the concept of continental drift and two new concepts; sea floor spreading and plate tectonics (the notion that the earth's crust consists of plates that are created at one edge and destroyed at the other).

Discoveries are made and interpretations developed so often that the scientific literature cannot keep up with them ; they are reported by preprint and wandering minstrel. At such a time any broad synthesis is likely to be short-lived, yet so many diverse observations can now be fitted into a coherent picture that it seems worthwhile to present it.

Before continental drift, sea-floor spreading and plate tectonics captured the imagination of geologists, most of them conceived the earth's crust as being a fairly stable layer enveloping the earth's fluid mantle and core. The only kind of motion normally perceived in this picture was isostasy the tendency of crustal blocks of float on a plastic man tie.

The horizontal displacement of any geologic feature by as much as 100 kilometers was considered startling. This view is no longer consistent with the geological evidence. Instead each new discovery seems to favor sea-floor spreading, continental drift and plate tectonics. These concepts are described elsewhere in this book.

Here I shall recapitulate them briefly to show how they are related to the actual features of the deep-ocean floor. According to plate tectonics the earth's crust is divided into huge segments afloat on the mantle. When such a plate is in motion on the sphere of the earth, it describes a circle around a point termed the pole of rotation (not to be confused with the entire earth's pole of rotation).

This motion has profound geological effects. When two plates move apart, a fissure called a spreading center opens between them. Through this figure rises the hot, plastic material of the mantle, which solidifies and joins the trailing edge of each plate. Meanwhile the edge of the plate farthest from the spreading center - the leading edge - pushes against another plate.

Where that happens, the leading edge may be deflected downward so that it sinks into a region of soft material called the asthenosphere, 100 kilometers or more below the surface. This process destroys the plate material at the same rate at which it is being created at its trailing edge.

Many of the fissures where plate material is being created are in the middle of the ocean floor, which therefore spreads continuously from a median line. Where the plates float apart, the continents, which are embedded in them, also drift away from one another. The most obvious consequence of this process on the ocean floor is the symmetrical seascape on each side of a spreading center.

As two crustal plates move apart (at a rate of one to 10 centimeters per year), the basaltic material that wells up through the spreading center between them splits down the middle. The upwelling in some way produces a ridge, flanked on each side by deep ocean basins and capped by long hills and mountains that run parallel to the crest.

The flow of heat from the earth's interior is generally high along the crest because dikes of molten rock have been injected at the spreading center. A spreading center may also open under a continent. If it does, it produces a linear deep such as the Red Sea or the Gulf of California.

If it continues to spread, or if the spreading center opens in an existing ocean basin, the same symmetrical seascape is ultimately formed. This symmetry extends to less tangible features of the ocean floor such as the magnetic patterns in the basalt of the slopes on either side of the mid-ocean ridge.

As the plastic material reaches the surface and hardens, it "freezes" into it the direction of the earth's magnetic field. The earth's magnetic field reverses from time to time, and as each band of new material moves outward across the ocean floor it retains a magnetic pattern shared by a corresponding band on the other side of the ridge.

The result is a matching set of parallel bands on both sides. These patterns provide evidence of symmetrical flows and make it possible to date them since they correspond to similar patterns on land that have been reliably dated by other means. The steepness of the mid-ocean ridge is determined by a balance between the rate at which material moves outward from the *spreading* center and the rate at which it sinks as it ages after *solidifying*.

The rate of sinking remains fairly constant throughout the ocean basin, and it seems to depend on the age of the crust. It can be calculated if the age of the oceanic crust (as indicated by the magnetic patterns) is divided into the depth at which a particular section lies.

Such calculations show that the crust sinks about nine centimeters per 1,000 years for the first 10 million years after it forms, 3.3 centimeters per 1,000 years for the next 30 million years, and two centimeters per 1,000 years thereafter. Not all the crust sinks; on the southern Mid-Atlantic Ridge the sea floor has remained at the same level for as long as 20 million years.

The rate at which the sea floor spreads varies from one 10 centimeters per year. Therefore fast spreading builds broad elevations and gentle slopes such as those of the East Pacific Rise. The steep, concave flanks of the Mid-Atlantic Ridge, on the other hand, were formed by slow spreading.

Whether the slopes are steep or gentle, the trailing edge of the plate at the spreading center is about three kilometers higher than the leading edge on the other side of the plate. The reason for this difference in elevation is not known. Heating causes some elevation and cooling some sinking, but the total relief appears much too great to be attributed to thermal expansion.

Cooling might account for the relatively rapid sinking observed during the first 10 million years, but continued sinking remains a puzzle. A decade ago scanty information suggested that the midocean ridge in both the Altantic and Pacific was continuous, with a few branches.

More complete surveys have revealed that crustal plates have ragges edges. Instead of extending unbroken for thousands of kilometers, a mid-ocean ridge at the trailing edges of two crustal plates forms a zigzag line consisting of many short segments connected by *fracture* zones to other *ridges*, trenches, young mountain ranges of crustal sinks. The fracture zones connecting the ridge segments are associated with what are called "*transform*" faults.

They provide important clues to the history of a plate. Because they form some of the edges of the plate, they delineate the circle around its pole of rotation, thereby indicating the direction in which it has been moving.

From what has been said so far it might appear that the spreading centers are fixed and stationary. The constantly repeated splitting of the new crust at the spreading center produces symmetrical continental margin', symmetrical magnetic patterns on the ocean floor, symmetrical ridge flanks and even symmetrical mountain ranges. More often than the spreading center itself moves. Oddly enough such movement gives rise to the same symmetrical geology.

All that is required in order to maintain the symmetry is that the spreading center move at exactly half the rate at which the plates are separating. If it moved faster or slower, the symmetry of the magnetic patterns would be destoyed.

Imagine, for instance, that the plate to the east of a spreading center remains stationary as the plate to the west moves. Since the material welling up through the fissure splits down the middle, half of it adheres to the stationary plate and the other half adheres to the moving plate.

The next flow of material to well up through the split thus appears half the width of the spreading center away from the stationary plate. The flow after that appears a whole width of the spreading center away from the stationary plate, and so on.

In effect the spreading center is migrating away from the stationary plate and following the moving one. If the speed of the spreading center exceeded half the speed of the migrating plate, however, a kind of geological Doppler effect would set in: the bands of the magnetic pattern would be condensed in the direction of the moving plate, and they would be stretched out in the direction of the stationary plate.

It might seem unlikely that the spreading center would maintain its even rate of speed and remain exactly between the two plates. W. Jason Morgan of Princeton University observes, however, that there is no impediment to see motion, provided only that the culprits where it is weakest (which is white split before, at the point where hot dike was originally injected).

A result the spreading center is always actly between two crustal plates where it moves or not. Moving spreading centers account some of the major features of the oct floor. The Chile Rise off the coast South America and the East Pacific are adjacent spreading centers, there is no crustal sink between them and new plate is constantly being on the inside edge of each rise, at the one of the centers must be moving, otherwise the basin between them manifold and thrust upward into a mount ranget or downward into a trench.

Similarly, the Carlsberg Ridge in the Indu Ocean and the Mid-Atlantic Ridge not separated by a crustal sink hence one of them must be moving. A moving center may have create the ancient Darwin Rise on the west edge of the Pacific basin and also modern East Pacific Rise.

As in the ocean of the Carlsberg Ridge and the Midatlantic Ridge, the existence of two spreading centers on opposite sides the ocean with no intervening sink has puzzled geologists. If such centres can move, however, it is posses that the spreading center in the west Pacific merely migrated all the across the basin, leaving behind ridges of the Darwin Rise.

In this one rise could simply have become other. Many other examples exist, Manik Talwani of the Lamont-Dohn Geological Observatory proposes that spreading centers move. As a plate forms at a spreading ceill it consists of two layers of mate an upper "volconic" layer and a and a low "oceanic" one.

Lava and feeder from the mantle form the volcanic lava its rocks are oceanic tholeite (or a morphosed equivalent), which is rich aluminum and poor in potassium. In oceanic layer is also some form of meta material. but its precise composit density and condition are not known.

Farther down the slope of the ridge plate acquires a third layer consisting sediment. The sediment comes from the contents and sifts down on all parts of basin, accumulating to a consider depth. It is mixed with a residue of hard parts of microorganisms that called calcareous ooze.

Below a certain depth (which varies among regions) material dissolves, and only red clay and other resistant components remain. For reasons only partly known the sediment is not uniformly distributed. At the spreading center the newly created crust is is of course bare of sediment, and within 100 kilometers of such a center the calcareous ooze is rarely thick enough to measure.

The ooze accumulates at an average rate of 10 meters for each million years. During which time the plate moves harizontally from 10,000 to 100,000 meters and sinks 100 meters. Where the red clay appears, it accumulates at a rate of less than one meter per million years.

The puzzle deepens when one considers that sediment on oceanic crust older the 20 million years stops increasing in thickness after it sinks to the depth where the calcareous ooze disolves. Indeed, in many places the age of the oldest sediment is about the same as the volcanic layer on which it lies.

It would therefore seem that almost all the deepocean sediment accumulates in narrow zones on the flanks of the mid-ocean ridges. If this correct, it has yet to be explained. The volcanic layer forms mainly at the spreading center.

Volcanoes and vents on the slopes of the mid-ocean ridge contribute a certain amount of oceanic theolite to it. It can be said in general that the thickness of the volcanice layer decreases as the spreading rate increases. If the crust spreads solwly, the material has time to accumulation.

Easy spreading reduces this time and therefore the accumulaion. The conclusion can be drawn that the rate at which the volcanic-layer material is discharged is nearly constant. These relations are based on only 10 observations, but they apply to 12 centimeters per year, and to thicknesses from 8 kilometer to 3.8 kilometers.

The total flow of volcanic material from all active spreading centres is about four cubic kilometers per year—four times the flow on the continents. Not the slightest sign of this volcanism on the ocean bottom can be detected at the surface of the ocean, with one possible exception: late in the 19th century a ship reported seeing smoke rising from the waters above the equatorial Mid-Atlantic Ridge.

The British oceanographer Sir John Murray remarked that he hoped the smoke signified the emergence of an island, since the Koyal Navy needed a coaling station at that point.

Like the volcanic layer, the oceanic layer forms, at the spreading center. Acoustical measurements of the thickness of this layer at spreading centers, on the flanks of midocean ridges and on the deep-ocean floor show, however, that at least part of the oceanic layer evolves slowly from the mantle rather than solidifying quickly and completely at the spreading center.

At the spreading center the thickness of the layer depends on how fast the ocean floor moves. In regions such as the South Atlantic, where the floor spreads at a rate of two centimeters per year, no oceanic layer forms within a few hundkilometers of the spreading centre.

Farther away from the spreading center the oceanic layer accumulates rapidly, reaching a normal thickness of four to five kilometers on the flank of of the mid-ocean ridge. A spreading rate of three centimeters per year is associated with an oceanic layer roughly two kilometers deep at the center that thickness by one kilometer in 13 million years.

A plate with a spreading rate of eight centimeters per year is three kilometers deep at the center and thickens by one kilometer in 20 million years. Thus the thinner the initial crust is, the faster the thickness increases as the crust spreads.

As a plate flows continuously from the spreading center, faulting, volcanic eruptions and lava flows along the length of the mid-ocean ridge builds its mountains and escarpments. This process can be most easily observed in Iceland, a part of the Mid-Atlantic Ridge that has grown so rapidly it has emerged from the ocean.

A central rift, 45 kilometers wide at its northern end, cuts the island parallel to the ridge. The sides of the rift consist of active, steplike faults. There are other step faults on the rift floor, which is otherwise dominated by a large number of longitudinal fissures. Some of these fissures are open and filled with dikes.

Fluid lava well wells up from the fissures and either buaies the surrounding mountains. valleys and foults or forms long, low "shield" volcanoes. Two hundred such young volcadoes, which have been erupting about one every five years over the past 1,000 years, dot the floor of she rift. Thirty of them are currently active.

Just as a balance between spreading and sinking shapes of the midocean ridges, so does a balance between lava discharge and spreading build undersea mountains, hills and valleys. High where spreading proceeds at two to 3.5 centimeters per year. In contrast, a spreading center that opens at a rate of five to 12 centimeters per year produces long hills less than 500 meters high.

This relationship is a natural consequence of the longterm constancy of the lava discharge. Over a short period of time, however, the lava discharge I may fluctuate or pulsate, a picture suggested by the fact that the thick volcanic layer associated with slow spreading can consist of volcanic mountains (which represent copious flow) separated by volleys covered by valleys covered by a thinner volcanic layer.

The volcanic activity and faulting that first appear near the spreading centers decrease rapidly as the plate ages and material moves toward its center, but volcanic in some form is never entirely absent. Small conical volcanoes are found on crust only a few hundred thousand years old near spreading centers, and active circular volcanoes such as those of Hawaii exist even in the middle of a plate.

It would appear that the great cracks that serve as conduits for dikes and lava flows are soon sealed as a plate ages and spreads, Volcanic activity is then concentrated in a few central vents, created at different times and places.

Many of these vents remain open for tens of millions of years, judging by the size and distribution of the different classes of marine volcanoes. First, the biggest volcanoes are increasingly big at greater distances from a spreading center, which means they must continue to erupt and grow as the crust ages and sinks, even when the age of the crust exceeds 10 million years.

In most places, in fact, a volcano needs at least 10 million years in order to grow large enough to become an island. Volcanoes that discharge lava at a rate lower than 100 cubic kilometers per million years never become islands because the sea floor sinks too fast for them to reach the sea surface. Other volcanoes drifting with a spreading ocean floor may remain active or become active on crust that is 100 million years old (as the volcanoes of the Canary Islands have).

Normally, volcanoes become inactive by the time the crust is 20 to 30 million years old. This is demonstrated by the existence of guyots, drowned ancient island volcanoes that were submerged by the gradual sinking of the aging crust, Guyots are found almost entirely on crust that is more than 30 million years old, such as the floor of the western equatorial Pacific.

Traditionally it has been thought that marine volcanoes spew lava from a magma chamber located deep in the mantle. Some volcanoes have a top composed of alkali basalt, slopes with transitional basalt outcrops and a base of oceanic thocilite, and it was therefore assumed that the lava in the magma chamber became differentiated into components that, rather like pousse-cafe, separated into several layers of different kinds of material, each of which followed the layer above it up the spout.

The emergence of plate tectonics and continental drift as respectable concepts have now brought this view of volcanic action into question. It remains perfectly possible for a volcano to drift for tens of millions of years over hundreds of kilometers while tapping a single magma chamber embedded deep in the mantle.

The motion of the plates, however, suggests another hypothesis. According to this view, the volcano and its conduit drift along with the crust as the conduit continually taps different parts of a relatively magma that is ready to yield various kinds of lava whenever a conduit appears.

In actuality the composition of the lava usually changes only slightly after the first 10 to 20 kilometers of drifting. Although the older hypothesis is still reasonable, the newer one must also be considered because it explains the facts equally well.

In addition to their characteristic volcanoes and mountains, spreading centers are marked by median valleys, which in places such as the North Atlantic or the northwestern Indian Ocean are deeper than the surrounding region. These rifts are commonly found in centers opening at a rate of two to five centimeters per year.

The deepest rifts, which may go as deep as 1,000 to 1,3000 meters below the surrounding floor, are associated with spreading at three to four centimeters per year. Only one valley is known to be associated with spreading at 5 to 12 centimeters per year.

Although rifts are found in all spreading centers, they usually do appear in conjunction with a slow center. Both of these features are also associated with volcanic activity.

The mid-ocean ridges, as we have noted, seldom run unbroken for more than a few hundred kilometers. They are interrupted by fracture zones, and the segments are shifted out of line with respect to one another. These fracture zones run at ridge and connect the segments. Where they lie between the segments they are termed ridge-ridge transform faults, which are the site of intense geological activity.

As the two edges of the fault side past each other they rub and produce earthquakes. The slope of a transform fault drops steeply from the crest of one ridge segment to a point halfway between it and then climbs to the top of the adjacent segment, reflecting the fact that the crust is elevated at the spreading center and subsides at some distance from it.

Like spreading centers, fracture zones have their own complex geology. In these areas the ridges stand as much as several kilometers high, and the troughs are equally deep. It appears that the same volcanic forces that shape the main ridges produce-the mountains and valleys of the faults.

As fracture zones open they slowly leak lava from hot dikes. At the same time the crust sinks away from the fault, line, and this balance produces high mountains. Beyond the spreading centers the fracture zones become the inactive remains of the earlier faulting.

The different rates at which these outer flanks of the mid-ocean ridge sink do produce some vertical motion as the scarps of the fracture zone decay. This may account for the few earthquakes in these areas. I should emphasize that it is not known if horizontal motiod is also absent from such dead fracture zones.

It is not necessary, however, to postulate such motion in order to explain existing observations. A fracture zone can become active again at any time, but if it does so, it becomes the side of a smaller new plate rather than part of the trailing edge of an old one. If the flank facture zones are as quiescent as they appear to be, then the plates forming the earth's crust are large and long-lived. If these fracture zones were active, on the other hand, it could only be concluded that each one marked the flank of a small, elongated plate.

The direction the plate is moving can be deduced from the magnetic pattern that runs at right angles to the fractures in the fracture zone. When the direction of plate motion changes, the direction in which the fracture zone moves also hanges.

This change in direction can be most clearly seen in the northeastern Pacific, where our knowledge is most detailed. On this part of the ocean floor the changes of direction have taken place at the same time in many zones, indicating that the entire North Pacific plate has changed direction as a unit. On the bottom of the Pacific and the North Atlantic the magnetic patterns are sometimes garbled.

Old transform faults may have vanished if short segments of spreading center have been united by reorientation. By the same token new transform faults may have formed if the change in plate motion has been too rapid to be accommodated by existing motions.

Thus fracture zones may be discontinuous. They may start and stop abtruptly, and the offset of the magnetic patterns may change from place to place along them without indicating any activity except at the former edges of plates. Some patterns are even harder to interpret, Douglas J. Elvers and his colleagues in U.S. Coast and Geodetic Survey discovered an abrupt boomerang shaped bend in the magnetic pattern south of the Aleutians.

The arms of this configuration, which Elvers calls the Great Magnetic Bight, are offset by fracture zones at right angles to the magnetic pattern. The Great Magnetic Bight seems to have required impossible forms of seafloor spreading and plate movement. However, Walter C. Pitman III and Dennis E. Hayes of the Lamont-Doherty Geological Observatory, among others, have been able to show that the configuration is fully understandable if it is assumed that the trailing edges of three plates met and formed a Y.

Similar complex patterns have now been found in the Atlanic and the Pacific. Indeed, if the transform faults are perpendicular to the spreading centers and two spreading rates are known, both the spreading rate of the third spreading center can be calculated even before it is mapped. One can also calculate the orientation and spreading rate for a third center that has already vanished In a trench.

As a crustal plate grows, its leading edge is destroyed at an equal rate. Sometimes this edge slides under the oncoming edge of another plate and returns to the asthenosphere. When this happens. a deep trench such as the Mariana Trench and the Tonga Trench in the Pacific is formed.

In other areas the movement of the creates young mountain ranges. Xavier Le Pichon of the Lamont-Geological Observatory concludes that the occurrence of one event or the other is a function of the rate at which plates are moving together.

If the rate is less than five to six centimeters per year, the crust can absorb the compression and buckles up into large mountain ranges such as the Himalayas. In these ranges folding and overthrusting deform and shorten the crust.

If the rate is higher, the plate breaks free and sinks into the mantle, creating an oceanic trench in which the topography and surface structure indicate tension. Several crustal sinks are no longer active. Their past, however, can be deduced from their geology.

Large-scale folding and thrust-faulting can be taken as evidence of the former presence of a crustal sink, although such deformation can also arise in other ways. Certain types of rock may also indicate the formation of a trench. The arcs of islands that lie parallel to trenches, for instance, are characterized by volcanoes that produce andesitic lavas, which are quite different from the basaltic lavas of the ocean floor.

The trenches themselves, and the deep-sea floor in general, are featured by deposits of graywackes and cherts. These rocks are commonly found exposed on land in the thick prisms of sediment that lie in geosynclines: large depressed regions created by horizontal forces resembling those generated by a drifting crustal plate.

Thus the presence of some or all of these types of rock may indicate the former existence of a crustal sink. This linking of marine geology at spreading centers with land geology at crustal sinks is becoming one of the most fruitful aspects of plate tectonics. Still, crustal sinks are by no means as informative about the history of the ocean floor as spreading centers are because in such sinks much of the evidence of past events is destroyed.

Even if the leading edge of a plate was once the side of a plate (or vice-versa), there would be no way to tell them apart. At the boundary between the land and the sea a presents itself. The sides of an oceanic trench move together at more than five centimeters per year, and it would seem that the sediment sliding into the bottom of the trench should be folded into pronounced ridges and valleys.

Yet virtually undeformed sediments have been mapped in trenches by David William School and his colleagues at the U.S. Naval Electronics Laboratory Center. Furthermore, the enormous quantity of deepocean sediment that has presumably been swept up to the margins of trenches cannot be detected on sub-bottom profiling records.

There are many ingenious (but unpublished) explanations of the phenomenon in terms of plate tectonics. One of them may conceivably be correct. According to that hypothesis, the sediments are intricately folded in such a way that the slopes and walls of trenches cannot be detected by normal survey techniques, which look at the sediments from the ocean surface and along profiles perpendicular to the slopes.

This kind of folding could be detected only by trawling a recording instrument across the trench much closer to the bottom or by crossing the slope at an acute angle. The concepts of sea-floor spreading and plate tectonics allow a quantitative evaluation of the interactions of many important variables in marine geology.

By combining empirical observation with theory it is possible not only to explain but also to predict the thickness and age of sediments in a given locality, the scale and orientation of topographic relief, the thickness of various crustal layers, the orientation and offsetting of magnetic patterns, the distribution and depth of drowned ancient islands, the occurrence of trenches and young mountain ranges, the characteristics of earthquakes, and many other previously unrelated and unpredictable phenomena.

This revolution in marine geology make some years to run its course. Ideas are changing, and new puzzles present themselves even as the old ones are solved. The only certainty is that the subject will never be the same again.

3

The Atmosphere of the Ocean

The atmosphere drives the great ocean circulations and strongly affects the properties of seawater; to a large extent the atmosphere in turn owes its nature to and derives its energy from the ocean. Indeed, there are few atmospheric phenomena for which the ocean is unimportant.

It is therefore hard to know where to start a discussion of the interactions of the atmosphere and the ocean, since in a way everything depends on everything else. One must break into this circle samewhere, and arbitrarily I shall begin by considering some of the effects of wind on ocean water.

When wind blows over water, it exerts a force on the surface in the direction of the wind. The mechanism by which it does so is rather complex and is far from being completely understood, but that it does it is beyond dispute. The ocean's response to this force is immensely complicated by a number factors.

The fact that the earth is rotating is of overriding importance. The presence of continental barriers across the natural directions of flow of the ocean complicates matters further. Finally there is the fact that water is a fluid, not a solid.

To simplify the picture somewhat, let us start by looking at what would happen to a slab of material resting on the surface of the earth. Let us further assume that the slab can move without friction. Consider the result of a sharp, brief impulse that sets the slab moving, say, due north Looked at by an observed rotating earth, any moving object is subject to a "*Coriolis acceleration*" directed exactly at a right angle to its motion.

The magnitude of the acceleration increases with both the speed of the object's motion and the vertical component of the earth's rotation, and in the *Northern Hemisphere* it is directed to the right of the motion. An acceleration at right angles to the velocity is just what is required to cause motion in a circle, and in the illustrate the center of the circle is due east of the original position of the original position of the *slab*.

A circular motion of this kind is called an inertial oscillation, and something of this nature may sometimes happen in the *ocean*, since inertial *oscillations* are frequently found when careful *observation* are made with current meters.

An inertial oscillation requires exactly half a pendulum day for a full circle. (A pendulum day is the time required for a complete revolution of a Foucault pendulum. Like a Coriolis effect, it depends on the vertical component of the earth's rotation and therefore varies with latitude, being just under 24 hours at the poles and increasing to several days close to the Equator.

To be precise, it is one sidereal-or star time-day divided by the sine of the latitude.) If there were a small amount of friction, the slab would gradually spiral to the center of the circle. Pushing it toward the north thus causes it to end up displaced to the east.

More generally, in the Northern Hemisphere particle is moved to the right of the direction in which it is impelled, and in the Sothern Hemisphere it is moved to the left. Let us turn to what happens to our frictionless slab if, instead of giving it a short impulse, we give it a steady thrust. Again assume that the force is toward the north.

Under the influence of this force the slab accelerates toward the north, but as soon as it starts to move it comes under the influence of the Coriolis effect and its motion is deflected (in the Northern Hemisphere) to the right-to the cast. As long as the slab has at least some component of velocity toward the north the force will continue to add energy to it and its speed will continue to increase.

After a quarter of a pendulum day, however, it will be moving due east. In this position the applied force (which is to the north) is pushing at a right angle to the velocity (east), opposing the influence of the Coriolis effect, which is now trying to turn the slab toward the south. If there has been no loss of energy because of friction, the slab is moving fast enough so that the Coriolis effect dominates, and it turns toward the south. Now there is a component of velocity opposing the applied force, which acts as a brake and takes energy from the motion.

At the end of half a pendulum day the process has gone far enough to bring the slab to a full stop, at which point it is directly east of its staving point. If is directly east of its starting point. If the force continues, it will again accelerate toward the north and the entire process is repeated, so that the slab performs a series of these looping (cycloidal) motions, each loop taking half a pendulum day to execute.

Overall, then, a steady force on a frictionless body resting on a rotating earth causes it to move at right angles to the direction of the force. What is happening is that the force is balanced-on the average-by the Coriolis effect. Now let us look at the situation when there is a certain amount of friction between the slab and the underlying surface.

Any frictional drag reduces the speed attained by the slab, reducing the Coriolis effect until it is no longer entirely able to overcome the driving force. As a result if the force is toward the north, the slab will move in a more or less northeasterly direction-more northerly if the friction is large, more easterly if it is small. A body of water acts much like a set of such slabs, one on top of the other.

Each slab to move largely independently of the others except for the frictional forces among them. If the top slab is pushed by the the wind, it will, in the Northern Hemisphere, move in a direction somewhat to the right of the wind. It will exert a frictional force on the second slab down, which will then be set in motion in a direction still farther to the right.

At each successive stage the force is somewhat reduced, so that not only does the direction change but also the speed is a bit less. A succession of such effects produces velocities for which the direction spirals as the depth increases. It is known as the Ekman spiral, after the pioneering Swedish oceanographer V. Walfrid Ekman, who first discussed it soon after the beginning of the century.

At a certain depth both the current and the frictional forces associated with it become negligibly small. The entire layer above that depth, in which friction is important, is termed the Ekman layer. Since there is negligible friction between the Ekman layer and the water lying under it, the Ekman layer as a whole behaves like the frictionless slab discussed above; its average velocity must be at a right angle to the wind.

The frictional mechanism, which involves turbulence, has proved to be extraordinarily difficult to study either theoretically or through observations, and surprisingly little is known about it. The surface flow does appear to be somewhat to the right of the wind.

Primitive theoretical calculation should be 45 degrees from the wind, but this theory is certainly inapplicable in detail. More complicated theoretical models have been attempted, but since almost nothing is known of the nature of turbulence in the presence of a free surface these models rest on weak ground.

An educated guess, supported by rather flimsy observational evidence, suggests that the angle is much smaller, perhaps nearer to 10 degrees. All that seems fairly certain is that the average *flow* in the Ekman layer must be at a right angle to the wind and that there must be some kind of spiral in the current directions.

We also believe the bottom of the Ekman layer lies 100 meters or so deep, within a factor of two or three. Of the details of the spiral, and of the turbulent mechanisms that determine its nature, we know very little indeed.

The Ekman layer *flow* has some important fairly direct effects in several parts of the world. Example, along the coasts of California and Peru the presence of coastal mountains tends to deflect the low-level winds so that they blow parallel to the coast.

Typically, in each case, they below toward the Equator, and so the average Ekman *flow* to the right off California and to the left off Peru-is offshore. As the surface water is swept away deeper water wells up to replace it. The upwelling water is significantly colder than the sun-warmed surface waters, somewhat to the discomfort of swimmers (and, since it is also well fertilized compared with the surface water, to the advantage of fishermen and birds).

The total amount of flow in the directly driven Ekman layer rarely exceeds a couple of tons per second across each meter of surface. That represents a substantial flow of water, but it is much lass than the flow in major ocean currents.

These are driven in a different way—also by the wind, but indirectly. To see how this works let us take a look at the North Atlantic The winds over this ocean, although they vary a good deal from time to time, have a most persistent characteristic: near 45 degrees north latitude or the re-abouts the westerlies blow strongly from west to east, and at about 15 degress the northeast trades blow, with a marked east-to-west component.

The induced Ekman now is to the right in each case, so that in both cases the water is pushed toward the region known as the Sorgasso Sea, with its center 30 degrees north. This "gathering together of the waters" leads not so much to a piling up (the surface level is only about a meter higher at the center than at the edges) as a pushing down. If it were not for the continental boundaries, the piling up would be much more important.

Because water tends to seek a level, the piled-up water would push north above 30 degrees and south below: the pushing force, like any other force in the Northern Hemisphere,, would cause a flow to its right, so that in the northern part of the ocean a strong eastward flow would develop and in the southern part a strong westward one.

On the earth as it now exists, however, these east-west flows are blocked by the continents; only in the Southern Ocean, around the Antarctic Continent, is such a flow somewhat free. In the absences of the continents the oceans, like the atmosphere, would be dominated by east-west motion.

As it is, only a residue of such motion is possible, and it is the pushing dawn rather than the piling up of water that is important. The downward thrust of the surface waters presses dawn an the layers of water underneath Far practical purposes water is incompressible, so that pushing it down from the tap farces it out at the aides.

It muse be remembered that this body of underlying water is rotating with the earth. As it is squeezed out laterally its radius of gyration, and therefore its moment of inertia, increase, and so its rate radius of gyration, and therefore its moment of inertia, increase, and so its rate of rotation muse slaw.

If it sows, however, the rotation no longer "fits" the rotation of the underlying earth. There are two possible consequences: either the water can rotate with respect to the earth or it can move to a different latitude where its newly acquired rotation will fit.

It usually does the latter. Hence a body of water whose rotation has been sowed by being squashed vertically will usually move toward the Equator, where the vertical component of the earth's rotation is smaller; an the other hand, a body whose rotation has been speeded by being bulged up to replace water that has been swept away from the surface will usually move toward the pales.

In the band of water a couple of thousand miles wide along latitude 30 degrees this indirectly wind-driven flaw moves water toward the Equator. Of course the regions of the ocean closer to the pales do not became empty of water; somewhere there must be a return flaw.

The returning water muse also attain a rotation that fits the rotation of the underlying earth, it muse gain counterclockwise rotation (or lose clockwise rotation). It does this by running in a strong current an the westward side of the ocean, changing its rotation by "rubbing its left shoulder" against the share.

The Gulf Stream is such a current; it is the return flow of water that we squeezed south by the wind-driven convergence of surface waters throughout the entire central North Atlantic. Mast great ocean currents seem to be indirectly driven in this way.

It is worth noting that these return currents muse be an the western side of the oceans (that is, off the eastern coasts of the land) in bath hemispheres and regardless of where the flaw is northward or southward. The reason is that the earth's angular velocity of rotation is maximum counterclockwise to an observer looking dawn at the North Pale and maximum clockwise at the South Pale.

Any south-flawidg return current in either hemisphere muse gain clockwise rotation (or lose counterclockwise rotation) if it is to fit when it arrives. It gains this rotation by friction an its right side, and so it muse keep to the right-that is, to the west-of the ocean.

On the other hand, a north-flowing return current muse keep to the leftagain the west. This description of the general winddriven circulation accords reasonably well with observations of the long-term charateristics of the ocean circulation.

What happens an a shorter term, in response to changes of the atmospheric circulation and the wind-farce pattern that results ? The characteristic time constant of the Ekman layer is half a pendulum day, and there is every reason to believe this layer adjusts itself within a day or so to changes in the wind field.

The indirectly driven flaw is much harder to deal with. Its time constant is of the order of years, and we have no clear understanding of haw it adjusts; the indirectly driven circulation may still be responding, in ways that are not clear, far years after an atmospheric change.

So far the discussion has been qualitative. To make it quantitative we need to know two things; the nature of the wind aver the ocean at each time and place and the amount of farce, the wind exerts an the surface. Meteorologists are getting better at the first question, although there are same important gaps in our detailed information, notably in the Southern Ocean and in the South Pacific.

Investigation of the second problem, that of the quantitative relation between the wind flaw and the farce an the surface, is becoming a scientific discipline in its own right. Turbulent flaw aver a boundary is a complex phenomenon far which there is no really complete theory even in simple laboratory cases.

Nevertheless, a great deal of experimental data has been collected an flaws aver solid surfaces, bath in the laboratory and in nature, so that from an engineering point of view at least the situation is fairly well understood. The force exerted on a surface varies with the roughness of that surface approximately with the square of the wind speed at some fixed height above it.

A wind of 10 meters per second (about 20 knots, or 22 miles per hour) measured at a height of 10 meters will produce a force of some 30 tons per square kilometer on a field of mown grass or of about 70 tons per square kilometer on a ripe wheat field. On a really smooth surface such as glass the force is only about 10 tons per square kilometer.

When the wind blows over water, the whole thing is much more complicated. The roughness of the water is not a given characteristic of the surface but depends on the wind itself. Not only that, the elements that constitute the roughness-the waves-themselves move more or less in the direction of the wind.

Recent evidence indicates that a large portion o f the momentum transferred from the air into the water goes into waves rather than directly into making currents in the water; only as the waves break, or otherwise dose energy, does their momentum become available to generated currents or produce Ekman layers.

Waves carry a substantia amount of both energy and momentum (typically about as much as is carried by the wind in a layer about one wavelength thick), and so the wavegeneration process is far from negligible. So far we have no theory that accounts in detail for what we observe.

A violently wavy surface belies its appearance by acting, as far as the wind is concerned as though it were very smooth. At 10 meters per second, recent measurements seem to agree, the force on the surface is quite a dot less than the force over mown grass and scarcely more than it is over glass; some observations in light winds of two or three meters per second indicate that the force on the wavy surface is less than it is on a surface as smooth as glass.

In some way the motion of the waves seems to modify the airflow so that air slips over the surface even more freely than it would without the waves. This seems not to he the case at higher wind speeds, above about five meters per second, but the force remains strikingly low compared with that over other natural surfaces. One serious deficiency is the fact that there arc no direct observations at all in those important cases in which the wind speed is greater than about 12 meters per second and has had time and fetch (the distance over water) enough to raise substantial waves. (A wind of even 20 meters per second can raise waves eight or 10 meters high-as high as a three-story building. Making observations under such circumstances with the dedicate instruments required is such a formidable task that it is little wonder none have been reported.)

Some indirect studies have been made by measuring how water piles up against the shore when driven by the wind, but there arc many difficulties and uncertainties in the interpretation of such measurements. Such as they are, they indicate that the apparent roughness of the surface increases somewhat under high-wind conditions, so that the force on the surface increases rather more rapidly than as the square of the wind speed.

Assuming that the force increases at least as the square of the wind speed, it is evident that highwind conditions produce effects far more important than their frequency of occurrence would suggest. Five hours of 60-knot storm winds will put more momentum into the water than a week of 10-knot breezes.

If it should be shown that for high winds the force on on the surface increases appreciably more rapidly than as the square of momentum to the ocean will turn out to be dominated by what happens during the decisional storm rather than by the long-term average winds.

It is tempting to try to infer high-wind behavior from what we know about dower wind speeds. Certainly the shapes of wavy surfaces appear nearly the same notwithstanding the size of the waves-as long as one disregards waves less than about five centimeters long, which are strongly affected by surface tension.

Yet, curious as it may seem, the only thing that makes one wind-driven wave field different in any fundamental way from another is surface tension, even though it directly affects only these very short waves.

Indeed, surface tension is the basis of the entire Bcaufort wind scale, which depends on the number and nature of whitecaps; only the fact that the surface tension is better able to hold the surface together at low wind speeds than at high speeds enables us to see a qualitative difference in the nature of the sea surface of different wind speeds.

Otherwise the waves would look just the same except for a

difference in scale. If we were sure we cold ignore surface-tension effects, then we could calculate the force the wind would exert at high wind speeds on the basis of data obtained at lower speeds, but one should be extremely cautious about such calculations, at least until some confirming measurements are available.

Whereas the ocean seems primarily to be driven by surface forces, the atmosphere is a neat engine that makes use of heat received from the sun to develop the mechanical energy of its motion. Any neat engine functions by accepting thermal energy at a comparatively high temperature, discharging some of this thermal energy at a lower temperature and transforming the rest into mechanical energy.

The atmosphere does this by absorbing energy at or near its base and radiating it away from much cooler high levels. A substantial proportion of the required heating from below comes from the ocean. The energy comes in two forms.

If cooler air blows over warmer water, there is a direct neat flow into the air. What is usually more important, though, is the vaporation of water from the surface into the air. Evaporation causes cooling, that is, it removes neat, in this case from the surface of the water.

When the moisture-laden air is carried to a high altitude, where expansion under reduced atmospheric pressure causes it to cool, the water vapor may vapor may recondense into water droplets and the neat that was given up by the surface of the water is transferred to the air. If the cloud that is formed evaporates again, as it sometimes does, the atmosphere gains no net thermal energy.

If the water falls to the surface as rain or snow, however, then there has been a net gain and it is available to drive the atmosphere. Typically the heat gained by the atmosphere through this evaporation-condensation process is considerably more than the neat gained by direct thermal transfer through the surface.

Virtually everywhere on the surface of the ocean, averaged over a year, the ocean is a net source of neat to the atmosphere. In some areas the effect is much more marked than in others. For example, some of the most important return currents, such as the Gulf Stream in the western Atlantic and the Kuroshio Current in the wester Pacific off Japan, contain very warm water and move so rapidly that the water has not cooled even when it arrives far north of the tropical and subtropical regions where it gained its high temperature.

At these northern latitudes the characteristic wind direction is from the west, off the continent. In winter, when the continents are cold, air blowing from them onto this abnormally warm water receives great quantities of neat, both by direct quantities of neat, both by direct thermal transfer and in the form of water vapour.

The transfer of neat and water vapor depends on a disequilibrium at the interface of the water and the air. Within a millimeter or so of the water the air temperature is not much different from that of the surface water, and the air is nearly saturated with water vapor.

The small differences are nevertheless crucial, and the lack of equilibrium is maintained by by the mixing of air near the surface with air at higher levels, which is typically appreciably cooler and lower in water vapour content.

The mixing mechanism is a turbulent one, the turbulence gaining its energy from the wind. The higher the wind speed is, the more vigorous the turbulence is and therefore the higher the rates of beat and moisture transfer are. These rates tend to increase linearly with the wind speed, but even less is known about the details of this phenomenon than about the wind force on water.

When the wind makes waves, it must transfer not only momentum but also important amounts of energy-that is not available to provide the turbulence needed to produce the mixing that would effect the transfer of neat and water vapors.

At fairly high wind speeds another phenomenon arises ;hat may be of considerable importance. I mentioned that when surface tension is no longer able to hold the water surface together at high wind speeds, spray droplets blow off the top of the waves.

Some of these drops fall back to the surface, but other evaporate and in doing so supply water vapor to the air. They have another important role. The tiny residues of salt that are left over when the droplets of seawater evaporate are small enough and light enough to be carried upward by the turbulent air.

They act as nuclei on which condensation may take place, and so they play a role in returning to the atmosphere the heat that is lost in the evaporation process.

The ocean's great effect on climate is illustrated by a comparison of the temperature ranges in three Canadian cities, all at about the same latitude but with very different climates. Victoria is a port on the southern tip of Vancouver Island, on the eastern shore of the Pacific Ocean; Winnipeg is in the middle of the North American land mass; St. John's is on the island of Newfoundland, jutting into the western Atlantic.

The most striking climatic difference among the three is the enormous temperature range at Winnipeg compared with the two coastal cities. The range at St. John's, although much less, is still greater than at Victoria, probably because at St. John's the air usually blows from the direction of the continent and the effect of the water is somewhat less dominant than at Victoria, which typically receives its air directly from the ocean.

St. John's is colder than Victoria because it is surrounded by cold water of the Labrador Current. The influence of the ocean is associated with its enormous thermal capacity. Every day, on the average, the earth absorbs from the sun and rcradiatcs into space enough heat to raise the temperature of the entire atmosphere nearly two degress Celsius (three degrees Fahrenheit).

Yet the thermal capacity of the atmosphere is equivalent to that of only the top three meters of the ocean, or only a few percent of the 100 meters or so of ocean water that is heated in summer and cooled in winter. The great bulk of ocean water, more than 95 percent of it, is so deep that surface heating does not penetrate, and its temperature is independent of season.

If the ocean lost its entire heat supply for a day but continued to give up heat in a normal way, the temperature of the upper 100 meters would drop by only about a tenth of a degree.

Compared with the land, the ocean beats slowly in summer and cools slowly in winter, so that its temperature is much less variable. Moreover, because air has so much less thermal capacity, when it blows over water it tends to come to the water temperature rather than vice versa.

For these reasons maritime climates are much more equable than continental ones. Although the ocean affects the atmosphere's temperature more than the atmosphere affects the ocean's, the ocean is cooled when it gives up heat to the atmosphere.

The density of ocean water is controlled by two factors, temperature and salinity, and evaporative cooling tends to make the water denser by affecting both factors : it lowers the temperature and, since evaporation removes water but comparatively little salt, it also increases the salinity. If surface water becomes denser than the water underlying it, vigorous vertical connective mixing sets in.

In a few places in the ocean the cooling at the surface can be so intense that the water will sink and mix to great depths, sometimes right to the bottom. Such occurrences are rare both in space and in time, but once cold water has reached great depths it is heated from above very slowly, and so it tends to stay deep for a long time with little change in temperature; there is some evidence of water that has remained cold and deep in the ocean for more than 1,000 years.

With this length of residence e not much of the heavy, cold water needs to be produced every year for it to constitute, as it does, the bulk o f the ocean water. The sinking of water cooled at the surface is one aspect of another important feature of the ocean: the flow induced by differences in density, which is to say the flow induced principally by temperature and salt content.

This thermohaline circulation of the ocean is in addition to the wind-driven circulation discussed earlier. In its thermohaline aspects the ocean itself acts as a heat engine, although it is far less efficient than the atmosphere.

Roughly speaking, the ocean can be divided into two layers a rather thin upper one whose density is comparatively low because it is warmed by the sun, and a thick lower one, a fraction of a percent denser and composed as water only a few degrees above the freezing point that has flowed in from those few areas where it is occasionally created.

Somewhere-either distributed over the ocean or perhaps only locally near the shore. And in other special places-there is mixing between these layers. The mixing is of such a nature that the cold deep water is mixed into the warm upper water rather than the other way around, that is, the cold water is added to the warm from the bottom.

Once the water is in the upper layer its motion is largely governed by the wind-driven circulation, although density differences still play a role. In one way or another some of this surface water arrives at a location and time at which it is cooled sufficiently to sink again and thus complete the circulation.

This picture can be rounded out by consideration of the effects of the earth's rotation, which are in some ways quite surprising. 'The deep water that mixes into the upper layer must have a net upward motion small to measure, only a few meters per year, but we infer its existence indirectly).

To make possible this upward flow there must be a compensating lateral inflow. Remember that on the rotating earth this lateral inflow results in an increase in speed of rotation, and so for it to continue to fit the rotation of the underlying earth the water must move toward the nearest pole; it must flow away from the equatorial regions.

Yet the source of this cold deep water is at high latitudes ! How does it get near the Equator to supply the demand ?

The answer is similar to the one for the wind-driven circulation: The cold water must flow in a western boundary current, in order to gain the proper rotation as it moves. There is some direct evidence of the inferred concentrated western boundary current in the North Atlantic, and there are hints of it in the South Pacific, but most of the rest is based on inference.

There seems to be no source of cold deep water in the North Pacific, so that the deep water there must come from Antarctic regions. We have seen that the atmosphere drives the ocean and that heat supplied from the ocean and that heat supplied from the ocean is largely instrumental in releasing energy for the atmosphere.

There is a great deal of feedback between the two systems. The atmospheric patterns determine the oceanic flows, which in turn influence where—and how much—heat is released to the atmosphere. Further, the atmospheric flow systems determine how much cloud cover there will be over certain parts of the ocean and therefore how-and where-the ocean will be heated.

The system is not a particularly stable one. Every locality has its abnormally cold or mild winters and its abnormally wet or dry summers. The persistence of such anomalies over several months almost certainly involves the ocean, because the characteristic time constants of purely atmospheric phenomena are simply too short.

Longer-term climatological variations such as the "*little ice age*" that lasted for about 40 years near the beginning of the 19th century are even more likely to have involved changes in the ocean's circulation. And then there are the more dramatic events of the great Pleistocene glaciations.

There are any number of theories for these events and, ince experts disagree, it is incumbent on the rest of us to refrain from dogmatic statements. Nevertheless, it does not seem impossible that the ocean-atmosphere system has a number of more or less stable configurations.

That is, there may be a number of different patterns in which the atmosphere can drive the ocean in such a way that the ocean releases heat to the atmosphere in the right quantity and at the right places to allow the pattern to continue.

Of course the atmosphere is extremely turbulent, so that its equilibrium is constantly being disturbed. If the system is stable, then forces must come into play that tend to restore conditions after each such disturbance.

If there are a number of different stable patterns, however, it is possible that a particulary large disturbance might tip the system from one stable condition to another. One can imagine a gambler's die lying on the floor of a truck running over a rough road; the die is stable on any of its six faces, so that in spite of bouncing and vibration the same face usually remains up-until a particularly big bump jars it so that it lands with a different face up, whereupon it is stable in its new position.

It seems not at all impossible that the ocean-atmosphere system behaves something like this, Perhaps in recent years we have been bouncing along with, say, a four showing. Perhaps 200 years ago the die flipped over to three for a moment, then flipped back to four. It could one day jounce over to a snake eye and bring a new ice age !

4

Deep Sea Environment

Contrary to what is often imagined, biology is not a unified science. Marine biologiests will surely agree with Jacob (1974), but whatever their interests, whether physiological, biochemical, ethological, ecological or biogeographical, they know they must endeavour to be more than biologists.

Proper *pursuance* of their studies demands at least some familiarity with correlated knowledge about the physical nature of marine environments. As Pantin (1968) says, *biological sciences* are *unrestricted* and their investigator must be prepared to follow their problems into any other science whatsoever. 'The *cradle* of life on earth is certainly the oceans', and throughout geological time sea water has been a benign medium for very *diverse* forms of plant and animal life.

Since the beginning of *Cambrian* times, about 600 million years ago, Durham (1967) estimates, there have been at least four million and probably as many as ten million species of (preservable) marine organisms. In the modern ocean there are at least 160,000 species of animals, making them nearly twice as numerous as the non-insect forms of animal life on land.

Moreover, certain forms, such as radiolarians, combjellyfishes, lamp-shells, arrow-worms, barnacles, cephalopods, beard-worms, echinoderms and tunicates live only in the sea. *Futaminifera*, *sponges*; cnidarians, bryozoans, sharks and rays are among those that are almost entirely marine.

Like Wordsworth's rocks, stones and trees, the ocean is 'rolled round in earth's diurnal course'. Even more than rocks and stones the ocean endures. 'The obvious thines that no one comments on are often the most remarkable; one of them is the constancy of the total volume of water through the ages.

The level of the sea, of course, has varied from time to time. During the ice ages, when much water was locked up in ice sheets on the continent, the level of the sea was lower than it is at present and the continental shelves of Europe and North America were laid bare. Often the sea has advanced over the coastal plains, but never has it covered all the land or even most of it.

The mechanism of this equilibrium is unknown; it might have been expected that water would be expelled gradually from the interior of the earth and that the seas would grow steadily, or that water would be dissociated into hydrogen and oxygen in the upper atmosphere and that the hydrogen would escape, leading to a gradual drying up of the seas.

These either do not happen or they balance each other. *Bullard* writes above of the fully formed ocean that can be seen through the study of *rocks* and *fossils*. To trace the origin of all this water, or to appreciate why out planet might better be called Ocean rather than Earth, we must first realize that water, air and life (hydrosphere, atmosphere and biosphere are made of elements that are not prevalent in the earth's crust or even in volcanic rocks that have come from deep within the earth.

We are led to study the elements in the entire Solar System and driven to conclude that water was not derived by condensation during the formation of the earth but came from subsequent '*degassing*' inside the newly formed earth. *Relics* of this process are apparent today in the *explosions* of *volcanoes*, for water seems to be part and *parcel* of *molten* rock (*magma*). The *expansion* of water vapour in the fierce heat below

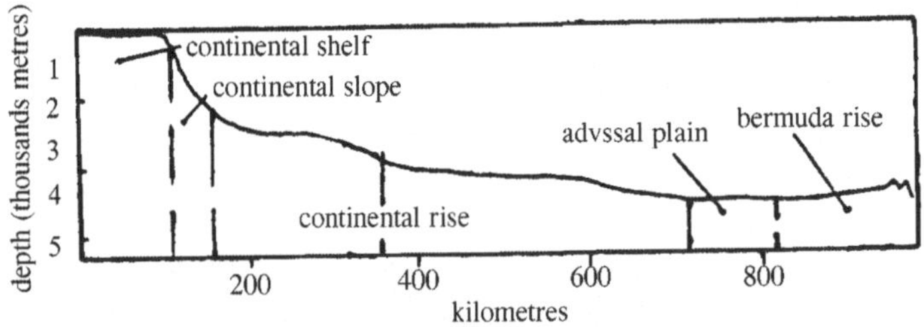

Figure 4.1: Profile or the deep-sea floor off the northeastern United States.

a plugged *volcanic* vent may eventually lead to an *awesome* explosion of steam, rocks and lava.

It seems clear that all or most of the ocean grew from the '*volcanic breath*' of the earth's *mantle*. Indeed, the volcanic bed of the ocean extends over some seven-tenths of the earth's surface. We turn first to the bed then to waters.

The Deep-sea Floor

The configuration of the deep-sea floor is revealed by scrutiny of soundings, and nearly all have been made in the past fifty years. Since the nineteen-twenties, when echo-sounders came into use, a vast and varied, yet orderly topography has been brought into view.

Survey of this submarine Iandscope with *echo-sounders* (and other sound sources) has also helped geologists to reveal the volcanic nature of the crust that bears the ocean. There are three fundamental parts of the ocean floor the continental margins, the ocean basin floors and the *midoceanic* ridge system.

Over most of the earth the continental margin is dapped by a continental shelf, which is the submerged perimeter of the continent, ever subject to marine erosion and sedimentation. The shelf cants gently seaward (gradient about 1 : 1,000) and at depths ranging from 20 to 550 metres (average 133 m) gives way to the steeper gradient (>1 : 40) of the *grandest* escarpments on earth, the continental slopes.

The continental shelves, which are generally supported by sedimentary *strata* or by *igneous* and *metamorphic* rocks, have a mean width of 78 kilometres and underlie 75 per cent of the total expanse of the ocean. Excluding the littoral or intertidal waters, the seas over the shelves form the *neritic* province of the *ocean*: the rest is oceanic province and also the province of this book.

But before leaving the shallow seas, which include the coral seas, it must be said that these waters hold a greater diversity of life and are much more productive than the deep ocean. For instance we know some 12,000 species of marine fishes and about 10,000 live in the shallow seas: the others are deep-sea species.

Over nine-tenths of the world's annual catch of fishes (about 50 million tonnes) consists of species that depend on the most productive waters over the continental *shelves*. By comparison with the riches shelf waters, the deep ocean is a deserted living space.

The continental slope descends to depths near 2,000 metres or more before merging with the gentler gradients (1 : 100-1 : 700) of the

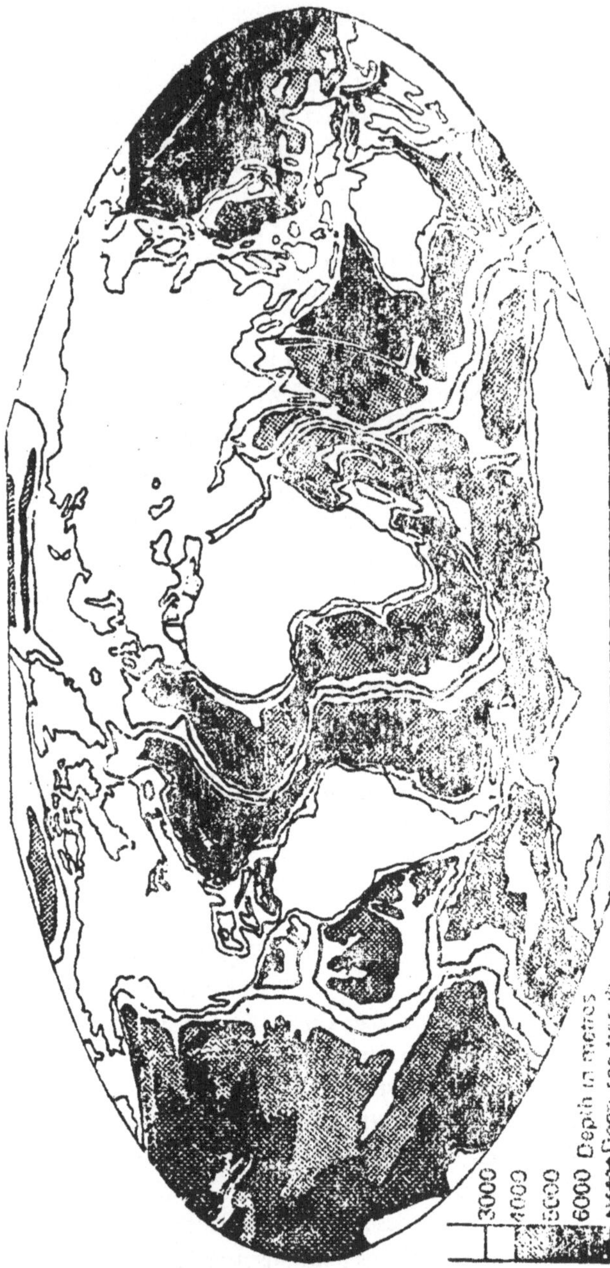

Figure 4.2: General bathymetric chart of the ocean.

continental rise. Off the northeastern United States for instance the transition between continental shelf and slope is about 100 km off shore. At the foot of the continental slopes which is nearly 160 km off shore, the depth is nearly 2,00 metres.

Towards the end of the *continental* rise, which is nearly 650 km from the shore, the depth is about 5,000 metress. This lowest reach of the continental margin averages about 4,000 metres in depth over the ocean. But over fringing areas of the western and northern Pacific Ocean, and off *Chile* and *Peru*, the continental *margin* descends into trenches with depths exceeding 6,000 metres.

Over most of the ocean the continental slopes and rises are covered with terrigenous or hemipelagic muds, mixtures of pelagic ooze and debris weathered from the continents and described as 'a sediment comprised of more than 30 per cent of continentally derived sand and silt grains; it is often green, black or slightly red, due to varying degrees of oxidation of the abundant organic matter'.

More than 50 per cent of the particles forming this sediment are coarser than 30 microns in diameter, and the rate of sedimentation, which is *appreciably* higher than that of any other deep-sea sediment, varies between depths of 5 and 100 centimetres per thousand years.

Nearness to the land and hencc the relatively rich shelf waters has much to do with the high content of organic matter in terrigenous muds, which in turn goes far to being the basis for the relatively great productivity of *bottom-dwelling* life over and on the continental margins.

In particular, the upper reaches of the continental slope are not only near to the land and shelf, but also comparatively near to sources of organic material from dead pelagic organisms. It is not surprising, then, that slopes and upper rises support more abundant populations than most of the deeper parts of the ocean.

Abyssal plains, typically the most level stretches of the deep-sea floor, are also covered and indeed formed by landderived sediments. They lie at the foot of continental rises and are widespread in the Atlantic and Indian Oceans and very extensive oil the continental margin of Antarctica. (Gradients range between 1 : 1,000 and 1 : 10,000.)

The sediments over these plans resemble the sands, silts and gravels recovered from submarine canyons. Submarine canyons such as the Hudson Canyon, the Congo Canyon and the *Ganges Canyon*, fissure the continental slopes throughout the world.

Most are only a few hundred metres deep but some cut 2,000

metres into the slope. All abyssal plains are connected by canyons or other channels to landward sources of sediment and down these fissures run fast *turbidity* currents charged with a great mass of sediment.

This sediment, which contains considerable amounts of organic matter, *spreads* over the plain. *Photographs* taken over the Sohm Abyssal Plain, south of the Great Banks of *Newfoundland* revealed very *muddy* bottom water, and it seems likely that some of the finest grained clays have not settled out from the most recent turbidity current'.

It is to be expected that some abyssal plains should be productive places for *benthic life*. The ocean basin floors include the parts of the deep-sea floor between the continental margins and the major oceanic ridge systems. Apart from the deep-sea trenches the ocean basins form the deepest reaches of the ocean, mostly with depths of 4,000 metres or more.

In the Atlantic Ocean, the main basins are the North American Basin (western North Atlantic), *Canaries* and *Cape Verde Basins* (eastern North Atlantic), *Brazil* and *Argentine* Basins (western South Atlantic), Angola, Cape and Agulhas Basins eastern South Atlantic) and the Atlantic-Antarctic Basin (southern South Atlantic).

More than half the area of these basins extends to depths of 5,000 metres or more, and much the same is true of the major basins of the Indian and Pacific Oceans. In the Northern Pacific Ocean, which is without a midoceanic ridge system, there is one vast North Pacific Basin, extending from the deep-sea trenches in the west to the continental margin of North America.

Of course in culinary (and relative) terms, the ocean basins look more like saucers than basins but their vast expanses are relieved here and there by islands and sea mounts, all the result of volcanic activity. 'Thousands of bountiful volcanic vents have poured out sufficient lava from the earth's mantle to build the massive underpinnings of oceanic islands, coral atolls and sea mounts.

However, millions of abyssal hills, knolls and peaks have been produced by other less sample vents which failed to produce enough to build to the surface of the sea before their activity was snuffed out.

At depths of 5,000 metres or more the ocean basins are covered with the sediment known as red clay and at shallower reaches with calcareous *oozes*. Red clay, which covers half the deep-sea floor of the Pacific and a quarter of each of the *Atlantic* and *Indian* Oceans, is: 'A *chocolate-brown*, extremely fine-grained sediment. It is composed of clay minerals, residue from dissolved *plankton shells*, *wind-borne* continentally derived silt, volcanic particles and in high latitudes red clay contains an admixture of ice-rafted pebbles, rocks and sand. Accumulation rates are the lowest of any deep-sea sediment, ranging from one-tenth to one millimetre per thousand years.

Indeed, red clay; which contain very little organic material, are the deserts of the deep-sea floor. Life on red clay consists largely of small invertebrates and are thinly spread.

The mid-ocean ridge system, which is a complex mountainous chain that winds round the world for a distance of 50,000 kilometres and forms a third of the deep-sea floor, is surely the most impressive major feature of our planet's physiography.

Here is the volcanic birthplace of the deep-sea floor, which is formed of vast tectonic plates that grow slowly outward from the mid-ocean ridge. The crest of the ridge system'...is cleft by a deep median rift valley. Deep gashes cut into the sea floor nearly at right angles to the crest and flanks of the ridge continue across the ocean basin floor until they are obscured beneath the sediments accumulated in the continental margins.

Sea mounts and islands lie in straight rows along these fracture zones and together with the linear scarps and ridges, which are parallel to the crest of the Mid-Ocean Ridge, they imposc a vivid fabric-like texture on the ocean floor.

The ridge is between 100 and 4,000 kilometres wide and from its foot-bills to the crest depths range from about 5,000 to 2,000 metres. The lower flanks are covered with red clay, the higher mountainous regions with calcareous oozes containing the remains of forminiferans and coccoliths.

Actually, the valleys of the system are filled with ponds of sediment, which show clearly on the records of powerful, low-frequency echo sounders. The peaks are just dusted with sediment. From ridge crest to ocean basin the covering of sediment gradually thickens.

Over its upper reaches, at least, there is presumably some variation in the rate of sedimentation, for the ridge system lies under waters of differing primary productivity (usually measured by the amount of carbon assimilated by the plant plankton under a square metre of the sea surface per day). Starting off east Greenland in the Jan Mayen area and proceeding through

Iceland and along the mid-Atlantic to the latitude of Gibraltar, the ridge passes under waters of very high to high productivity. Proceeding under the deep blue Sargasso Sea, where productivity is low, the ridges

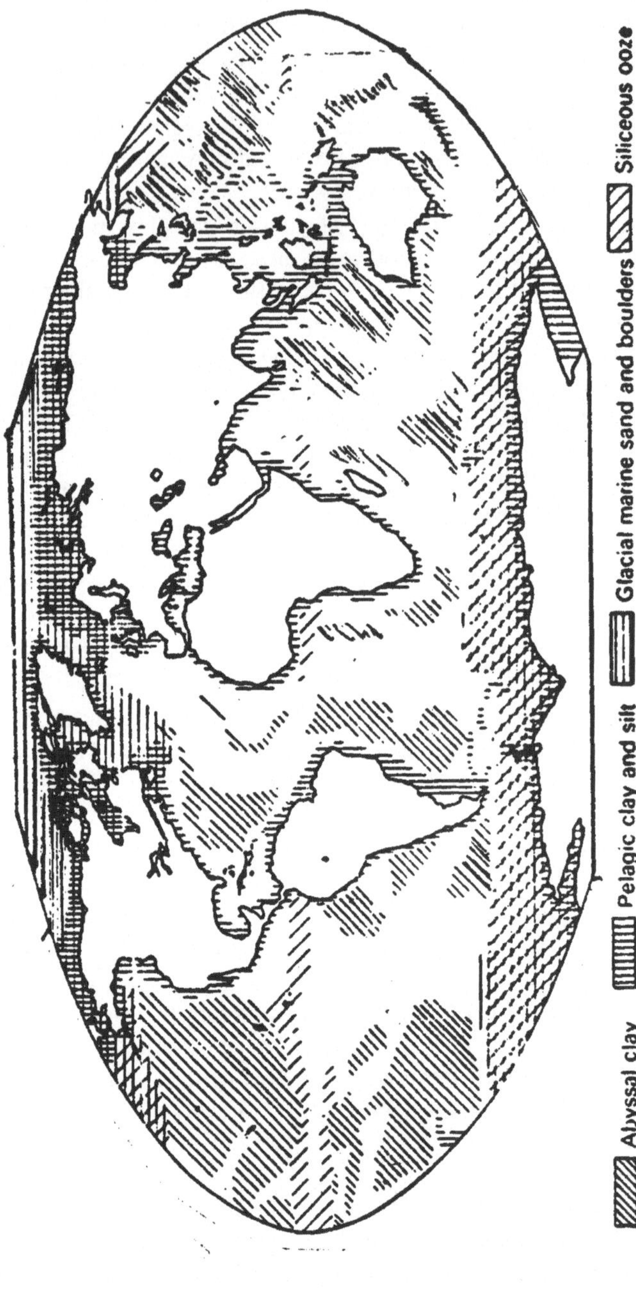

Figure 4.3: Distribution of deep-sea sediments the white areas represent calcarous oozes.

ranges under highly *productive* waters up to equatorial regions, but through most of the South Atlantic productivity falls to low values and the ocean is again deep blue.

Level with Cape Horn the ridge turns east and then northeast into the Indian Ocean to about latitude 30°S. Over this stretch the ridge is under highly productive seas, but as the ridge turns north to the east of Malagasay there is a belt of low productivity. The ridge continues northwards to the equator then northwestward into the Gulf of Aden and the Red Sea.

Over this stretch the waters increase in productivity from moderate to very high values. *Retracing* out giant steps along this part of the Indian oceanic ridge, the system continues *southeastward* and then eastward across the ocean until it arrives roughly midway between Australia and Antarctica.

This expanse passes under moderately productive waters, then enters high regions between New Zealand and Antarctica. South of new Zealand the ridge continues eastward but soon turns east-northeast then northward into the South Pacific, where productivity is low. In the equatorial region the ridge is once more under more productive waters and over its northward continuation towards the Gulf of California the seas become even richer.

The significance of this varying path of productivity in relation to animal life on the ridge has yet to be unravelled. Even so, deep-sea cameras have shown biologists aspects of life on the ridge system that could never have been revealed by dredge or trawl. The volcanic heart of the ridge is seen in broken *pillars* of *basalt* along the *rift valley*, where hot lava is *chilled* by the sea.

Here life is rare. The peaks of the ridge are covered with attached organisms, such as sponges, sea-fans, sea-pens and bryzoans. On the ponds of sediment in the valleys there arc era *cucumbers*, *brittle-stars*, *sea-urchins*, *bristle-worms*, *acorn-worms*, *sea snails* and *crabs*, *fishes*, such as *rat-tall*, *cruise* over the ponds.

The deepest parts of the ocean are in trenches at depths below 6,000 metres. Most tronches have V-shaped sides and a level floor. Thirty-one have been listed, and most lie along the margins of the Pacific Ocean: others indent the borders of the northern Indian Ocean and in the Atlantic follow the outer loops of the *Caribbean* and *Scotia Arcs*. *Deepsea* trenches are elongated and narrow depressions with lengths ranging from a few hundred to over 2,000 kilometres and mean widths from 25 to 120 kilometres.

Starting from New Zealand and moving clockwise round the Pacific, the main trenches and their maximum depths (in metres in parentheses) are : the Kermadec Trench (10,047), Tonga Trench (10,800), New Hebrides Trench (9,165), Philippine Trench (10,497) Mariana Trench (11,524), Ryukyu Trench (7,507), Idzu-Bonin Trench (9,810), Japan Trench (8,412), Kurile-Kamchatka Trench (10,542), Aleutian Trench (7,679), Middle American. Trench (6,662) and the Peru-Chile Trench (8,055). The main trenches of the Indian Ocean are the Chagos Trench (5,408), Java Trench (7,450), Amirante Trench (9,074), Mauritus Trench (5,564) and the Diamantina Trench (8,230). In the Atlantic lie the Puerto Rico Trench (8,385), Cayman Trench (7,930), Dominican Trench (ca. 6,200), Romanche Trench (7,856) and South Sandwich Trench (8,428). Most trenches, then, are parallel to island arcs of parts of the continents with coastal cordillera. It is now evident that such trenches are formed along collision lines between tectonic plates.

Though the deepest parts of the ocean, trenches are not necessarily the most barren parts. The deepest levels are filled with land-derived sediments, which may be rich in organic material and several trenches underlie waters of high productivity. *Invertebrate* life may thus be relatively *abundant*, and indeed, *diverse*.

Bruun called these animals the hadal fauna, for present exploration indicates that each trench contains a proportion of (*endemic*) species that have yet to be found elsewhere.

OCEANIC WATERS: THE PELAGIC ENVIRONMENT

Water, Salt and Heat Balance

Physical *oceanographers* study water, salt and beat balance in the ocean, and so do physiologists in living organisms. Both ocean and organisms tend to maintain steady states. One that is often taken for granted, the principle of *conservation* of volume, follows from the fact that water is no more than *slightly compressible*.

Thus, the fact that water flows out of basins such as the Mediterranean and Red Sea with no change in sea level means that water must be flowing in at the same rate.

Elsewhere the *conservation* of volume has profound effects on the productivity of the ocean. For instance, in the Antarctic Ocean and off parts of the western sea board of the African and American continents, surface waters are displaced and water rich in nutrient salts moves up to fill their place.

We shall see later that the upwelling leads to prolific crops of plant plankton. The sea gains water from the land, rain and melting ice and loses it through evaporation and freezing. Most of the earth's rain water comes from the very surface of the ocean (carrying much particulate matter) and much finds its way back to its source.

Clearly, salinity increased by *evaporation* and reduced by precipitation. Indeed, if the mean values of surface salinity and the difference between evaporation and *precipitation* (in cm) are plotted against latitude, there is a close parallel between the two curves.

Salinity, which is the total amount of dissolved material in parts per thousand (%) of sea water, is at a minimum (ca, 34.5%) near the Equator, rises to a maximum (35.8) in about latitudes 20°N and 20°S and then decreases to 34.0% or less towards high latitudes.

Though the salinity varies, the proportion of the main ions in sea water is almost constant, which C.R. Dittmar discovered by making careful analyses of 77 water samples collected all over the world by HMS *Challenger.* Thus, percentage values are; chloride 55-26; sulphate 7-68; magnesium 0.76; calcium and strontium 1.20 ; potassium 1.12; and sodium 30.58.

This uniformity of relative composition is due to constant mixing and circulation and it is vital to marine plants and animals which all have near-oceanic cell sap or body fluids. If any one of the main ions changed in proportion from place to place, marine organisms would need to be ever using energy reserves to maintain a *steady* inner state.

Even to, some animals do contain concentrations of certain ions that differ considerably from those in sea water. For instance, relative to sea water, magnesium ions are lower in concentration in the body fluids of many *crustaceans* and *chordates* but higher in some bivalves, *gastropods* and *cephalopods*.

Potassium ions, which are particularly vital for nervous and muscular systems, are concentrated by molluscs and crustaceans. In the body fluid of the squid, *Loligo,* the concentration of potassium is more than twice that of sea water. There is also the principle of conservation of salt, which '...asserts that the total amount of dissolved salts in the ocean is constant.

When one first learns that the rivers of the world centribute to the sea a total of about 3×10^{12} kg of dissolved solids per year, the conservation of salt seems to be *contradicted.* In principle it is, but in practice it is contradicted only to a negligible extent. The amount of salt in the oceans is about 5×10^{19} kg and therefore the amount brought in each year by rivers increases the ocean *salinity* by about one part in three million per year. But we can only measure the salinity of sea water to an accuracy of about 20.003%, or about 300 parts in three million taking the mean ocean salinity as 35%.

In other words, the oceans are increasing in salinity each year by an amount which is three hundred times smaller than our best *accuracy* of measurement. So fall all practical purposes we can assume that the average *salinity* of the oceans is constant at least over *periods* of tens or even hundreds of years'.

The surface of the sea covers 71 per cent of the earth and thus intercepts most of the sun's heat that falls on our planet. Even so, most of the ocean is cold, for though tropical latitudes gain much heat, cold waters, especially in *polar regions*, sink and fill the ocean basins.

Radiant energy from the sun reaches the earth directly or as radiation scattered by the *atmosphere*, particularly by clouds (sky radiation). Atthe sea surface, some of this energy is scattered : the rest enters the sea, is absorbed and raises the *temperature* of the water. At already intimated, the intensity of solar energy falling on a unit area of surface from a *beam* of given cross-section decreases from equator to poles (as the cosine of the latitude).

At a given latitude the diurnal and seasonal range in the sun's elevation will have a differential radiant effect like that of latitudinal variation. Again, when the sun is directly overhead (90 elevation) a unit area of sea surface will receive more radiant beat from a given beam than at *slanting* elevations (and the amount decreases as the size of the angle of elevation).

Concerning the reflection of direct radiant energy at the sea surface, the lower the elevation of the sun, and the more disturbed the water surface, the greater the amount of reflection. For sky radiation, which comes from all directions and varies mainly with cloud cover, about a tenth is reflected.

The sea surface loses heat through long-wave radiation to the atmosphere, through heat lost by evaporation and through heat conducted away from the surface, either into the water or out of the, water. If these three loss quantities are Qb, Qe and Qh respectively and Qs is the rate of flow of solar energy through the sea surface, then the heat balance is

$$Qs = Qb + Qe + Qh$$

The outstanding thermal *feature* of the *ocean*, as already hinted,

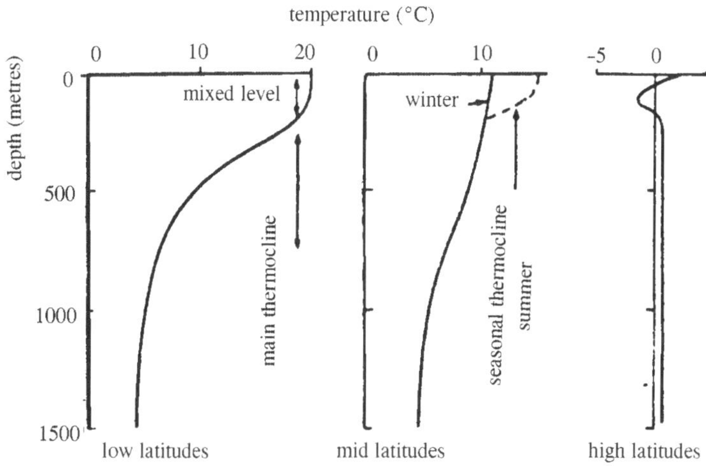

Figure 4.4: Typical mean temperature profiles in tropical, temperate and cold latitudes of the open ocean.

is that there is an upper-warm layer of water, mainly in tropical and subtropical latitudes, floating, as it were, on a cold ocean. Anton Bruun, who believed the isotherm for 10°C to have wide significance in marine *biogeography*, called the warm water above this *isotherm* the thermosphere and the cold underlying waters the *psychrosphere*.

In the Atlantic and Pacific Oceans the thermosphere extends between latitudes 50°N and 50°S and to depths between 300 and 1,000 metres. If the warm and cold water spheres are so defined, the former would seem to occupy no more than one-tenth of the entire volume of the ocean.

Indeed, *three-quarters* of this volume has temperatures between 0° and 6°C (and *salinities* between 34.6% and 34.8%). The mean temperature of the entire ocean 3.5°C (and the mean salinity 34.7%). The temperature structure of the ocean has, of course a more complex pattern. A profile of temperature through the warm and cold water spheres traces a sigmoid curve.

The upper most, vertical part of the curve shows an isothermal surface layer ranging from about 10 to 200 metres in thickness. Temperatures in this layer range between 30° and 15°C, depending on season and latitude.

In a zone below this, extending between depths of 300 and 1,000 metres, temperatures fall rapidly to values near 5°C, then in the rest of the water column the temperature decreases slowly to levels between

1° and 2°C at 4,000 metres, the mean depth of the ocean. The surface layer is mixed to *isothermal* , consistency by the wind, and is thus called the '*mixed layer*'.

It becomes thicker in winter, especially in middle latitudes In the western North Atlantic, for, instance, the mean depth of the mixed layer is between 40 and 120 metres in winter and between 10 and 60 metres in summer. The layer is separated from cooler underlying waters by a *thermocline*, a layer in which there is a rapid decrease of temperature with depth.

The depth of maximum decrease is the axis of the thermocline and is marked by the upper bend of the sigma. This discontinuity layer, for reasons to be given, is called the '*seasonal*' *thermocline*. The epither is not entirely apt, for over much of the subtropical belts the '*seasonal*' *thermocline* persists throughout the year.

Hence productivity of the plant plankton is so limited the subtropical regions are the largest and most deserted part of the ocean. The zone between 300 and 1,000 metres, where there is a second rapid decrease in temperature, is known as the permanent thermocline. Below are the cold, deep and bottom waters.

Poleward from the subtropical belts there are marked changes, in temperature profiles. In temperate waters the thermocline below the mixed layer develops only in the summer: hence the term '*seasonal*'. The permanent thermocline is also much less marked, and one reaching polar waters, thermoclines have vanished.

Indeed, there is little change in temperature from to *bottom*. In the coldest polar waters there is an increase from negative values (-1.9°C to 0°C) to slightly values at depths below 200 metres.

The ocean is immense and water absorbs great quantities of heat with relatively little change in temperature. Except for liquid *ammonia*, the heat capacity of water is the highest of all solids and liquids. Thus, after leaving the surface layer, great quantities of beat are moved by the circulation from one part of the ocean to another. (The transfer of water properties through currents is termed '*advection*', to distinguish it from transfer through diffusion.)

Moreover, there are extreme ranges or sudden changes in temperature in the ocean, which in this respect (and others) is a more benign environment than the atmosphere. On land the most abundant and ubiquitous vertebrates are birds and mammals, which are warm-blooded and able to regulate their body temperature.

In the sea the warm-blooded homeothermal whales seals and

penguins, which had land-dwelling ancestors, range from polar to *tropical regions*. The only inveterate warm-blooded dwellers of the ocean among the vertebrates are members of the tuna family (Thunnidae) and *makoshark* family (*Isuridae*).

The *bluefin tuna*, which has some power of temperature regulation. ranges from warm waters off the Bahamas to cool sea off Norway. Even so, many marine organisms are *eurythermal*, able to exist over a wide range of temperature.

The most remakable are the diverse invertebrates and fishes that migrate up and down each day between cool deep waters (near 10°C) to surface waters in the tropics with temperatures in excess of 20°C. There are planktonic organisms that live in the ocean from polar to tropical regions.

But any one of the these species may consist of temperature races, each adapted to a relatively narrow range of temperature, the entire complex covering the span of environmental temperatures. Temperature tolerances of marine organisms range from the seeurythermal (*generalist*) kinds- to *specialists* that exist within narrow limits of temperature and are described as *stenothermal*.

Density

Density in the ocean is fundamental to marine science. For physical oceanographers, a synoptic survey of density helps them to discover the origins, *equilibrium* levels and spread of water masses. The density of marine organisms matches or is a little more than that of the sea, and *biologists* are thus led, inter alia, to investigate the buoyancy relations of diverse plants and animals.

For animals, a crucial metabolic advantage of weightlessness in winter is that they can stay at a preferred level with the minimum expenditure of energy. *Density* which is expressed in grams per cubic *centimetre*, depends on pressure as well as on salinity and temperature. Pressure in water increases by one atmosphere for each increase in depth of to metres, and water is slightly compressible.

Thus at the surface, sea water of salinity 35% and temperature 5-0°C has a density of 1.012813, which at a depth of 4,000 meteres and *hydrostatic* pressure of 400 atmospheres is increased by compression to a value of 1.04849.

Since physical *oceanographers* usually compare water masses at the same depth or over the same interval of depth, densities are reduced to atmospheric (i,e. hydrostatic pressure, p = 0), but salinities and temperatures are taken as measured at the depths involved. In the open ocean values of density range from about 1.024 to 1.030g/cm^3. Naturally, the saltier the water, the more its density, while warm water is less dense than cold.

More precisely, the rate of increase of density with salinity at atmospheric pressure is about 8 × 10^{-4} gm/cm^3 per 1%, The rate of decrease of density with increasing temperature is more involved and ranges from 5 × 10^{-5} per 1°C change at 0°C to 34 × 10^{-8} per 1°C change at 30°C.

The ocean is more than 800 times denser than the atmosphere, and is thus more buoyant by the same factor. Sea water sustains, in more than one sense, a marvellous diversity of organisms from bacteria to blue whales. It is hardly fortuitous that '*protoplasm*', which arose in the sea, is only a little denser than its birth fluid, or that the cell sap of plants and the body fluids of animals have a near-oceanic salt balance.

Marine animals almost entirely depend, directly or indirectly, on the microscopic plants in the *plankton*, which have buoyant and motile means to stay in surface waters, where light is strong enough for *photosynthesis*. Beside supporting whales, seals and fishes, all with firm muscular bodies and heavy skeletons, the *buoyant* properties of the sea have led to its exploitation by forms that consist largely of a fragile, gelatious skeleton. *Medusae jellyfishes*, *siphonophores* and *pelagic tunicates* are among such forms.

Since marine animals have much the same compressibility as the sea, their change of density with depth will match that of their environment. Gases, of course are highly compressible, and animals that depend on a gas-filled float for neutral buoyancy have evolved means of regulating their density against changes of pressure. Changes of pressure have less obvious effects on organisms.

Certain fishes and planktonic animals of coastal waters respond in various ways to quite small changes in pressure, and it will be interesting to discover if the same is true of their relatives in the deep sea. Changes of pressure have effects on the activities and *enzyme* systems of marine animals. Certain deep-sea species *tolerate* wide ranges of pressure; others seem to be less tolerant.

WATER MASSES AND CIRCULATION

Through tracing the origin and distribution of each oceanic water mass, physical oceanographers have helped marine *biologist* to understand better the distribution of deep-sea *organisms*. Water masses keep their identity and support certain *characteristic* communities of *invertebrates* and fishes.

Water masses have individual ranges of temperature, salinity and density, and in 1918 the *Norwegian oceanographer*, Bjorn Helland-Hansen, realized how these properties could be used effectively to define a water mass. Besides *plotting* the values of temperature and salinity against the depths of sampling at any particular station, Helland-Hansen found that characteristic thermohaline curves are produced when one property is plotted against the other.

Such as curve is known as a TS diagram, and there is an advantage in using temperature, salinity (and density) as identification marks of water masses. Near the surface, as we saw, these properties may be changed by variations in solar radiation, evaporation, precipitation and so forth but away from the surface they are unchanged, except through mixing processes.

The are '*conservative properties*'. Eeven so, other features, such as oxygen content or concentration of nutrients (e.g. phosphates), can help in identifying water masses. When using these fearures one has to remember that they are '*non-conservative*' properties: their concentrations are changed by living organisms.

If there are enough stations in depth and area for synoptic survey, one can see where a water mass begins and ends. That each water mass has a characteristic TS diagram may be appreciated when the TS curves for an ocean are plotted on one graph. Wider understanding comes from comparing the oceans, which have certain water masses in common.

Thus, the Atlantic Ocean, India Ocean and South Pacific Oceans contain water masses that are given these names : Antarctic Bottom Water, Antarctic Intermediate Water, Subantarctic Water and Central Water. Apart from the last kind, these water masses, as implied by their names, are formed in antarctic and subantarctic regions of the Southern Ocean.

Their origin is near the surface and, together with water masses formed near the surface in high latitudes of the North Atlantic and North Pacific, they fill about three-quarters of the ocean, which as we saw, is predominantly cold.

We begin then, in the Southern Ocean, which merges widely with the three other oceans. After moving into the Atlantic Ocean, which has been well explored, we will then compare and contrast the Atlantic with the Pacific and Indian Oceans.

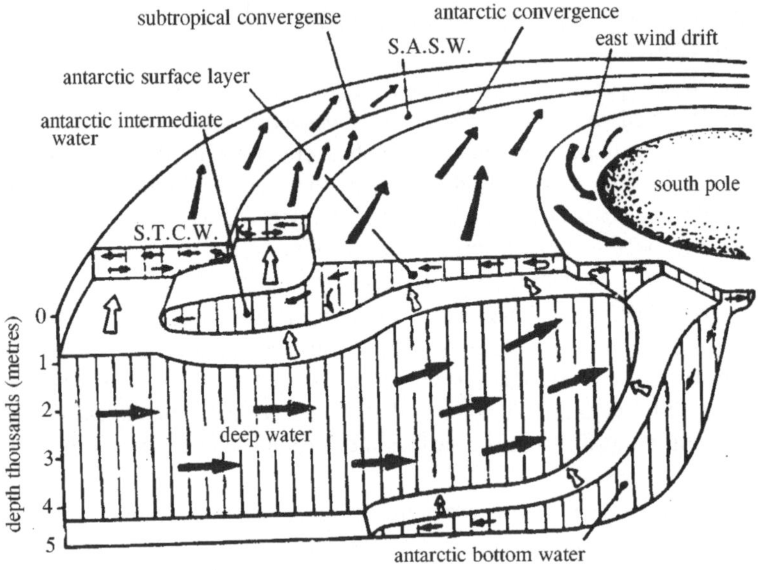

Figure 4.5: Three dimensional representation of the water masse and circulation of the Southern Ocean.

During the winter the surface waters around Antarctica become colder and saltier, and by summer, when the days are longer and ice melts, become warmer and less saline. In winter surface temperatures are between-1.9°C and 1°C, rising to between-1°C and 4°C in summer.

Winter conditions are particulary severe over the shelf of the Weddell Sea, where temperatures reach-1.9°C and the formation of **sea** ice leads the water of relatively high salinity (34.6%). Such water has a high density (1-0279), and after mixing with *Circumpolar Water*, it sinks down the *continental slope* and *flows* away from Antarctica over deeper reaches of the ocean floor.

This is Antarctic Bottom Water and it moves northward and eastward into the basins of the Southern Atlantic, Indian and Pacific Oceans. In the Atlantic this water type has been traced as far north is 40°N, about the latitude of Spain.

There is evidence of Subpolar Bottom Water off eastern Greenland and in the Norwegian Sea, but this water clearly nothing like the volume of Antarctic Bottom Water.

North of a narrow east wind drift near the land, surface waters off Antarctica are driven clockwise round the continent as a broad west wind drift. Due to the force inherent in the earth's rotation (*Coriolis Force*), there is a northerly component; in this drift.

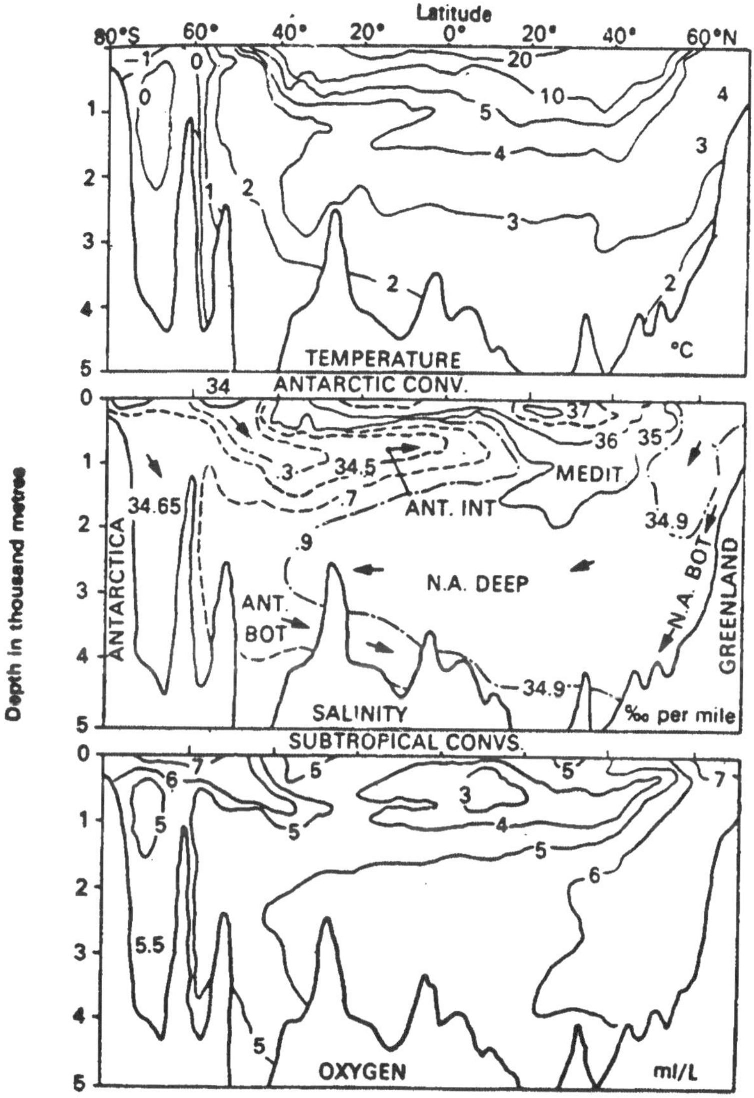

Figure 4.6: South to north longtudinal secton of water characteristics along the western trough of the Atlantic Ocean.

Over southerly reaches, the properties of *Antarctic Surface Water*, which has a thickness of 100 to 250 metres, vary with the seasons (winter temperatures reach-1.9°C and salinities nearly 34.5%), but during their oblique drift to the north these waters absorb summer heat and at latitudes between 60°S and 50°S temperatures are close to 2°C and salinities below 34%. Between these latitudes and along a narrow circumpolar front called the Antarctic Convergence, Antarctic Surface Water of higher temperature (4°C or more) and begins to sink.

On the way down it mixes strongly with deeper and warmer waters that are rising above Antarctic Bottom Water and after finning its level at about 1,000 metres, continues north as Antarctic Intermediate Water (temperature 2°C, salinity 33.8%). In the Atlantic this water mass crosses the Equator in the west.

North of the Equator in the east a smaller intermediate water mass is formed by the sinking of Mediterranean water to 1,000 metres or more as it flows into the Atlantic. The warm deep water is not formed in the Southern Ocean but far to the north in the surface waters of the North Atlantic.

South of Greenland at about latitude 60°N relatively saline waters that are chilled in winter, sink and then flow south between depths of 1,500 and 4,000 metres as the very voluminous North Atlantic Deep Water Mass. North of the Antarctic Convergence at about latitude 40$ there is a second circumpolar front, the Subtropical Convergence, where cool Subantarctic Water meets a warmer mass of water.

Here, over a much broader front than met at the Antarctic Convergence, water sinks to levels between Antarctic Intermediate Water, and the surface mixed layer to form South Atlantic Central Water. North Atlantic Central Water is formed along another broad front at about 40 N in the northwestern Atlantic.

These Atlantic Central Waters, which extend to depths of 300 metres on either side the Equator and deepen to 600-900 metres at mid-latitude, have temperature ranging from about 17 to 7°C and salinities from 36.5 to 34.5%. It will be seen that the Central Water Masses form most of the thermosphere.

The Southern Subtropical Convergence may be taken also as the southern boundary of the *Atlantic*, *Indian* and *Pacific Oceans*. The rest of the ocean is formed of '*seas*'. One group, such as the Arctic Sea, the Bering Sea, the Sea of Okhotsk, the Gulf of Mexico, the Caribbean Sea, the Mediterranean Sea the Red Sea, the Sea of Japan and the South China Sea, are partly enclosed by land or island arcs, and thus have restricted openings into the main ocean.

The term '*sea*' is given also to certain unconfined parts of the ocean that have individual *oceanographic* features. The Barents Sea, the *Norwegian* Sea, the Arabian Sea and the Tasman Sea are among such seas.

Conditions in the Pacific Ocean and Indian Ocean may now be seen in comparison and contrast to the above outline of water masses in the Southern Ocean and Atlantic Ocean, Antarctic Bottom Water and Antarctic *Intermediate* Water move into southerly parts of the Pacific and Indian Oceans.

Intermediate Water in both oceans flows north to meet Equatorial Water Masses, soon to be described. Intermediate Water informed also in the northern Pacific, evidently by vertical mixing in the subantarctic region, not by the sinking of surface water.

In the northwestern Indian Ocean an intermediate water mass between depths of 1,000 and 1,500 metres may be traced to the sinking of warm and saline waters (salinity 36%, temperature. 15°C) that flow out of the Red Sea.

There is little or no formation of deep water in the Pacific Ocean, and from a level of 2,500 metres downwards the Deep and Bottom Water (temperature 1° to 3°C, salinity 34.6 to 34 8%) must come entirely from the Antarctic Circumpolar Current. This is also the source of some of the deep water in the Indian Ocean; as in North Atlantic Deep Water, which enters at depths below 2,000 metre in the southwest.

Two more deep-water masses are formed within the ocean itself. North Indian Deep Water forms in the Arabian Sea from Rod Sea water and a much smaller outflow from the Gulf of Oman. The Red Sea Water moves towards *Africa* and may betraced as far south as 5° to 6° S. Further south, between 10° and 16°S, North Indian Deep Water mixes with *Antarctic Intermediate* Water and Antarctic Bottom Water and is transformed into South Indian Deep Water (temperatures 3.0 to 1.0°C, salinities 34.78 to 34.60%).

The Central water Masses in the South Pacific and South India Ocean arise, of course, at the Southern Subtropical Convergence. In the North Pacific Central Water is formed along a front at about latitude 30°N. North of this is a broad ocean-spanning mass of Subarctic Water of low salinity (33.5 34.5%) and rather low temperatures (2 to 4°C). In both oceans the Central Water Masses lie between depths of about 100 and, 1,000 metres and have temperatures ranging from 17 to 4°C, salinities from 36.3% to 34.2%.

Between the Central Water Masses of the Pacific and north of the Central Water in the Indian Ocean is a vase Equatorial Water Mass. There is no counterpart in the Atlantic Ocean. Pacific Equatorial Water extends right across the ocean, decreasing in width towards west and reaching a depth about 800 metres. It has temperatures of about 15° to 5°C, salinities of about (35.3 to 34.7%).

Indian Equatorial Water which has a small range of *salinity* (35.2 to 34.9%), extends across the ocean to the north of latitude 10°S and reaches a depth of about 1,000 metres, Indian Central Water merges with *Antartic Intermediate* Water at a depth of some 1,000 metres. In the pacific and *Indian Ocean*, *Equatorial* and *Central Waters* form most of the *thermosphere*.

The uppermost part consists of the surface mixed layer. This ends a brief survey of the oceanic water masses seen in terms of temperature, salinity and density. Water masses maintain their thermohaline (and other) features, which was well seen when observations made in the Atlantic during 1925 to 1927 by the German *Meteor* Expedition were compared with those made during the international *Geophysical Year* (IGY, 1957-58) on the ships of the Woods Hole Oceanographic Institution USA and the National Institute of Oceanography (UK).

Relevant comparisons of the two sets of observations showed that the distributions of temperature, salinity and dissolved oxygen were almost identical. Marine biologists who know a particular area through repeated observations find also that communities of deep sea animals may maintain their identity.

Diverse species seem to bound to the physical and biological conditions of water masses: others transcend these conditions. After thirty years, it seems astonishing that values of dissolved oxygen were still the same in certain part of the Atlantic.

Through a given '*volume*' of the ocean, the circulation moves at a certain rate and carries a certain quantity of dissolved oxygen, which is used by resident organisms in the processes of life and decay, Does the correspondence between the Meteor and IGY measurements imply that in some parts of the ocean there is a steady state in the quantity of dissolved oxygen ?

Is the supply of oxygen so great compared to the oxygen requirements of the organism that methods of oxygen analysis are unable to detect the withdrawal of oxygen by life ? At mid-depths in some parts of the ocean the oxygen content is minute but life abundant. Life in these oxygen minimum layers will be considered later.

Convergences, where surface waters rich in oxygen sink into the depths, have been called the lungs of the ocean. The atmosphere is the main source of oxygen dissolved in sea water. The plants in the *plankton* also produce oxygen during *photosynthesis*, and at times the surface layer may be supersaturated with this gas. The oxygen content of water is expressed as the number of millilitres (ml) of oxygen gas dissolved in one litre (1) of seawater at NTP. Values range from 0-8 ml/l.

Down from the convergences the circulation of the water masses carries oxygen to nearly all parts of the ocean below the surface layer. The exceptions are the Black Sea and Cariaco Trench (in the *Caribbean Sea*) where subsurface layers are devoid of oxygen and carry hydrogen sulphide, sure signs of stagnant conditions.

As a water mass sinks and finds its level in the ocean, the contained oxygen is used by living organisms and in the oxidation of organic detritus. Once it has left the surface a water mass can only gain oxygen by mixing with another water mass of higher oxygen content.

If the circulation is sluggish a water mass will lose much oxygen to its life after travelling several thousand miles. But how fast is *sluggish*? Natural radiocarbon (C^{14}) is the most useful of the radionuclide tracers of oceanic circulation.

The sea surface gains radiocarbon from the atmosphere. Thus, the concentration of C^{11} in part of a water mass will depend on how long this part has been below the surface (the *residence* time) and on the rate of gain or loss of C^{14} to local water masses. To use this method, then, one must make certain *assumptions* about the exchange of C^{44} between the atmosphere and ocean and about mixing between water masses.

In a survey of the distributions of C^{14} in the Pacific and Indian Oceans much emerged. Deep waters were less active than those near the *surface*, showing, as one would expect, their greater age. In the Pacific, for instance, the activity of the deep water *decreased* from south to north, which reflects the ageing of the water as it moves north.

The northerly component in the deep circulation was calculated to have an average rate of 0.05 cm/sec (43 meters per day). Since the deep water moves so slowly *and* originated in *antartic region*, it is hardly surprising that values of oxygen content at levels of 2,000 metres or more have fallen from about 4.5 ml/l in the South Pacific to between/0.5 and 3 ml/I in the *North Pacific*, Indeed, in the eastern Pacific between 10 and 20 N there is a *pronounced* oxygen minimum layer with values down to less than 0.1 ml/l between 200 and 1,000 metres.

Here productivity is high and it seems that the requirements of life, combined with slow circulation, are the major causes for the oxygen minimum layer. As already implied, the distribution of radiocarbon can be used to calculate mean residence times for the various water masses. For deep *Pacific water* the residence time is about 1,000 to 1,600 years, which is approximately twice that of deep water in the Atlantic and Indian Oceans.

In Atlantic deep-water values of dissolved oxygen (3 to 6.5 ml/I) are higher than these in *Pacific deep water*, which seems reasonable in view of the less sluggish circulation of the former. But deep currents are not invariably slow. At all events, the slow pace of the deep waters may be appreciated in contrast to surface waters, which have a residence time of 10 to 23 years and a lively circulation.

PATTERNS OF CIRCULATION NEAR THE SURFACE

Circulation in the upper waters is turned by part of the sun's energy that falls on the sea. *Evaporation* at the surface, which may be facilitated by the stirring motions of *microscopic* plants and animals in the surface film, yields potential energy in the form of water vapour. Minute particles of salt and organic material also leave the surface film, elected it seems by *breaking bubbles*, Water vapour and particles are swirled into the atmosphere, where the particles form the nuclei for the *condensation* of water vapour which releases latents heat, the main source of energy for atmospheric circulation.

Winds that blow over the sea raise waves and drive ocean currents. The wind-driven circulation of the ocean thus differs from the *thermohaline* circulation of the water masses, which as we saw, is maintained by the pull of gravity on dense water types that sink and then flow along stratified levels of *equilibrium*. The wind-driven circulation consists essentially of currents that flow horizontally in the upper few hundred metres of the ocean.

Due to the force inherent in the earth's rotation (*Coriolis Force*), these currents move along lines to the right of the wind direction in the northern hemisphere and to the left in the southern. The patterns of wind-driven circulation in the three main oceans are broadly similar, as one might expect.

In equatorial regions the Trade Winds drive a current system that A. Defant called 'the backbone of the circulation'. Near or at the equator there is a westerly flowing South Equatorial Current that it kept in motion by the southeast Trades. To the north of the equator a

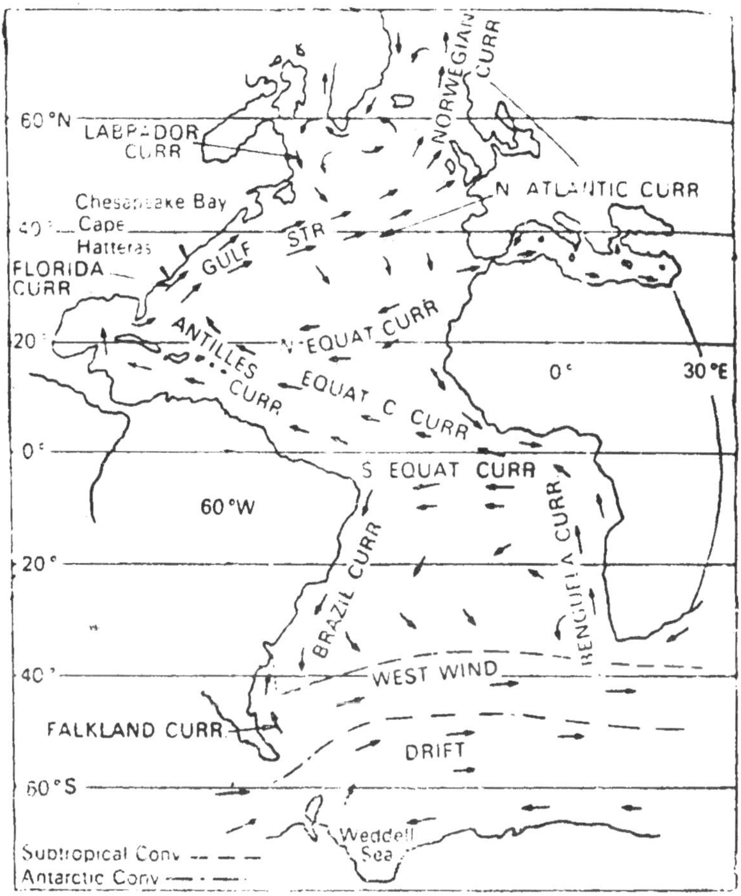

Fig. 6.7. Surface circulation of the Atlantic Ocean.

parallel, westerly flowing North Equatorial Current/ is driven by the northeast Trades. Both currents cross the ocean and pile up water that returns between them as an Equatorial Counter Current.

This current spans the entire width of the *Pacific Ocean* but is *prominent* only over the eastern half of the Atlantic. There is a parallel, triple current system in the *equatorial* Indian Ocean from November to March, when northeast Trade Winds (northeast monsoon maintain the North Equatorial Current, which is close to the equator (with the change to the southwest monsoon from April to September, the North Equatorial Current reverses direction and the Equatorial Counter Current is no longer distinguishable).

The Trade Winds not only drive the equatorial currents but also

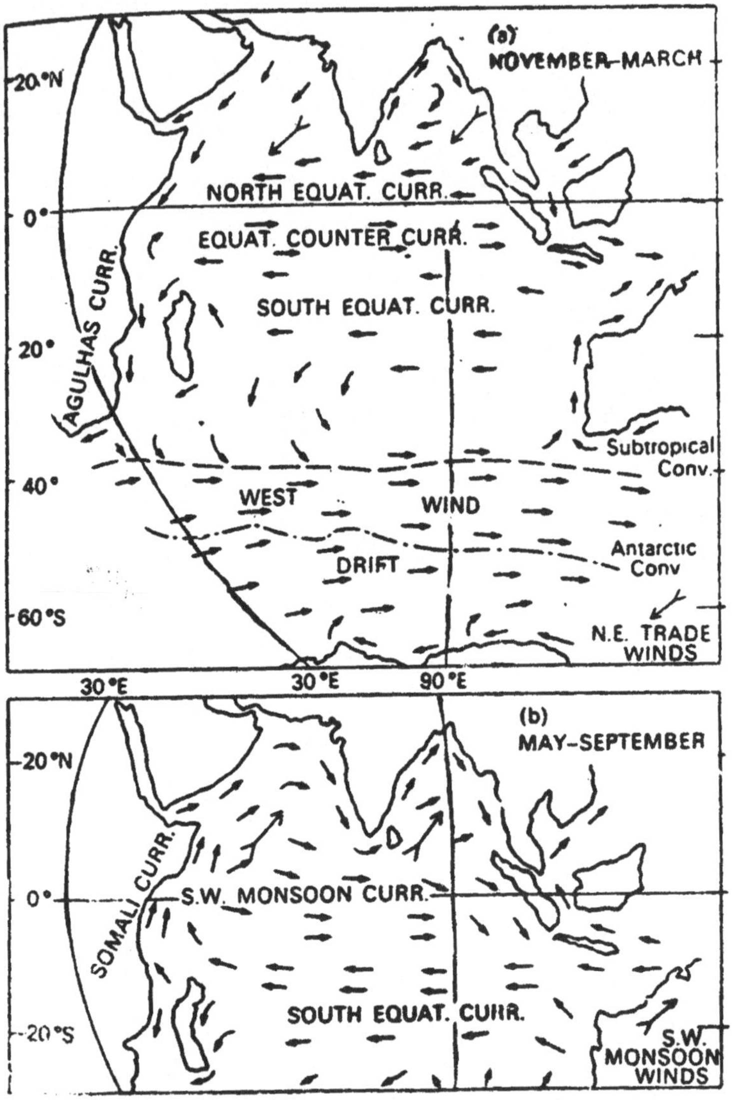

Figure 4.8: Surface circulation of the Indian Ocean.

their continuation as vast gyres that encircle the subtropical regions : hence the evocative phrase '*the backbone of the circulation*', seems justified. These oceanic gyres thus turn clockwise in the northern parts of the Atlantic and Pacific (the Asiatic land mass precludes the formation of a gyre in the northern Indian Ocean) and anticlockwise in the southern parts of all three oceans. The gyres overlie the Central Water Masses

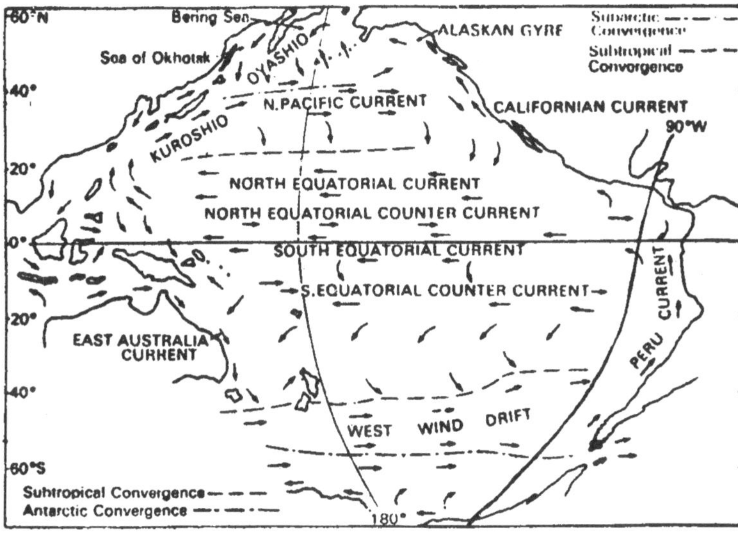

Figure 4.9: Surface circulation of the Pacific Ocean.

and, indeed, may extend into these waters. The North Atlantic gyre includes the *Sargasso Sea*, the westerly edge of which is the fast-flowing Gulf *Stream* and largely the *continuation* of the *Florida* Current that springs from the Gulf of Mexico. Speeds in the Stream, which reach 250 cm/sec (5 knots), are among the highest recorded in oceanic currents.

Detailed surveys have shown that the Gulf Stream consists of narrow streams that trace a *sinuous* northeasterly path, and *occasionally* great eddies are detached to turn in the Sargasso Sea for mouths at a time. The *Stream breaks* away from the American coast at Cape Hatteras and near the *Grand Banks* of *Newfoundland*, where it broadens into the North Atlantic current, it impinges on cold water from the Labrador Current.

Part of the North Atlantic current moves eastward across the ocean and then turns south east Spain to complete the gyre in the North Equatorial Current: the other part flows northeasterly and eventually becomes part of the circulation of the Greenland, Norwegian and Arctic Seas.

The western boundary current of the South Atlantic gyre is the south-flowing Brazil Current but it is not so fast as the Gulf Stream. The eastern flow of the gyre moves across the ocean with the west wind drift in subantarctic waters, and on heading north is edged by the Benguela Current off Southeast Africa.

In the North Pacific the counterpart of the Gulf Stream is the *Kuroshio*, which flows past Japan and then turns east as the Kuroshio Extension. Like the Gulf Stream, the Kuroshio changes its position from time to time and reaches maximum speeds of 250 em/sec (5 knots). Again, the Kuroshio Extension, like its counterpart, the North Atlantic current, meets cold waters (in the south flowing *Oyashio*).

In both regions the mixing of warm and cold waters leads to high productivity and profitable fisheries. The Kuroshio Extension flows east as the North Pacific Current, which edges the cool subarctic waters and on nearing America parts turns south, as the California Current, part northeast to feed the gyre in the Gulf of Alaska.

In the South Pacific the easterly flow of the gyre moves with the west wind drift in subantarctic waters and after turning north, forms part of the Peru Current. There are undercurrents below parts of the wind-driven circulation. Below the Gulf Stream there is a counter-flowing undercurrent with speeds of 9-18 cm/sec but it is not always present.

This was discovered by plotting the movements of Swallow neutral-buoyancy floats, which also revealed that deep currents in the North Atlantic are not invariably sluggish and steady. In the Bermuda area, where slow deep currents were expected, the flow at a depth of 2.000 metres averaged 6 cm/sec (maximum 20 cm/sec) and at 4,000 metres the average was 12 cm (maximum 42 cm/sec).

Off Portugal measurements at 1,500 to 4,000 metres indicated currents of 1 to 2 cm/sec (maximum 5 cm/sec), which seems more in keeping with earlier estimations of deep water movement in the Atlantic. Undercurrents are prominent below the equatorial systems and the first was discovered in the Pacific, where, 'The Equatorial Undercurrent is almost as large in volume transport as the North or South Equatorial Currents and it lies only 100 metres or less below the sea surface along the equator.

Yet it was not discovered until 1952. The outstanding discovery from current surveys, which was announced by Cromwell, Montgomery and Stroup, '...was that near the equator and embedded in the well-known westward flowing South Equatorial Current, there was a previously undiscovered eastward flowing current between 70 and 200 metres depth'.

An intensive study by Knauss of Scripps Institution of Oceanography revealed many details of the current. It is a thin ribbon, only 0.2 km thick, but 300 km wide, extending from about 2°N to 2°S. This ribbon certainly stretches over the eastern half of the Pacific and may well be

12,000 km in length. The speed in the eye of the current is up to 150 cm/sec and the volume of water transported approaches that of the Gulf Stream. 'In other words, it is a major ocean current which was unknown before 1952 and had not even been predicted by theory'.

There are also Equatorial Undercurrents in the eastern half of the Atlantic Ocean and the Indian Ocean (from about 60°E to 90°E). The speed of the Indian Equatorial Undercurrent is only about half that of its counterpart in the other two oceans. The wind-driven circulation has profound effects on the lives of deep-sea animals.

The upward transport of *nutrient* salts from subsurface levels to the productive, plant bearing surface layer is *quickened* along the edges of swift current (e.g. the Gulf Stream), or along lines of current divergence, or slowed in the great *subtropical gyres* that turn above a more or less permanent thermocline.

As we shall see, the outstanding patterns of plant productivity are reflected down to all levels is the ocean, certainly affecting the abundance and the community structures of deep-sea faunas. Each night, the productive surface waters are the feeding grounds of diverse that move up from the upper mid-waters. These waters also form the nursery grounds for the young stages of many pelagic and some bottom dwelling deep-sea animals.

During their *planktonic* existence the young may be widely dispersed by the lively wind-drived circulation and eventually some will grow into recruits for their parental populations. The quickest parts of the circulation may well carry the young away from the parental grounds but some, as they metamorphose and *descend*, may recurr in the *undercurrents*. Gyres and swirls will, of course, tend to keep planktonic forms within the confines of their circulation.

If the ocean may be likened to a marine organism. the living units must above all evolve the right kind of organization and staying power to survive in the great organism's circulation.

LIGHT IN THE OCEAN

Short-wave energy streaming from the' sun heats and illuminates the ocean. Light penetrating the sea is both scattered and absorbed. Both processes are involved in the submarine attenuation of light which increases exponentially with depth and varies with the wave length.

Virtually all of the energy in waves shorter than the visible (ultra-violet) or longer than the visible (*infra-red*) is absorbed in the top metre of the sea.

At a depth of 10 metres most of the energy is in the blue-green part of the spectrum, though there is still a trace of visible red light. Thus, *reddish organisms* appear dark or black at depths below 10 metres, for at these levels there is little or no red light to be reflected by there organisms. It is thus not altogether surprising that diverse mid water invertebrates have adopted *vanishing* coats of red pigment.

Blue-green rays are still detectable near a level of 1,000 metres in the clearest oceanic waters, but no more than 5 per cent of the light energy penetrates to 50 metres. Even so, the light is strong enough for plant *photosynthesis* at depths down to 150 metres in the most *transparent* regions, where between 50 and 100 metres there is also *enough light* to allow divers to work.

The twilight zone of the ocean thus falls between the productive (euphotic) gone and the greatest reach of blue-green sunlight, which is probably close to 1,200 metres. The *diversity* of animal life in this upper midwater (*mesopelagic*) zone, greatly exceeds that in the vaster, deeper midwater (*bathypelagic*) zone, where there is no trace of *sunlight*.

The *twilight zone* is full of animals that migrate daily to the more productive waters that move overhead. The most complex animals, notably decapod crustaceans, squid and fishes, have very sensitive eyes, able, more probably, to detect daily changes in light level and so regulate their vertical *migrations*. The twilight zone is also full of luminescent animals and with few exceptions, the light produced is blue-green and close in wavelength to the ambient solar light.

Furthermore, eyes are most sensitive to blue-green rays, which seems almost inevitable in this *marvellously integrated* twilight world. Just below the surface, where the sun's rays are reflected and refracted, the field of light is diffused and complex. At deeper levels most of the radiation is downward and approaches the zenith with increasing depth.

At depths between 300 and 400 metres in clear oceanic waters the field of light is likely to be symmetrical around the zenith, and the polar diagram looks rather like the cross-section of a fish. Indeed, by matching this ambient field of light with the light of their own photophores, certain fishes of the twilight zone vanish from the view of predators.

Life Zones and Life Forms

We must now be evident that water masses and pelagic forms of life are disposed in horizontal strata in the ocean. Pelagic organisms drift and move in submarine space: they are adapted for life at all levels between the air/sea interface and the interface between sea and substrate. *Benthic organisms* live on the ocean floor. For many millions of years, certainly from *Cambrain* times (600 million years ago), the vast *pelagic* and *benthic* living spaces have been the scenes for a succession of *evolutionary* plays known as adaptive tradiations.

Today, according to Thorson (19/1), there are about 160,000 species of marine animals, of which 98 per cent are benthic and 2 per cent pelagic. Perhaps about 5 per cent of the total number of marine animals live in the deep sea, where the proportions of pelagic forms is perhaps greater.

At all events this proportion certainly differs in large groups with both pelagic and benthic representatives. There are considerably more benthic, deep-sea cnidarians, polychaete worms, crustaceans and molluscs than of related pelagic forms. But pelagic deep-sea fishes are about as diverse as bottom-dwelling kinds.

Pelagic organisms, which range in size from bacteria to the largest whales, are broadly classed as planktonic or nektonic forms. Plankton (from the Greek *plankton,* neuter of *planktos,* wandering) consists of diverse organisms that are *non-motile* or have limited powers of movement: they thus drift, or tend to drift, with the sea. Pelagic bacteria are classed as *bacterioplankton*, *pelagic plants* as *phytoplankton* and *pelagic* animals as *zooplankton*.

Bacteria and the plants are microscopic forms, and so are some of the animals, such as the Protozoa and the early larval stages of invertebrates. Most adult members of the zooplankton range in size from millimetre-long copepods to large jellyfishes (e,g. *Cyanea* over a metre in diameter. The most ubiquitous forms are *copepod crustaceans*: other important groups are *cnidarians*, *ostracod crustaceans*, *pteropod molluscs*, *arrow-worms*, and the *pelagic tunicates*.

Members of the nekton (from the Greek *nekton,* neuter of *nektos,* swimming) have sufficient powers of locomotion to make their way against currents. *Cetaceans*, *seals*, *turtles*, *fishes* and *squid* are classic forms of *nektonic* animals. But where does the plankton end and the nekton begin?

The commonest deep-sea fishes belong to the genus *Cyclothone* and the smallest species range from 25 mm to 50 mm in length. Several species of euphausiid shrimps fall within this size range, or even exceed it, and the group as a whole is often regarded as planktonic. Large—*euphausiids* must have just as good powers of movement as small *Cyclothone.*

Indeed, certain of the deep-sea prawns, which are larger than euphausiids, prey on *Cyclothone*. It seems reasonable then, to have a category called the micronekton, which would consist largely of decapod crustaceans and the smallest cephalopods and fishes.

At all events, nektonic animals are larger than say, 15 mm and they belong to groups with plenty of muscle. Such animals, which need to maintain large, energy-consuming *muscles*, are mostly *omnivores* or *carnivores*. Many *planktonic animals*, *notably copepods* and the *pelagic tunicates*, are entirely or largely *herbivorous*.

Animals that move or float on the sea surface have the collective name pleuston. The movers are *water-striders (Halobates spp.)* of the insect order *Hemiptera*: the floaters have some kind of gas-filled buoyancy chamber and include various cnidarians (e,g. *Physalia, Velella, Porpita* and certain sea-anemones), stalked barnacles, purple snails *(lanthina spp.)* and nudibranch molluscs (e.g. *Glaucus)*.

Their headquarters are on the warmer parts of the ocean, which seem very remote from the levels of deep-sea life. Each day, though, many animals of the upper mid waters move into the surface layer and some, as we shall see, feed close to the surface, where they may well fall prey to the cnidarians, especially to *Physalla,* the *Portuguese* man-of-war.

Organisms that live in the uppermost few centimetres of the sea form the neuston. There are bacteria, tiny species of phytoplankton (nanoplankton) and diverse planktonic animals. Relatively few species of neustonic animals stay near the surface throughout the entire day, but from time to time they are joined by others, especially during the night.

In *subtropical* and *tropical* regions many members of the neuston (e.g. pontellid copepods, *arrow-worms*, *pelagic tunicates* and *larval stages* of *crustaceans* and fishes) may be *suffused* with blue or purple *pigments*.

Again, life close below the surface seems remote from that in the depths, but young stages of upper mid water (mesopelagic) animals, such as larval sergestid prawns and lantern-fishes, may form part of the neuston. Furthermore, neuston nets catch adult lantern-fishes (e.g. *Gonichthys coccoi, Symbolophorus veranyi. Myctophum punctatum),* which evidently take some neustonic food during their nightly stay in the surface waters.

Indeed, land-dwelling insects that have been blown out to sea and eventually come to rest on the surface film may make up much of the food of certain lantern-fishes. Concerning the *neuston*, one must remember though, that it is concentrated in a 'very thin layer and must thus be no more than a subsidiary source of surface-dwelling food for nektonic animals, particularly in tropical and subtropical waters. In these regions the overall impression one gains of the near surface (0-10 cm) zone (compared to the layer from the surface to 30 metres) is that of a poor feeding ground with a rather low density of invertebrates and fishes.

The uppermost waters of the open ocean are known as the epipelagic zone. Here, in the subtropical and tropical belts is the swim of flying *squid*, *flying-fishes*, *skippers*, *sauries*, *grey sharks*, *thresher-sharks*, *mako sharks*, *tuna-fishes* and *billfishes*. The sharks, tunas and billfishes are Gullivers compared to the Lilliputian fishes in the waters of the deep sea world. Many thousands of the largest lantern-fishes and stomiatoid fishes are needed to equal the weight of a large bluefin tuna or a blue marlin.

What is the lower limit of the epipelagic zone? Tuna fishes live in the upper 200 metres and are sometimes concentrated near the '*seasonal*' thermocline but this varies in level between about 10 to 250 metres. Planktonic plants live in the surface layer and sunlight is strong enough for photosynthesis down to 150 metres in the clearest oceanic waters. Not far below this depth small luminous fishes with silvery sides (e.g. the stomiatoids such as *Bonapartia, Vinciguerria* and *Valencienneiius* begin to appear in nets towed at successively deeper levels below the surface.

We shall accordingly, and somewhat arbitrarily, take the lower limit of the epipelagic zone to about 150 metres, which is also close to the mean depth of the outer edge of the continental shelf where shallow seas give way to deep seas.

If the mesopelagic zone is regarded as a twilight environment, then the transition between this zone and the dark underlying bathypelagic zone is the threshold of light. Measurements of underwater light by Clarke (1970) and his *colleagues* have shown that in very clear oceanic waters sensitive instruments will detect sunlight down to about 1,200 metres.

There are not enough measurements to give a reliable estimate of the mean depth of light penetration in the entire oceanic province, but this is likely to be close to 1,000 metres. In *subtropical* and *tropical* waters the *mesopelagic* zone contains the main *thermocline*, but everywhere below this zone temperatures at a given level are virtually uniform and range between 5°C and negative values.

The *bathypelagic* zone is thus uniformly cold and dark (apart from flashes of *bioluminescence*). Considering that the headquarters of deep-sea animals are below the warm oceanic belts, what are the biological features of the *twilight-thermoline-mesopelagic* and the dark-cold-bathypelagic zones.

Full treatment of the mesopelagic and bathypelagic faunas comes later in this book : here we look briefly at copepods and fishes, the two ends of oceanic food chains. At depths below 1,000 metres there is a distinct and rather diverse bathypelagic fauna of calanoid copepods, distinguishable from *mesopelagic* and *epipelagic* kinds. some of which are related forms.

Concerning the fishes, the transition between the mesopelagic and bathypelagic zones is marked by certain dark-coloured species of lantern-fishes of the genera *Lampadena* and *Taaningichthys*. Lantern-fishes, most of which migrate daily between their daytime levels and -the upper waters, are classic mesopelagic animals.

Ceratioid angler-fishes, dark-coloured species of bristle-mouth fishes *(Cyclothone),* whale-fishes and gulper-eels, which are non-migrators, are typical dwellers at bathypelagic levels. This is not to say that they are entirely confined to the bathypelagic zone.

The vertical ranges of certain black species of *Cyclothone* and angler-fishes (e.g. *Melanocetus* and *Cryptopsaras)* may extend into lower mesopelagic levels. The transition between the two midwater zones, whether physical or biological, is by no means abrupt.

Besides housing many kinds of vertical migrators and the reflections of some as sound-scattering layers (which do not occur at bathypelagic levels), the *mesopelagic zone* is also, as already stated, full of luminous animals.

At depths below 1,000 metres luminous flashes become much less frequent. Indeed the specific diversity of life and the amount of life (biomass) are much reduced at bathypelagic compared to mesopelagic levels. For instance, for every species of the bathypelagic fish fauna (about 150 spp.) there are six mesopelagic species.

The biomass of zooplankton decreases markedly between the surface layer and 1,000 metres but at deeper levels the decline is less rapid. Beyond 2,000 metres there is a gradual and steady exponential fall in bimass. In the deeper parts of the bathypelagic zone below 4,000 metres there seems to be a distinct abysopelagic fauna, which contains, inter alia, members of the copepod family Spinocalanidae.

Species of this family live also near the deep-sea floor as part of a benthopelagic fauna, which ranges from these millimetre-sized copepods to certain fishes (*macrourids*) and *cirrate octopods* that reach lengths of about a metre. Part-time members of the benthopelagic fauna include pelagic forms (e.g. *medusae* and *jellyfishes*) and also some benthic species (e.g. *amphipods*). Animals of the deep-sea floor, like their benthic relatives on the shelf, live partly or entirely above the interface between sea and land (epifauna) or within the upper layer of sediment (infauna).

The infauna consists largely of minute (*melobenthic*) forms (e.g. *forminifera* and *nematode* worms) and small species of burrowing bivalves, crustaceans and polychaete worms. The epifauna is not only represented by members of the taxa that flourish on the continental *shelves*, but there are others that are *predominantly* deep-sea forms, notably the *glass-sponges*, *beardworms* (*Pogonophora*) and elasipod *sea-cucumbers*.

Down the continental slope and rise and moving deeper into the ocean basins there is a decline in the biomass and species diversity of the benthos. The decline is most marked in most of the *epifauna* but is much more *gradual* in the relatively small forms of the infauna.

Some specialists differentiate a bathyal fauna, extending down the slope to about 2,000 metres, from an abyssal fauna at deeper levels. *Critical survey* of these faunas is beyond the scope of this book.

5

The Nature of Oceanic Life

We plan to take the reader on a brief tour of marine life from the surface layers of the open sea, down through the intermediate layers to the deep-sea floor, and from there to the living communities on continental shelves and coral reefs.

Like Dante, we shall be able to record only a scattered sampling of the races and inhabitants of each region and to point out only the general *dominant* factors that *typify* each *domain*; in particular we shall review some of the conditions, principles and interactions that appear to have molded the forms of life in the sea and to have established their range and compass.

The organisms of the sea are born, *live*, *breathe*, *feed*, *excrete*, *move*, *grow*, *mate*, *reproduce* and *die* within a single *interconnected* medium. Thus interactions among the marine organisms and interactions of the organisms with the chemical and physical processes of the sea range across the entire *spectrum* from simple, adamant constraints to complex effects of many subtle *interactions*.

Far more, of course, is known about the life of the sea than we shall be able even to suggest, and there are yet to be achieved great steps in our knowledge of the living entities of the sea. We shall mention some of these possibilities in may concluding remarks.

A general discussion of a living system should consider the ways in which plants elaborate basic organic meterial from inorganic substances and the *successive* and often highly intricate steps by which organisms then return this material to the inorganic *reservoir*. The discussion should also show the forms of life by which such processes are conducted. we shall briefly trace these processes through the regions we have indicated, *returning* later to a more detailed discussion of the living forms and their constraints.

Some organic material is carried to the sea by rivers, and some is *manufactured* in shallow water by attached plants. More than 90 percent of the basic organic material that fuels and builds the life in the sea, however, is *synthesized* within the lighted surface layers of open water by the many varieties of *phytoplankton*. These sunny pastures of plant cells are gazed by the *herbivorous zoo-plankton* (small planktonic animals) and by some small fishes.

These in turn are prey to various carnivorous creatures, large and small, who have their predators also. The debris from the activities in the surface layers *settles* into the *dimly lighted* and *unlighted midlayers* of the sea, the twilight mesopelagic zone and the midnight *bathypelagic* zone, to serve as one source of food for their strange *inhabitants*.

This process depletes the surface layers of some food and particularly of the vital plant nutrients. or fertilizers, that become trapped below the surface layers, where they are unavailable to the plants. Food and nutrients are also actively carried downward from the surface by vertically migrating animals.

The deplated *remnants* of this constant "*rain*" of detritus continue to the sea floor and support those animals that live just above the bottom (*epibenthic animals*), on the bottom (*benthic animals*) and burrowed into the bottom. Here filter-feeding and burrowing (deposit feeding) animals and bacteria re-work the remaining refractory particles.

The more active animals also find repast in mid-water creatures and in the occasional falls of carcasses and other larger debris. Except in unsual small areas there is an abundance of oxygen in the deep water, and the solid bottom presents advantages that allow the support of a denser population of larger creatures than can exist in deep mid-water.

In shallower water such as banks, atolls, continental shelves and shallow seas conditions associated with a solid bottom and other regional modifications of the general regime enable rich populations to develop. Such areas constitute about the percent of the total area of the ocean. In some of these regions added food results from the growth of larger fixed plants and from land drainage.

With the above bare recitation for general *orientation* we shall now discuss these matters in more detail.

The cycle of life in the sea, like that on land, is fueled by the sun's visible light acting on green plants. Of every million photons of sunlight reaching the earth's surface, some 90 enter into the net production of basic food. Perhaps 50 of the 90 contribute to the growth of land plants and about 40 to the growth of the single-celled green plants of the sea, the phytoplankton.

It is this minute fraction of the sun's radiant energy that supplies the living organisms of this planet not only with their food but also with a *breathable atmosphere*. The terrestrial and marine plants and animals arose from the same sources, through similar evolutionary sequences and by the action of the same *natural laws*.

Yet these two living systems differ greatly at the stage in which we now view them. Were we to imagine a terrestrial food web that had developed in a form limited to that of the open sea, we would envision the land populated *predominantly* by short-lived simple plant cells gazed by small insects, worms and snails, which in turn would support a sparse predaceous population of larger insects, birds, frogs and lizards.

The population of still larger carnivores would be a small fraction of the populations of large creatures that the existing land food web can nurture, because organisms in each of these steps pass on not more than 15 percent of the organic substance.

In some important respects this imaginary condition is not unlike that of the dominant food web of the sea, where almost all marine life is sustained by microscopic plants and nearmicroscopic herbivores and carnivores, which pass on only a greatly diminished supply of food to sustain the larger, more active and mote complex creatures.

In other respects the analogy is substantially inaccurate, because the primary marine food production is carried out by cells dispersed widely in a dense fluid medium.

This fact of an initial dispersal imposes a set of profound general conditions on all forms of life in the sea. For comparison, the concentration of plant food in a moderately rich grassland is of the order of a thousandth of the volume of the gross space it occupies and of the order of half of the mass of the air in which it is immersed.

In moderately rich areas of the sea, on the other hand, food is hundreds of times more dilute in volume and hundreds of thousands of times more dilute in relative mass. To crop this meager broth a blind herbivore or a simple poa in a filsering structure would need to process a weight of water hundreds of times the weight of the cell it eventually captures.

In even the densest concentrations the factor exceeds several thousands, and with each further step in the food web dilution increases. Thus from the beginnings of the marine food web we see many adaptations accommodating to this dilution: eyes in microscopic herbivorous animals, filters of *exquisite design*, *mechanisms* and *behavior* for discovering local *concentrations*, complex search gear and, on the bottom, attachments to elicit the aid of moving water in carrying out the task of filtration.

All these adaptations stem from the conditions that limit plant life in the open sea to *microscopic dimensions*. It is in the sunlit near-surface of the open sea that the unique nature of the dominant system of marine life is irrevocably molded. The near-surface, or mixed, layer of the sea varies in thickness from tens of feet to hundreds depending on the nature of the general circulation.

Here the basic food production of the sea is accomplished by single-celled plants. One common group of small *phytoplankton* are the cocolithophores, with calcareous plates, a swimming ability and often an oil *droplet* for food storage and buoyancy. The larger microscopic phytoplankton are composed of many *species belonging* to several groups: naked algal cells. diatoms with complex shells of silica and actively swimming and *rotating flagellates*. Very small forms of many groups are also abundant and collectively are called *nannoplankton*.

The species composition of the phytoplankton is everywhere complex and varies from place to place, season to season and year to year. The various regions of the ocean are typified, however, by dominant major groups and particular species. Seasonal effects are often strong, with dense blooms of *phytoplankton* occurring when high levels of plant nutrients suddenly become usable or available, such as in high *latitudes* in spring or along coasts at the onset of *upwelling*.

The concentration of phytoplankton varies on all dimensional scales, even down to small patches. It is not immediately obvious why the dominant primary production of organic matter in the sea is carried out by microscopic single-celled plants instead of free-floating higher plants or other intermediate plant forms.

The question arises: Why are there no pelagic "*trees*" in the ocean ? One can easily compute the advantages such a tree would enjoy, with its canopy near the sup face in the lighted levels and its trunk and roots extending down to the *nutrient-rich* waters under the mixed layer. The answer to this fundamental question probably has several parts.

The evolution of plants in the *pelagic realm* favored smallness rather than expansion because the mixed layer in which these plants live

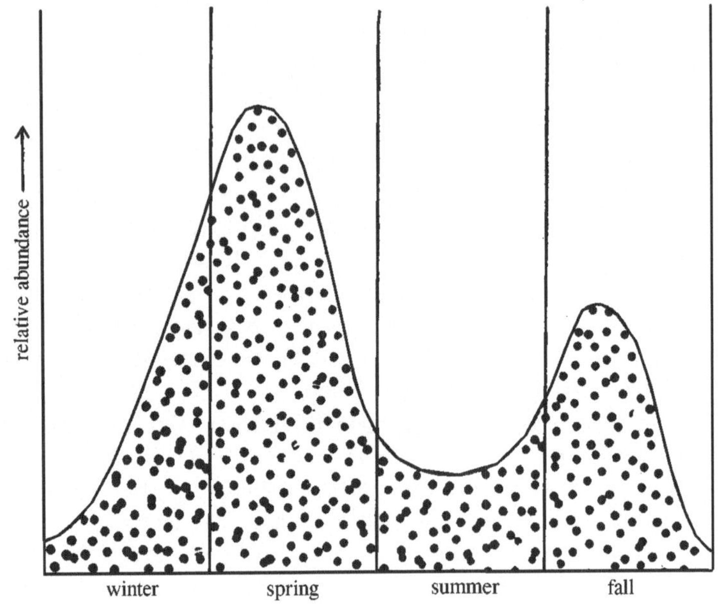

Figure 5.1: Species Composition and Abundance of the phytoplankton varies from season to season, Particularly at high latitudes.

is quite homogeneous; hence small incremental extensions from a plant cell cannot aid it in bridging to richer sources in order to satisfy it several needs.

On land, light is immediately above the soil and nutrients are *immediately* below; thus any extension is of immediate benefit, and the development of single cells into higher erect plants is able to follow in a stepwise evolutionary sequence. At sea the same richer *sources* exist but are so far apart that only a very large a ready-made plant ;could act as a bridge between them.

Although such plants could develop in some other environment and then adapt to the *pelagic* conditions, this has not come about. It is difficult to see how such a plant would propagate anyway certainly it could not propagate in the open sea, because the young plants there would be at a severe disadvantage.

In the sea small-scale differential motions of water are rapidly damped out, and any free-floating plant must often depend on molecular diffusion in the water for the uptake of nutrients and excretion of wastes.

Smallness and *self-motion* are then *advantageous*, and a gross structure of cells cannot exchange nutrients or wastes as well as the same cells can separately or in open *aggregations*.

In addition the large-scale circulation of the ocean continuously sweeps the pelagic plants out of the region to which they are best adapted. It is essential that some individuals be returned to renew the populations. More mechanisms for this essential return exist for single-celled plants than exist for large plants, or even for any conventional spores, seeds or juveniles.

Any of these can be carried by oceanic gyres or diffused by large-scale motions of *surface eddies* and *periodic counterblow*, but single-called plant, can also ride *submerged* counter-currents while temporarily feeding on food particles or perhaps on dissolved *organic material*. Other *mechanisms* of *distribution undoubtedly* are also occasionally important. For example, living marine plant cells are carried by storm-borne spray, in bird feathers and by wellfed fish and birds in their undigested food.

No large plant has solved the many problems of development, dispersal and reproduction. There are no pelagic trees, and these several factors in concert therefore restrict the open sea in a profound way. They confine it to an initial food web composed of microscopic forms, whereas larger plants live attached only to *shallow bottoms* (which comprise some 2 percent of the ocean area).

Attached plants, unlike free-floating plants, are not subject to the aforementioned limitations. For attached plants all degree of water motion enhance the exchange of nutrients and wastes. Moreover, their normal population does not drift, much of their *reproduction* is by budding, and their spores are adapted for rapid *development* and settlement.

Larger plants too are sometimes found in nonreproducing terminal accumulations of drifting shore plants in a few special convergent deep-sea areas such as the *Sargasso Sea*. Although species of phytoplankton will populate only regions with conditions to which they are adapted, factors other than *temperature*, *nutrients* and *light levels undoubtedly* are important in determining the species composition of *phytoplankton* populations.

Little is understood of the mechanisms that give rise to an abundance of particular species under certain conditions. *Grazing* herbivores may consume only a part of size range of cells, allowing certains and types to dominate *temporarily*. Little is understood of the mechanisms it give rise to an abundance of *particular* species under certain conditions chemical by-products of certain species probably exclude certain other species. Often details of individual cell behavior are probably also important in the introduction and success of a species in a particular area. In some cases we can impose what these mechanisms area.

For example, both the larger diatoms and the larger flagellates can move at appreciable *velocities* through the water. The diatoms commonly sink *downward*, ereas the flagellates actively swim upward toward light.

These are probably patterns of behavior primarily for increasing exchange, but the interaction of such unidirectional motions with random turbulence or systematic connective moon is not simple, as it is with an inactive particle.

Rather, we would expect diatoms to be statistically abundant in upward-moving water and to sink out of the nearsurface layers when turbulence upward convection is low. *Conversely*, *flagellates* should be startically more abundant in downwelling eater and should concentrate near the surface in low *turbulence* and slow ownward water motions. These effects them to exist.

Off some continental pasts in summer flagellates may evenaly collect in high concentrations. As they begin to shade one another from the light, each individual struggles closer to the lighted surface, *producing* such a high density that large areas of the water the turned red or brown by their pigments.

The concentration of *flagellates* these "*red tides*" sometimes becomes to great for their own survival. Several species of flagellates also become highly toxic as they grow older. Thus they some both produce and participate in a mass death of fish and invertebrates that has been known to give rise to such a high yield of *hydrogen sulfide* as to *lacken* the white houses of *coastal cities*.

Large diatom cells, on the other hand, depend a disproportionately greater time upward-moving regions of the water and an unlimited time in any region there the upward motion about equals their own downward motion. *Diatom cells* are thus statistically abundant in upwelling water. and the distribution of diatoms probably is often a reflection of the *turbulent-convective* regime of the water.

Sinking and the dependence of the larger diatoms on upward convection and turbulence for support aids them in reaching *upwelling* regions, where *nutrients* are high; it helps to explain their dominance in such regions and such other features of their distribution as their high proportion in rich *ocean* regions and their frequent inverse *occurrence* with *flagellates*.

Differences in adaptations to the *physical* and *chemical* conditions, and the release of chemical products, probably reinforce such relations. In some areas, such as parts of the *equatorial* current system and shallow seas, where lateral and *vertical circulation* is rapid, the species composition of phytoplankton is perhaps more simply a result of the inherent ability of the species to grow, survive and reproduce under the local conditions of *temperature*, *light*, *nutrients*, *competitors* and *herbivores*.

Elsewhere, second-order effects of the detailed cell behavior often dominate. Those details of behavior that give rise to concentrations on any dimensional scale are particularly important to all subsequent steps in the food chain. All phytoplankton cells eventually settle from the surface layers. The depletion of nutrients and food from the surface layers takes place continuously through the loss of *organic material*, *plant cells*, *molts*, *bodies of animals*, *fecal pellets* and so forth, which release their content of chemical nutrients at various depths through the action of *bacteria* and other organisms.

The periodic downward migration of zooplankton further contributes to this loss. These nutrients are "*trapped*" below the level of light adequate to sustain photosynthesis, and therefore the water in which plants must grow generally contains very low concentrations of such vital substances.

It is this condition that is principally responsible for the comparatively low total net productivity of the sea compared with that of the land. The regions where trapping is broken down or does not exist-where there is upwelling of nutrient-rich water along coasts, in parts of the *equatorial* regions, in the wakes of islands and banks and in high latitudes, and where there is rapid *recirculation* of nutrients over shallow shelves and seas-locally bear the sea's richest fund of life.

The initial factors discussed so far have placed an *inescapable* stamp on the form of all life in the open sea, as irrevocably no doubt as the properties and distribution of *hydrogen* have dictated the form of the universe.

These factors have limited the dominant form of life in the sea to an initial microscopic sequence that is relatively unproductive, is stimulated by upwelling and mixing and is otherwise altered in species composition and distribution by *physical*, *chemical* and *biological* processes on all *dimensional* scales.

The same factors also limit the populations of higher animal and have led to unexpectedly simple adaptations, such as the sinking of larger diatoms as a tactic to solve manifold problems of enhancing nutrient and waste exchange, finding nutrient remaining in the surface waters a repopulating.

The grazing of the phytoplankton principally conducted by the herbirous members of the zooplankton, a heterogeneous group of small animals the carry out several steps in the food was as herbivores, carnivores and detri (debris-eating) feeders. Among the important members of the zooplankton in the *arthropods*, *animals* with external skeletons that belong to the same broad group as insects, crabs and shrimps.

The *planktonic* arthropods include the abundant copepods, which are in a sense the marine equivalent of insects. Copepods arc represented in the sea by some 10,000 or more species that act not only as herbivores, carnivores or detrital feeders but also as external or even internal parasites! Two or three thousand of these species live in the open sea.

Other important arthropods are the shrinmplike *emphausiids*, the strongest vertical migrators of the zooplankton. They compose the vast shoals of krill that occur in high latitudes and that constitute one of the principal foods of the baleen whales.

The zooplankton also include the strange bristle-jawed chaetognaths, or *arrow-worms*, *carnivores* of *mysterious* origin and *affinities* known only in the *marine environment*. Widely distributed and abundant, the chaetognaths are represented by a surprisingly small number of species. perhaps fewer than 50.

Larvae of many types, *worms*, *medusae*, *ctenophores*, *gastropods*, *pteropods* and *heteropods*, *salps*, *unpigmented flagellates* and many others are also important components of this milieu, each with its own remarkably complex and often bizarre life history, behavior and form.

The larger zooplankton are mainly carnivores, and those of herbivorous habit are restricted to feeding on the larger plant cells. Much of the food supply, however, exists in the form of very small particles such as the nannoplankton, and these appear to be available almost solely to microscopic creatures.

The immense distances between plant cells, many thousands of times their diameter, place a great premium on the development of feeding mechanisms that avoid the simple filtering of water through fine pores.

The power necessary to maintain a certain rate of flow through pores or nets increases *inversely* at an exponential rate with respect to the pore or mesh diameter, and the small planktonic herbivores, detrital feeders and carnivores show many adaptations to avoid this energy loss. Eyesight has developed in many minute animals to make possible selective capture.

A variety of *webs*, *bristles*, *rakes*, *combs*, *cilia* and other structures are found, and they are often sticky. *Stickiness* allows the capture of food that is finer than the interspaces in the filtering structures, and it greatly reduces the expenditure of energy.

A few groups have developed extremely fine and apparently quite effective nets. One group that has accomplished this is the Larvacea. A larvacian produces and inhabits a complex external "*house*," much larger than its owner, that contains a system of very finely constructed nets through which the creature maintains a gentle flow.

The *Larvacea* have apparently solved that problem of energy loss in filtering by having proportionately large nets, fine strong threads and a low rate of flow. The composition of the zooplankton differs from place to place, day to night, season to season and year to year, yet most species are limited in distribution, and the members of the *planktonic communities* commonly show a rather stable representation of the modes of life.

The zooplankton are, of course, faced with the necessity of maintaining breeding assemblages and, like the *phytoplankton*, with the necessity of establishing a *reinoculation* of parent waters. In addition, their behavior must lead to a *correspondence* with their food and to the pattern of large-scale and small-scale *spottiness* already imposed on the marine realm by the phytoplankton.

The swimming powers of the larger zooplankton are quite adequate for finding local small-scale patches of food. That this task is accomplished on a large scale is indirectly demonstrated by the observed correspondence between the quantities of zooplankton and the plant nutrients in the surface waters.

How this large-scale task is *accomplished* is understood for some groups. For example, some *zooplankton* species have been shown to descend near the end of suitable conditions at the surface and to take temporary residence in a submerged countercurrent that returns them upstream.

There are many large and small puzzles in the distribution of zooplankton. As an example, dense concentrations of phytoplankton are often associated with low populations of *zooplankton*. These are probably rapidly growing blooms that *zooplankton* have not yet invaded and grazed on, but it is not completely clear that this is so. Chemical repulsion may be involved.

The concentration of larger zooplankton and small fish in the surface layers is much greater at night than during the day, because of a group of strongly swimming members that share their time between the surface and the mesopelagic region.

This behavior is probably primarily a tactic to enjoy the best of two worlds: to crop the richer food developing in the surface layers and to minimize mortality from predation by remaining always in the dark, like timid rabbits emerging from the thicket to graze the nighttime fields, although still in the presence of foxes and ferrets.

Many small zooplankton organisms also make a daily migration of some vertical extent. In addition to its primary purpose daily vertical migration undoubtedly serves the *migrating* organisms in a number of other ways. It enables the creatures to adjust their mean temperature, so that by *spending* the days in cooler water the amount of food used during rest is reduced.

Perhaps such processes as the rate of egg development are also controlled by these tactics. Many land animals employ hiding behavior for similar kinds of adjustment. Convincing arguments have also been presented to show that vertical *migration* serves to maintain a wide range of tolerance in the migrating species, so that they will be more successful under many more conditions than if they lived solely in the surface layers.

This migration must also play an important part in the distribution of many species. *Interaction* of the daily migrants with the water motion produced by daily land-sea breeze alternation can hold the migrants offshore by a kind of "*rectification*" of the *oscillating* water motion.

More generally, descent into the lower layers increases the influence of *submerged countercurrents*, thereby enhancing the opportunity to return upstream, to enter upwelling regions and hence to find high nutrient levels and associated high phytoplankton productivity.

Even minor details of *behavior* many strongly contribute to success. Migrants spend the day at a depth corresponding to relatively constant low light levels, where the movement of the water commonly is different from that at the surface. Most of the *members* rise some what even at the passage of a shadow.

Should they be carried the shadow of an area rich in phytoplankton, they migrate to shall depths, thereby often decreasing or halting their drift with respect to rich region to which they will ascend night.

Conversely, when the surfaceters are clear and lean, they will much deeper and most often drift related faster. We might simplistically view the distribution of zooplankton, and phytoplankton for that matter, as the consequence of a broad inoculation oceans with a spectrum of species, with a certain *adaptive* range of finces and a certain variable ran feeding, reproducing and migration behavior.

At some places and at some the behavior of a species, inter even in detailed secondary ways the variable conditions of the ocean its other inhabitants, results in temporary, seasonal or persistent success. There are a few exceptions to the croscopic dimensions of the herb in the pelagic food web.

Among the herrings and herring-like fisher able to consume phytoplankton as stantial component of their diet. Sum adaptation gives these fishes *accompany* times the food supply of the *fivorous* groups. It is therefore no rise that the partly herbivorous comprise the bulk of the world's.

These larger creatures of the sea commonly move in schools, shoals and herds. In addition to meeting the needs of mating such grouping is advantageous in both defensive and predatory strategy, much like the cargo-ship convoy and submarine "*wolf pack*" of World War II. Both *defensive* and *predatory assemblages* are often complex. Small fishes of several species commonly school together.

Diverse predators also form loosely cooperative groups, and many species of marine birds depend almost wholly on prey driven to the surface by submerged predators. At night, schools of prey and predators are almost always *spectacularly* illuminated by *bioluminescence* produced by the *microscopic* and larger *plankton*.

The reason for the ubiquitous production of light by the *micro-organisms* of the sea remains *obscure*, and suggested *explanations* are controversial. It has been suggested that light is a kind of inadvertent byproduct of life in transparent organisms. It has also been hypothesized that the emission of light on *disturbance* is advantageous to the plankton in making the predators of the plankton *conspicuous* to their predators ! Unquestionably it does act this way.

Indeed, some fisheries base the detection of their prey on the *bioluminescence* that the fish excite. It is difficult, however, to defend the thesis that this effect was the direct factor in the original development of bioluminescence, since the effect was of no advantage to the individual microorganism that first developed it.

Perhaps the luminescence of a microorganism also discourages

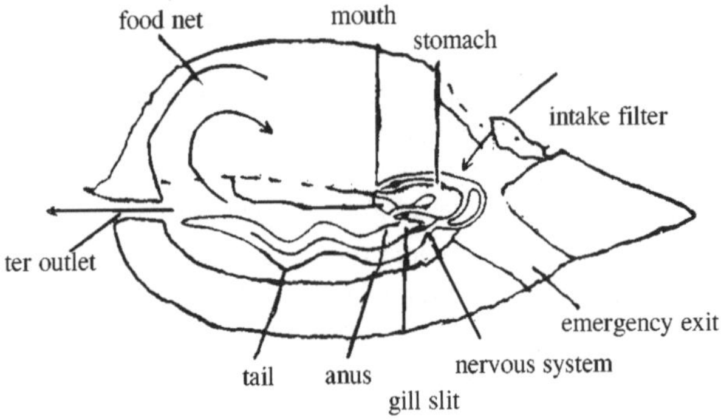

Figure 5.2: Ryacian is representative of a group of small planktonic herbivores.

attack by the light-avoiding zooplankton and is of initial survival benefit to the individual. As it then became general in the population, the effect of revealing plankton predators to their predators would also become important.

The fallout of organic material into the deep, dimly lighted mid-water supports a sparse population of fisher and invertebrates. Within the *mesopelagic* and *bathypelagic* zones are found some of the most curious and bizarre creatures of this earth. These range from the highly developed and *powerfully predaceous* intruders, toothed whales and sword-fishes, at the climax of the food chain, to the remarkable *squids*, *octopuses*, *euphausiids*, *lantern fishes*, *gulpers* and *anglerfishes* that inhabit the *bathypelagic* region.

In the mesopelagic region, where some sunlight penetrates, fishes are often countershaded, that is, they are darker above and lighter below, as are surface fishes. Many of the creatures of this dimly lighted region participate in the daily migration, swimming to the upper layers at evening like bats emerging from their caves.

At greater depths, over a half-mile or so, the common inhabitants are often darkly pigmented, weakbodied and frequently adapted to unusual feeding techniques. Attraction of prey by luminescent lures or by mimicry of small prey, greatly extensible jaws and expansible abdomens are common. It is, however, a region of Lilliputian monsters, usually not more than six inches in length, with most larger fishes greatly reduced in musculature and weakly constructed.

There are some much larger, stronger and more active fishes and squids in this region, although they are not taken in trawls or seen from submersibles. Knowledge of their existence comes mainly from specimens found in the stomach of sperm whales and swordfish. They must be rare, however, since the slow, conservative creatures that are taken in trawls could hardly coexist with large numbers of active predators.

Nevertheless, populations must be sufficiently large to attract the sperm whales and swordfish. There is evidence that the sperm whales possess highly developed long-range bunting sonar. They may locate their prey over relatively great distances, perhaps miles, from just such an extremely sparse population of active bathypelagic animals.

Although many near-surface organisms are luminescent, it is in the *bathypelagic* region that *bioluminescence* has reached a surprising level of development, with at least two-thirds of the species producing light. Were we truly marine-oriented, we would perhaps be more surprised by the almost complete absence of biological light in the land environment, with its few rare cases of *fireflies*, *glowworms* and *luminous bacteria*. Clearly bioluminescence can be valuable to higher organisms, and the creatures of the *bathypelagic realm* have developed light-producing organs and structures to a high degree.

In many cases the organs have obvious functions. Some fishes, squids and euphausiids possess *searchlights* with *reflector*, lens and iris almost as complex as the eye. Others have complex patterns of small lights that may serve the functions of recognition, schooling control and even *mimicry* of a small group of *luminous plankton*.

Strong flashes may confuse predators by "*target alteration*" effects, or by producing residual images in the predators' vision. Some squids and shrimps are more direct and discharge luminous clouds to cover their escape.

The luminous organs are arranged on some fishes so that they can be used to countershade their silhouettes against faint light coming from the surface. Luminous baits are well developed. Lights may also be used for locating a mate, a problem of this vast, sparsely populated domain that has been solved by some *anglerfishes* by the development of tiny males that live parasitically attached to their relatively hugemates.

It has been shown that the vertebrate eye has been adapted to detect objects in the lowest light level on the earth's surface—a moonless, overcast night under a dense forest canopy-but net lower. Light levels in the bathypelagic region can be much lower.

This is most probably the primary difference that accounts for the absence of bioluminescence in higher land animals and the richness of its development in the ocean forms. The densest populations of *bathypelagic* creatures lie below the moot productive surface regions, except at high latitudes, where the dearth of winter food probably would exhaust the meager reserves of these creatures. All the bathypelagic populations are sparse, and in this region living creatures are less than one hundred-millionth of the water volume.

Nevertheless, the zone is of immense dimensions and the total populations may be large. Some genera, such as the feeble; tiny bristle-jawed fishes, are probably the most numerous fishes in the world and constitute a gigantic total biomass. There are some 2,000 species of fishes and as many species of the larger invertebrates known to inhabit the bathypelagic zone, but only a few of these species appear to be widespread.

The *barriers* to distribution in this widely interconnected mid water region are not obvious. The floor of the deep sea constitutes an environment quite unlike the mid-water and surface environments. Here are sites for the attachment of the larger invertebrates that filter detritus from the water.

Among these animals are *representatives* of some of the earliest multicelled creatures to exist on the earth, glass sponges, sea lilies (crinoids)—once thought to have been long extinct—and lamp shells (brachiopods). At one time it was also thought that the *abyssal* floor was sparsely inhabited and that the populations of the deepocean floor were supplied with food only by the slow, meager rain of terminal detrital food material that has passed through the surface and bathypelagic populations.

Such *refractory material* requires further passage into filter feeders or through slow bacterial action in the sediment, followed by consumption by larger burrowing organisms, before it becomes available to active free-living animals. This remnant portion of the food web could support only a very small active population.

Recent exploration of the abyssal realm with a baited camera throws doubt on the view that this is the exclusive mechanism of food transfer to the deep bottom. Large numbers of active fishes and other creatures are attracted to the bait almost immediately.

It is probably true that several rather independent branches of the food web coexist in support of the deep-bottom creatures : one the familiar rain of fine detritus, and the other the rare, widely separated falls of large food particles that are in excess of the local feeding capacity of the broadly diffuse bathypelagic population.

Such falls would include dead whale, large sharks or other large fishes and fragments of these, the multitude of remnants that are left when predators attack a school of surface fish and now, undoubtedly, garbage from ships and kills from underwater explosions.

These sources result in an influx of high-grade food to the sea floor, and we would expect to find a population of active creatures adapted to its prompt discovery and utilization. The baited cameras have demonstrated that this is so.

Other sources of food materials are braided into these two extremes of the abyssal food web. There is the rather subtle downward diffusion of living and dead food that results initially from the daily vertical migration of small fish and zooplankton near the surface.

This migration appears to impress a *sympathetic* daily migration on the mid-water populations down to great depths, for below the levels that light penetrates. Not only may such vertical migration bring feeble *bathypelagic* creatures near the bottom but also it accelerates in itself the flux of dead food material to the bottom of the deep sea.

There must also be some unassignable flux of food to the abysaal population resulting from the return of juveniles to their habitat. The larvae and young of many abyssal creatures develop at much shallower levels. To the extent that the biomass of *juveniles* returning to the deep regions exceeds the biomass of spawn released from it, this process, which might be called "*Faginism*", *constitutes* an input of food.

Benthic animals are much more abundant in the shallower waters off continents, particularly offshore from large rivers. Here there is often not only a richer near-surface production and a less hazardous journey of food to the sea floor but also a considerable input of food conveyed by rivers to the bottom. The deep slopes of river sediment wedges are typified by a *comparatively* rich population of *burrowing* and *filtering* animals that utilize this fine organic material.

All the great rivers of the world save one, the Congo, have built sedimentary wedges along broad reaches of their coast, and in many instances these wedges extend into deep water. The shallow regions of such wedges are highly productive of active and often valuable marine organisms. At all depths the wedges bear larger populations than are common at similar depths elsewhere.

Thus one wonders what inhabits the fan of the *Congo*. The great river, because of a strange *invasion* of a *submarine* canyon into its month, has built no wedge but rather is depositing a vast alluvial fan in the two mile depths of the *Angola Basin*. This great deep region of the sea floor may harbor an *unexplored* population that is *wholly* unique.

In itself the pressure of the water at great depths appears to constitute no insurmountable barrier to water-breathing animal life. The depth limitations of many creatures are the associated conditions of low *temperature*, *darkness*, *sparse food* and so on.

It should perhaps come as no surprise, therefore, that some of the fishes of high latitudes, which are of course adapted to cold dark waters, extend far into the deep cold waters in much more southern latitudes. Off the coast of Lower California, in water 1,200 to 6,000 feet deep, baited cameras have found an abundance of several species of fishes that are known at the near surface only far to the north. 'these include giant arctic sharks, sablefish and others.

It appears that some of the fishes that have been called arctic species are actually fishes of the dark cold waters of the seas, which only "*outcrop*" in the *Arctic*, where cold water is at the surface.

We have discussed several of the *benthic* and *epibenthic* environments without pointing out some of the unique features the presence of a solid interface entails. The bottom is much more variable than the mid-water zone is. There are as a result more *environmental niches* for an organism to occupy, and hence we see organisms that are of a wider range of form and habit. Adaptations develop for hiding and ambuscade, for mimicry and controlled patterns. *Nests* and *burrows* can be built, lairs occupied and defended and booby traps set.

Aside from the wide range of form and function the benthic environment elicits from its inhabitants, there are more fundamental conditions that influence the nature and form of life there. For example, the *dispersed* food material settling from the upper layers becomes much concentrated against the sea floor.

Indeed, it may becomes further concentrated by lateral currents moving it into depressions or the troughs of *ripples*. In the mid-water environment most creatures must move by their own energies to seek food, using their own food stores for this motion. On the bottom, however, substantial water currents are present at all depths, and creatures can await the passage of their food.

Although this saving only amounts to an added effectiveness for predators, it is of critical importance to those organisms that filter water for the fine food material it contains, and it is against the bottom interface that a major bypass to the *microscopic* steps of the dominant food web is *achieved*.

Here large organisms can grow by consuming microscopic or even submicroscopic food particles. *Clams*, *scallops*, *mussels*, *tube worms*, barnacles and a host of other creatures that inhabit this zone have developed a wide range of extremely effective filtering mechanisms.

In one step, aided by their attachment, the constant currents and the concentration of detritus against the interface, they perform the feat, most unusual in the sea, of growing large organisms directly from *microscopic food*. Although the *benthic environment* enables the creatures of the sea to develop a major branch of the food web that is emancipated from successive microscopic steps, this makes little difference to the *food economy* of the sea.

The sea is quite content with a large population of tiny organisms. From man's standpoint, however, the shallow benthic environment is an unusually effective producer of larger *creatures* for his food, and he widely utilizes of these resources.

Man may not have created an ideal environment for himself, but of all the environments of the sea it is difficult to conceive of one better for its inhabitants than the one marine creatures have created almost exclusively for themselves: the *coral islands* and coral reefs. In these exquisite, immense and wellnigh unbelievable structures from and adaptation reach a zenith.

An adequate description of the coral reef and coral atoll structure, environments and living communities is beyond the scope of this article. The general history and structure of atolls is well known, not only because of an inherent fascination with the magic and beauty of coral islands but also because of the wide admiration and publicity given to the prescient deductions on the origin of atolls by Charles Darwin, who foresaw much of what modern exploration has affirmed.

From their slowly sinking foundations of ancient volcanic mountains, the creatures of the coral shoals have crected the greatest organic structures that exist. Even the smallest atoll far surpasses any of man's greatest building feats, and a large *atoll* structure in actual mass approaches the total of all man's building that now exists.

These are living monuments to the success of an extremely intricate but balanced society of fish, invertebrates and plants, capitalizing on the basic advantages of benthic populations already discussed. Here, however, each of the reef structures acts almost like a single great isolated and complex benthic organism that has extended itself from the deep poor waters to the *sunlit richer* surface.

The trapping of the advected food from the surface currents enriches the entire *community*. Attached plants further add to the economy, and there is considerable direct consumption of plant life by large invertebrates and fish. Some of the creatures and relationships that have developed in this environment are among the most highly adapted found on the earth. For example, a number of the important reef building animals, the corals, the great tridacna clams and others not only feed but also harbor within their tissues dense populations of single-celled green plants.

These plants photosynthesize food that is then directly available within the bodies of the animals; the plants in turn depend on the animal waste produets within the body fluids, with which they are bathed, to derive their basic nutrients. Thus within the small environment of these plant-animal composites both the entire *laborious* nutrient cycle and the microscopic food web of the sea appear to be *substantially bypassed.*

There is much unknown and much to be discovered in the structure and ecology of coral atolls. Besides the task of unraveling the complex relationships of its inhabitants there are many *questions* such as: Why have many potential atolls never initiated effective growth and remained submerged almost a mile below the surface?

Why have others lost the race with *submergence* in recent times and now become shallowly submerged, dying banks? Can the nature *of* the circulation of the ancient ocean be deduced from the distribution *of* successful and unsuccessful atolls ? In there circulation within the coral limestone structure that adds to the nutrient supply, and is this related to the curious development of coral knolls, or coral heads, within the lagoons?

Finally, what is the potential of cultivation within these vast shallow—water bodies of the deed open sea? There is, of course, much to learn about all marine life the basic processes of the food web, productivity, populations, distributions and the mechanisms of reinoculation, and the effects of intervention into these processes, such as pollution, artificial upwelling, transplantation, cultivation and fisheries.

To learn of these processes and effects we must understand the nature not only of strong simple actions but also of weak complex interactions, since the forms of life or the success of a species may be determined by extremely small second- and third-order effects. In natural affairs, unlike human codes, de minimis curat lex—the law is concerned with trivial.

Little is understood of the manner in which speciation (that is, the evolution of new species) occurs in the broadly intercommunicating pelagic environment with so few obvious barriers Important yet unexpected environmental niches may exist in which temporary isolation may enable a new pelagic species to evolve. For example, the top few millimeters of the open sea have recently been shown to constitute a demanding environment with unique inhabitants. Further knowledge of such microcosms may well yield insight into speciation.

As it has in the past, further, exploration of the abyssal realm will undoubtedly reveal undescribed creatures including members of groups thought long extinct, as well as commercially valuable populations. As we learn more of the condition that control the distribution of species of pelagic organisms, we shall become increasingly competent to read the pages of the earth's *marine-biological*, *oceanographic* and *meterological* history that are recorded in the sediments by organic remains.

We shall know more of primordial history, the early production of a breathable atmosphere and petroleum production. Some of these deposits of sediment cover even the period of man's recorded history with a fine time resolution. From such great records we should eventually be able to increase greatly our understanding of the range and interrelations of weather, ocean conditions and biology for sophisticated and enlightened guidance of a *broad spectrum* of man's activities extending from meteorology and hydrology to oceanography and *fisheries*.

Learning and guidance of a more specific nature can also be of great practical importance. The diving ***physiology*** of marine mammals throws much light on the same physiological processes in land animals in *oxygen stress* (during birth, for example).

The higher flowering plants that inhabit the marine salt marshes are able to tolerate salt at high concentration, desalinating seawater with the sun's energy. Perhaps the *tiny molecule* or DNA that commands this process is the most precious of marine-life resources for man's uses. Bred into existing crop plants, it may bring salt-water agriculture to reality and nullify the creeping scourge of *salinization* of agricultural soils.

Routine upstream reinoculation of preferred species of phytoplankton and zooplankton might stabilize some pelagic marine populations at high effectiveness. Transplanted marine plants and animals may also animate the dead saline lakes of continental interiors, as they have the Salton Sea of California.

The possible benefits of broad marine-biological understanding are endless. Man's aesthetic, adventurous, recreational and practical proclivities can be richly served. Most important, undoubtedly, is the intellectual promise: to learn how to approach and understand a complex system of strongly interacting biological, physical and chemical entities that is vastly more than the sum of its parts, and thus how better to understand complex man and his *interactions* with his complex planet, and to explore with *intelligence* and open eyes a huge portion of the earth, which continuously teaches that when understanding and insight are sought for their own sake, the rewards are more *substantial* and *enduring* than when they are sought for more limited goals.

6

ACTIVE ANIMALS OF THE DEEP-SEA FLOOR

Photographs made by *automatic cameras* that have been dropped to the deep-ocean floor have confirmed a finding that was first suggested by evidence gathered from baited traps some years ago. A deep-sea *population* of large, active animals thrives in what was generally assumed to be a province inhabited mainly by small, feeble creatures such as worms, snails sponges.

The thousands of pictures make it clear that much of the deepsea floor teems with numerous species of *scavengers*: *vigorous* invertebrates and fishes, including some gigantic sharks, that are supported by a marine food web whose extent and complexity is only beginning to be perceived. The celebrated expedition of H.M.S. *Challenger in* the 1870's laid to rest the old idea that the deep waters of the open ocean were a lifeless desert.

The *Challenger's* trawls and dredges brought to the surface and to the attention of biologists a vast collection of deep-mid-water and bottom-dwelling creatures from even the deepest ocean trenches. The inventory included some of the most some of the most *grotesque* forms into which higher animals have ever been molded by adaptation to extreme conditions, and several animals that had been thought to be long extinct.

In this country much has been added to that inventory and to our understanding of deep-living animals. The investigations were conducted, however, by means of *trawls* and *dredges*, by direct observation from deep-diving *submersible* vehicles and by inspection of *photographs* made by cameras lowered on cables from ships, and it is *characteristic* of these methods that they *ordinarily* sample only the stationary or slow-moving animals of the deep-sea communities; the deeper the investigation is, the more difficult and the less effective it is.

The gave rise to the prevalent assumption of a few years ago that the ocean bottom was *sparsely inhabited* by weak creatures specially adapted to live on the only food material then thought to be available at great depths: a terminate food web supported by the thin but constant rain of detritus that sifts down from the surface layers and that is metabolized by primitive filter feeders or bacteria and deposit feeders in the bottom ooze.

A proper *reconnaissance* of the active deep-sea creatures whose presence was revealed by the baited traps required new tools. Over the past seven years *Meredith Sessions*, *Richard Shutts* and the authors, working at the Scripps Institution of Oceanography, have designed and constructed robot motion picture and still cameras and other instruments with which to explore the *bottom* and to study the nature, *distribution* and *behavior* of its *inhabitants*.

We find, first of all, that the population of sea-floor invertebrates is by no means sparse and that many of its species are far from weak. And they are not alone. Their domain is shared by a population of scavenging fishes and crustaceans adapted for the prompt discovery and consumption of large falls of food; the bodies of dead animals descending from above, mid-water *creatures* that happen to approach the bottom and juveniles of their own species that return to the deeps from the *shallower* water where they undergo their early development.

The cameras we have devised for the ocean-floor study are free-fall devices connected to a recovery buoy, a flood-light and a bait holder. Released at the surface, the camera falls to the bottom and remains there, anchored by the bait holder for between 12 and 48 hours, making still *photographs* or short bursts of *motion* pictures at five-to 15-minute *intervals*.

The bait is in the foreground of each frame and the camera's view is either vertical or oblique. At the end of the mission the bait ballast is released and the camera and its buoy rise to the surface, where a radio transmitter *broadcasts* a signal that aids in *recovery*. The free-fall technique allows a research ship to ,conduct various other missions while a number of cameras it has distributed keep *functioning* on the sea floor.

And the work can be done from rather simple, inexpensive vessels, provided only that they have *reasonable navigation* and *sonic-sounding*

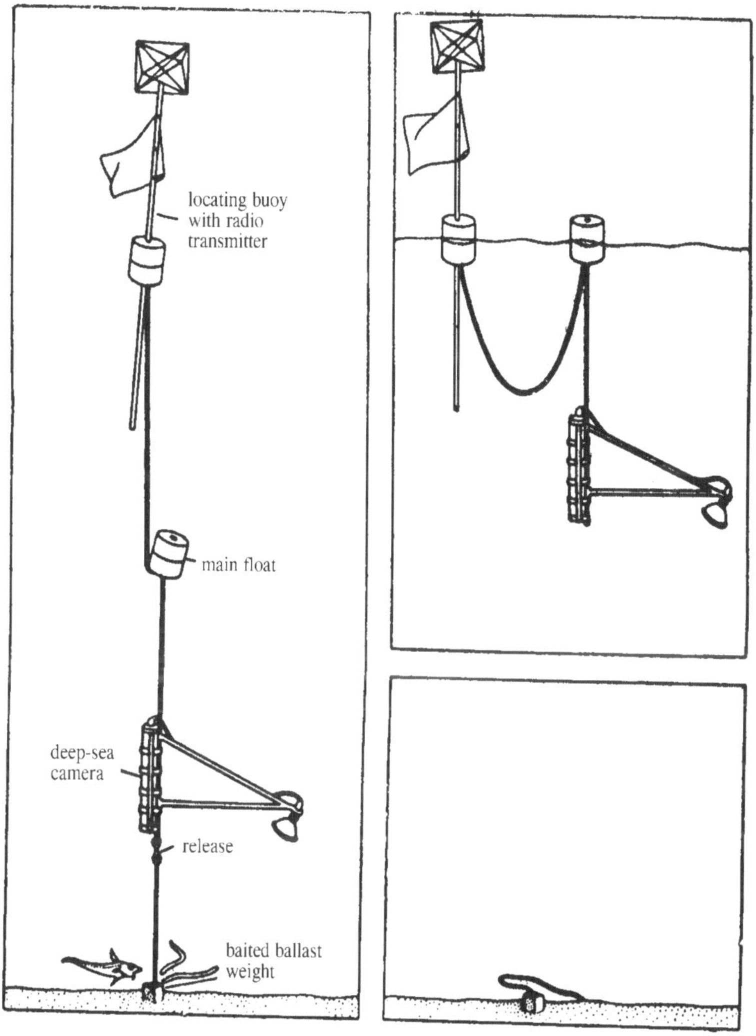

Figure 6.1: Free-fall Camera is dropped to the ocean bottom, where it is held in position by a baited ballast weight and a float made of foamed plastic.

equipment. In a typical drop the camera is released in water that is between 400 and 7,000 meters deep. *Greater depths* call for a special camera housing and flotation gear because of the immense pressures.

The camera operates during the descent, which may take as long as several hours, but ordinarily not much is seen in photographs made on the way down except for the "*snow*" of small particles, which are ubiquitous in the midwaters of the sea, and a few fleeting small crustaceans.

Sometimes the very first photographs on the bottom, made a few minutes, after the camera reaches it, show great activity, with fishes and invertebrates already tearning at the bait. More commonly, however, the first scenes show only *brittle stars*, *large shrimps*, *amphipods* (small *crustaceans*) and perhaps a fish or two.

On more than half of the missions at least one fish has been photographed within 30 minutes of the camera's arrival on the bottom, even at the greater depths. (Curiously the first photographs sometimes record a fish of a species that is not seen again in the sequence, as though the camera had invaded the territory of a creature that was not a part of the population of active *scavengers* and wanted nothing to do with the subsequent activity.)

Usually the number of fish gathered around the bait increases slowly, reaching a maximum after a few hours. Often the scene develops into one of furious activity, with several species of fish competing for the bait, thrashing and tearing at it and sometimes attacking one another. *Shrimps*, *brittle stars*, *amphipods* and other invertebrates *encroach* on the melee.

In almost half of the sequences from drops down to 2,000 meters the party ends abruptly after three to eight hours, when some creature, usually a large shark, moves in, (frightens off the other fish and consumes the bulk of the bait. In any case the time comes when most of the bait has been e ten.

The fish depart, and slowly *crabs*, *sea urchins*, *snails* and other such *creatures* arrive to complete the task of *sanitizing* the sea floor. Sometimes the direction of the near bottom currents has been determined and it can be seen that these latecomers to the banquet plot upstream toward the bait-an indication that they are probably following a scent.

The fishes also probably depend on scent for close—in detection of the bait; on some occasions we could relate the *number* of fish gathered around the *bait* to the strength of the current, which suggests that an increased current had carried the *scent* more widely.

Like *wide-ranging* scavengers on land, however, fish that are farther away are probably led to the area of the bait by other cues. They may sense the *successive collapse* of loosely established *territories* as the scavengers that held them move closer to the bait, each invading the area once held by an absent *neighbor*.

The western *prairie wolf*, vultures and other terrestrial *scavengers*

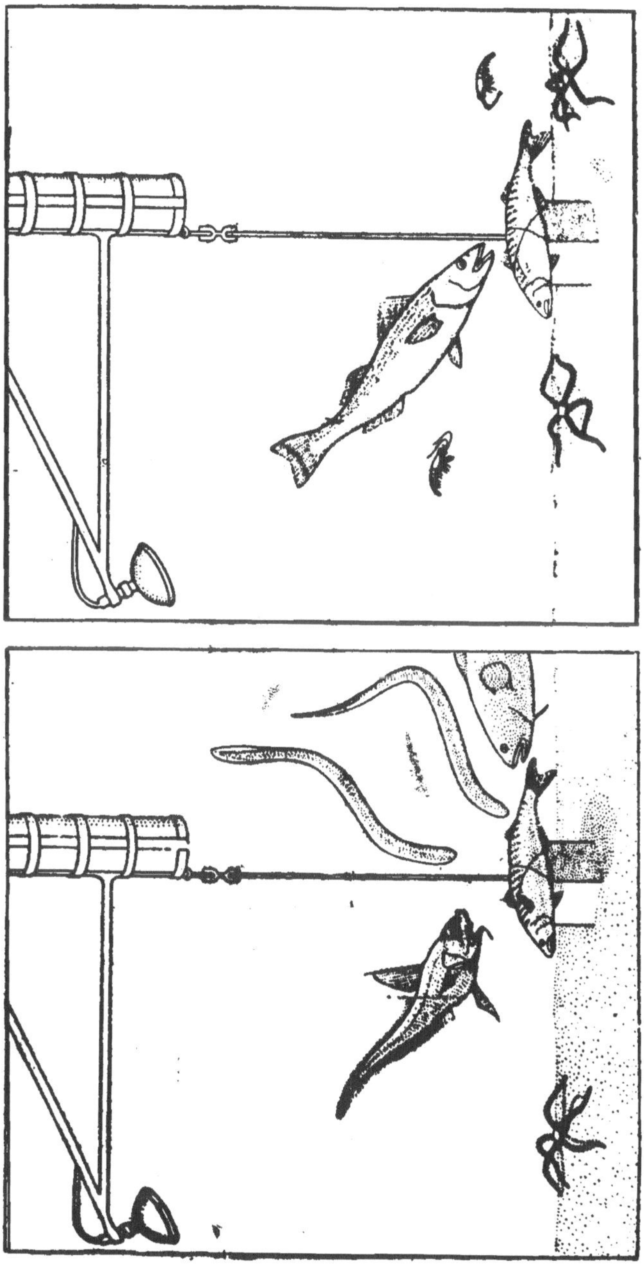

Figure 6.2: One likely sequence of events following the arrival of a baited camera system on the ocean floor is shown in the idealized drawing on these two pages.

respond to just such a territorial collapse to converge on *large kills*. Surprisingly, we find particularly *abundant* bottom populations in regions of the Pacific where the surface *populations* are the least abundant, and vice versa. For example, under the least productive surface waters of the North *Pacific Gyre*, on an *austero* bottom paved with manganese nodules nearly 6,000 meters down, more than 40 large fish and shrimps were attracted by the bait within a few hours; at least four species were represented.

Moderately productive areas of the Indian Oeean the California Current system and biologically poor areas around the Hawaiian Islands have also shown remarkably large numbers of deep-sea creatures. On the other hand, only 4,000 meters down under the most productive oceanic waters of the world, in the Antarctic over a bottom of soft organic ooze, the bait was visited by only a few eelpouts, brotulids and rattail fish (grenadiers), along with some small crustaceans, the louselike isopods.

The *brotulids* (fishes distantly related to cods) remained almost motionless for hours, nibbling gently at the bait. Camera drops along the underwater ridges of the Line Islands, a highly *productive equatorial* area of the *Pacific*, revealed only a few eels. Photographs from the bottom below the rich Peru Current showed very few fish but large numbers of invertebrates: furious masses of amphipods that stripped the bait in a few hours.

The explanation for such a puzzling distribution must lie in the nature of this part of the marine food web. These abyssal roving scavengers must depend for their sustenance in substantial part on falls of large food particles.

Such particles include fish and marine mammals that have died, fragments of forage from surface-feeding schools of fish, vertically migrating creatures, garbage from ships and (nowadays) animals killed by under-water explosions, ships' propellers and whaling. Falling food material can support a population of deep scavengers only if the food descends to the bottom, and it may be that the midwater population below highly *productive* regions is *sufficiently dense* and continuous to consume such food on the way down, Regions of low productivity, on the other hand, may support such sparse and discontinuous mid-water populations that a substantial proportion of dead *surface creatures* do fall all the way to the sea floor.

And them on the floor even a meager fall can support a sizable population, whose scavenging can be much more intensive than that of

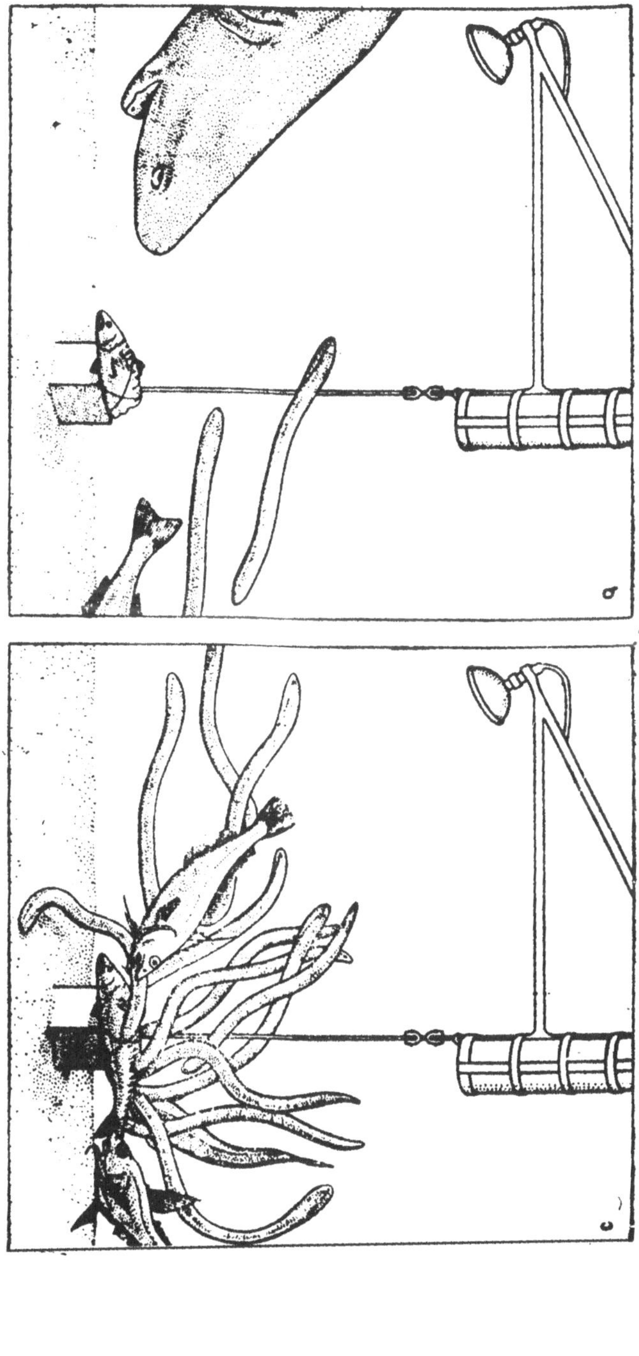

Figure 6.3: Bait increases slowly, reach in a maximum after a few hours.

fish living on the relatively brief passage of falls through the immense volume of the mid waters.

Somewhat different explanations are possible, perhaps in combination with this mid-water-population effect. The western north-central Pacific, where so many fish were photographed over a *manganese-nodule* bottom, is an area through which tuna and other large surface fishes and whales and other *cetaceans periodically* migrate.

Just as terrestrial deserts are traps for aged, infirm or injured creatures, so may this marine desert be a trap. The number of large migrants that succumb in traversing its unproductive surface waters may be sufficient to support the bottom population.

We know nothing of the "natural" end of the largest fishes and cetaceans; it could well be that these vast areas of low productivity inflict the final stress on aging and infirm members of the populations of great marine *creatures*, *exhausting* their *ultimate* reserves.

Deep below areas of high productivity, on the other hand, the principal descending food may be rather small particles, sufficient to support a sizable and continuous population of mid-water creatures as well as throngs of small bottom scavengers that do not need to rove far for sustenance.

Moreover, in such waters the large near-surface animals have plentiful food and are not in such a precarious situation as the schools of large migrants crossing the great marine deserts. Areas of high productivity might therefore fail to support the larger scavengers of the deep-floor; few active, roving fish would be searching for large food falls such as our bait represents.

Some of the fishes now being observed for the first time at great depths at low latitudes turn out to be species that are well known in near-surface waters; at high latitudes. The flatnose codling, the sablefish and the arctic sleeper shark are common inhabitants of the bottom off the coast of southern *California* and *Lower California*; the *sablefish*, which is found in commercially valuable numbers off the coast of Washington, British Columbia and Alaska, is particularly abundant on the deep-sea floor of the Southern California Bight thousands of miles to the south. On the basis of the incidence of this species in a *random* series of pictures made with unbaited comeras, we have estimated that there are 800.000 *tons* of *sablefish* at depths of between 800 and 1,500 meters in the southern *California* waters; they seem to be of the same race as the *commercially harvested* variety far to the north.

At least along the Pacific coast of North America, then, some species that are generally considered arctic fishes apparently represent mere near-surface outcroppings of populations that inhabit the cold, deep waters of *continental* borders to the south. If that is true of other coasts as well, the size and extent of a number of fish populations may be dramatically larger than has been thought. The total numbers of large shrimps in particular must be *immense*, since they are almost always attracted to the bait at all depths and in all regions we have sampled.

In one of our sequences a small brown' shark appears in the bottom waters of the Santa *Barbara* Basin, which contain virtually no dissolved oxygen. We have also photographed dead mid-water fish on the bottom there. The combination suggests another sources of food in some deep waters. Perhaps anoxic basins serve as traps for *unsuspecting* vertically migrating animals that have never encountered pockets of suffocating water.

A scavenger adapted for short forays into such a basin could find a rich harvest. Perhaps the brown shark is so adapted, able to survive a brief period of oxygen deficit. Sometimes no fish appear in our pictures: the bait is completely consumed by vast numbers of invertebrates such as shrimps and swarming amphipods.

Motion pictures from the Santa Cruz Basin off southern California shows the amphipods accumulating until the bait is totally covered and the surrounding water is nearly saturated by a rolling mass of these crustaceans.

In that sequence one sablefish came near the bait but left immediately, *gaping* as if to rid itself of amphipods. Is it possible that where there are swarms of aggressive invertebrates such as *amphipods*, fish are not able to compete for the small amount of food that reaches the bottom?

Amphipods can sustain themselves on small food particles, but they are also capable of quickly and completely devouring the much larger pieces that fall to the ocean floor. Deep-living octopuses are other *invertebrates* that tend to *monopolize* the bait.

In one motion-picture sequence made at about 4,000 metres a small octopus squats on the bait, keeping the grenadiers at tentacle's length, and in an unusual sequence made with a still camera off *Cedross Island* in *Lower California* two octopuses fend off a single *grenadier* from the bait.

The bait is often taken over *aggressively* and completely *innumerable hagfish*, primitive eyeless and jawless chordates that dril into dead creatures and consume them from the inside out. Hagfish thrive at a depth of from 200 meters to nearly 2,000 meters. At first we were puzzled by the *reluctance* the Gorgon's-head tangle of *hagfish* and feed on the bait.

Closeup motion pictures gave the answer: the hagfish enclose the bait in a thick cocoon of slime that other fishes apparently find distressing. On a number of occasions fish emerge from the feeding mass making frantic efforts to clear their gills of slime.

The spectacular ability of the hagfish to exude slime has long been known; the exudation of a single hagfish can convert a large container of water into a slimy gel. Their employment of this defense mechanism to sequester food, however, had not been suggested.

Some of the scavenging bottom fishes display a feeding capability that could scarcely be predicted from an examination of their jaw and tooth structure. The grenadiers are quite capable of tearing out the abdomen of a bait fish; sablefish shake large baits as terriers do and spin furiously to twist off mouthfuls of food.

The large sharks that frequent the deep-ocean floor have been photographed to depths of about 2,000 meters. Their behavior in approaching the bait appears to be mediated in part by a sense of smell: the fish execute slow, deliberate geometrical maneuvers that apply combine to establish a complex a pattern.

On some occasions, when bait holder has been hung somewhat as a rough bottom, the sharks are unable to discover it. Clearly they accustomed only to food resting on sea floor; when they connot find it, snudge and bite at rocks or other por objects under the bait. Even search for bait that is on the ocean usually requires more than one before the bait is found.

Several are sequences end just as the shark position to seize the bait, with the dead ahead within the width of park's jaws. Yet the next sequence, five minutes later, may show the untouched and the shark still end in a slow, deliberate search. Like as. hagfish are unable to discover the w en it is a meter or so above bottom, whereas eels and grenadiers no difficulty locating bait that is above the bottom.

Knowledge of feeding limitations will help in the development of better techniques for some deep-water fisheries, where the depredations of shark and hagfish greatly limit the catch. One of the shyest fishes we have photographed, and perhaps one of the deepest-living, is the brotulid. In a number of photographs from the deepest locations brotulids lurk at the outer edge of a group of grenadiers.

In one motion picture series a brotulid hovers like a motionless blimp through sequence after sequence, facing the feeding grenadiers. Unlike most of the deep-water fishes, the brotulids have very reduced eyes, and it may be that their behavior is related to diminished visual acuity.

Creatures living more than several hundred meters below the surface are maneuvering in a profound darkness that is lighted only by the faint glow or brighter brief flashes of bioluminescent. Only fishes with a highly developed visual system can be expected to be guided by visual cues. Brotulids may be responding not to the presence of the bait but to the sound of the feeding fish.

Many sequences yield fresh insights into feeding behavior. A crab gingerly lifts some sea urchins off the bait, holds them away from its body like a spider ejecting a distasteful insect from its web and drops them.

Sheltered by the empty bait holder, a small spiny lobster flails its antennae in a strong current, apparently grasps a small swimming crustacean between the antennae and conveys it to its mouth by some movement too quick for us to make out.

As grenadier goes after small food particles in the sediment with a sudden explosive thrust into the bottom, throwing a cloud of sediment through its gills. The uniformly large size of most of the fish photographed at great depths presents something of a puzzle.

Very few small fish are ever seen. The grenadiers photographed at from 750 to 6,000 meters in the Pacific, Antarctic and Indian oceans are all large, nature fish, some measuring more than a meter in length. We have so far recovered no free grenadier eggs or juvenile fish from collections made off California anywhere between the surface and the bottom, although females with ripe ovaries have been collected near the bottom.

All the arctic sleeper shark photographed off souther California and Lower California have been very large, but most of the photographs have shown only a small portion of their total length, which we can only estimate as being between five and eight meters. They also must be quite common, since they have been photographed in nearly half of our missions off California down to 2,000 meters; on a number of occasions when more than one large shark was *photographed* during a mission, we could tell from distinguishing scars and other markings that the sharks were different *individuals*.

It is probable that the *juveniles* of these deep-living fishes inhabit much *shallower* depths than the adults. The young of the sablefish, for example, are *numerous* in many places at depths of 100 meters or so. It may be that the rarity of *juveniles* is merely the result of great adult longevity and low fecundity.

On the other hand, *juveniles* of many species must return to the deep bottom *environment*, indeed, their return may constitute a *meaningful importation* of food from the more productive upper layers for the nourishment of the total adult population.

We usually think of the relation between juveniles and adult stocks only in terms of *replacement*. Juveniles may also be important as prey; indeed, in some freshwater environments, the young of a species are a *principal prey* of adults of the same species. To the degree that this process, which has been called *Faginism*, is important to the food economy of the deep-sea populations, we would of course expect to observe a paucity of *juveniles* in the populations: most of them are *quickly* consumed by their elders.

The baited camera suffers from some limitations common to many simple *exploratory* tools. Its sample is highly selective. *Quantification* and even *identification* can be doubtful. There are several ways to deal with these problems. One can, for example, set out *fishlines* and traps in order to retrieve *specimens* for sure identification.

A particularly promising means of quantification is an unbaited drifting *camera* that lightens itself until it rises just a few meters above the bottom. It drifts with the current, making *overlapping* photographs and meanwhile recording the direction and *distance* of drift. Such a camera has been successfully operated in waters about 1,000 meters deep.

We have plans to develop a drifting camera that will remain submerged for several months, making photographs along a drift track as long as 200 kilometers.

The drifting camera should yield a meaningful census of the creatures that have been observed by *stationary* baited cameras and thus help us to assess the potential food *harvest* from the *deepocean* floor and to understand the *ramifications* of this remarkable branch of the marine food web. Meanwhile vast areas await investigation with the baited camera. A series of *photographic* "*section*" across the continental shelves along all the major land masses and down the slopes to the abyss would fill many gaps in our knowledge of bottom-dwelling animals and should reveal entirely new fishery resources.

Among the environments that are of special interest to oceanographers and marine biologists are the floor of the Arctic. Ocean, the deep delta of the Congo River, the *Antarctic slope*, the deeps of the Mediterranean, the top of *seamounts* and *mid-ocean ridges* and the slope and bottom of *deep occanic trenches*.

Since the free-all cameras can be operated from *inexpensive*, *unspecialized* craft, they are particularly suitable for studies by investigators in underdeveloped countries who want to know more about the creatures and the *potential* deep *fisheries* off their coast.

7

Oceanic Plants

During the long and arduous antarctic voyages of HMS *Erebus* and HMS *Terror* between 1839 and 1853, Sir James Clark Ross had Dr Joseph Hooker with him as naturalist to the expedition.

Dr Hooker was no doubt well aware of the Royal Society's instructions for the expedition, but he must have been particularly impressed by a letter from Alexander von Humboldt to the First Lord of the Admiralty. The letter drew attention to the far-reaching *significance* of the work of the German *microscopist* Dr Ehrenberg, on the fine structure of certain rocks.

Dr Ehrenberg had shown that the beds of '*rotten stone*' found in various parts of the world were made of immense deposits of diatom frustules and the skeletons of *Radioaria* and *sponges*; and from other *observations* on living diatom and *Radioaria* had concluded that similar *rocks* ought to be forming in the present age-at the bottom of the sea.

During the summer the *antarctic seas* teem with diatoms. Rocker saw signs of their presence almost everywhere; as brown stains on the icebergs and pack ice, as a wash of pale ochre's colour in the brhsh and pancake ice and as a *mucous scum floating* in the ice-free waters. He saw with Ehrenberg that the diatoms with their *indestructible* siliceous *coverings* must sink to form sediments on the sea floor after they die, but he also became aware of the unique importance of the living diatoms in the economy of the seas. They could be found in the stomachs of small Crustacea and other planktodic creatures.

They were the invisible plant life of the ocean '...a microscopic herbag,...probably maintaining in the South Polar Ocean that balance between the vegetable and animal kingdom which prevails over the surface of our globe'. Hooker's remarkable observations and predictions were soon followed by the independent *discoveries* of the Danish botanist Anders Sandoe Orsted.

During a voyage from Denmark to the West Indies in 1847, Orsted found that microscopic algae were the cause of discoloured water in aquaria and was led to collect sea water samples for microscopic examination. Once again he saw microscopic algae, and like Hooker,

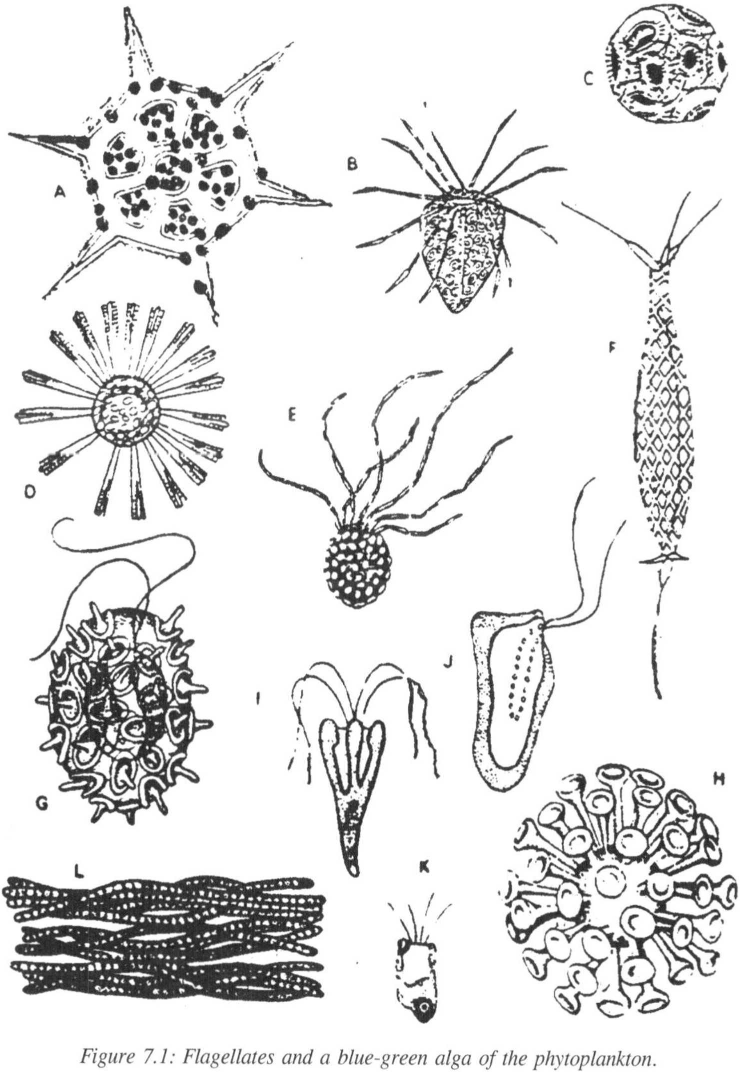

Figure 7.1: Flagellates and a blue-green alga of the phytoplankton.

discerned that these minute plants must be the main primary source of food for marine animals.

Under the microscope the sculptured patterns in the siliceous cell walls of diatoms are both *beautiful* and *distinctive*. From the middle of the ninteenth century onwards many naturalists delighted in studying these patterns; and they described more and more new species.

In 1883 von Stein monographed another group of microscopic plants, the peridinians or *Dinoflagellata*. They too were evidently of importance as food, for much of the meterial studied came from the stomachs of the transparent barrel-like salps of the plankton.

During the *Challenger* Expedition, Sir John Murray was able to show that the calcareous coccospheres and rhabdoliths of deep-sea deposits are actually parts of the skeletons of minute plants (*Coccolithophores*) that live in the surface waters of the ocean.

Soon after 1880 Victor Hensen began to study the biology of the drifting life of the ocean, the *plankton* as he called it Hensen particularly wanted to get some measure of the production of nutrient material by the plants (the *phytoplankton*).

He reasaned/that a conical silk net of a particular size drawn vertically/through the upper *plant-bearing* layer of the sea should catch all the plants in the cylindrical column of water through which it would pass. Having counted the plants it would than be possible to calculate how many were living below a unit of sea surface.

But later on Hans Lohmann pointed out that very *small* and important members of the phytoplankton, such as the *coccolithophores*, passed through the meshes of the finest silk nets. This fine nanoplankton fraction could only be obtained by means of special filters or by *centrifuging* samples of sea water so as to throw the tiny cells out of suspension.

PLANTS GROUPS

Lohmann convincingly revealed the plant-like nature of the Coccolithophoridae: within the cells are one or two brown bodies containing chlorophyll. Like the *dinoflagellates*, the *coccolithophorids* are propelled by two *protoplasmic flagella* and both have a tendency to move towards the light (*phototaxis*).

Reproduction, as in all groups of the phytoplankton, is by binary fission, though there is evidence of sexual means. *Coccolithophorids*, otherwise known as calcareous flagellates, are so called from the minute calcareous plates (*coccoliths*) that form around them and which vary in size from 1 to 35 microns (1 micron, 1/,=0.001 mm). The numbers and ornamentation of the plates differ from species to species but may also vary within a species. Coccoliths may be lacking, and if formed the cells may be without flagella.

Indeed, the form of coccolith and the nutritional mode of the motile individuals .may differ considerably from those of non-motile individuals of the same species. Much has been learned of coccolith structure and taxonomy through the use of electron-microscopes. But 'essential details of the *morphology*. Life *history*, *physiology* and *ecology* of the *coccolithophorids* are still unknown'.

There is much to be gained, both in pure and applied biology, from better knowledge of these minute plants which, after all, are known from Jurassic times and are the main constituent of chalk deposits of the *Cretaceous*. Most of the calcareous flagellates range in size from 5 to 25 microns. *Micro-flagellates*, which belong to several classes of algae, are even smiller.

They have one or more flagella and many species contain green or yellow-brown photosynthetic pigments.

Some are so small (1-2 microns) and delicate as to be almost beyond detection. Mary Parke, who has established pure cultures of several species in the Plymouth Marine Laboratory, has done much to elucidate their structure, life cycles and taxonomy.

When this diverse and elusive assemblage of microorganisms is better known, we should, above all, hope to gain closer appreciation of their significance in oceanic productivity and their importance as food for minute members of the zooplankton and for pelagic turicates.

Dinofligellates, known as *micro-fossils* from *Silurian* times, are considerably larger than calcareous flagellates and microflagellates. Most species tall in the size range from 10 to 1,000 microns the largest are species of *Noctiluca*.

There are two main groups, amoured and unarmoured. Armoured species form a transparent cell wall of *cellulose* than soon divides into *platelets pierced* by minute holes. The pattern and armature of the platelets vary from species. The cell wall of *unarmoured* species is thin and *undivided*.

There are two flagella and in many forms one *flagellum* is housed in a groove around the cell: the other is attached so that it trails backwards. The *grooved* flagellum rotates the cell, while the other drives it forwards. In some species both flagella arise at one end of the organism.

The many plant-like *dinoflagellates* contain yellow, brown or *greenish*

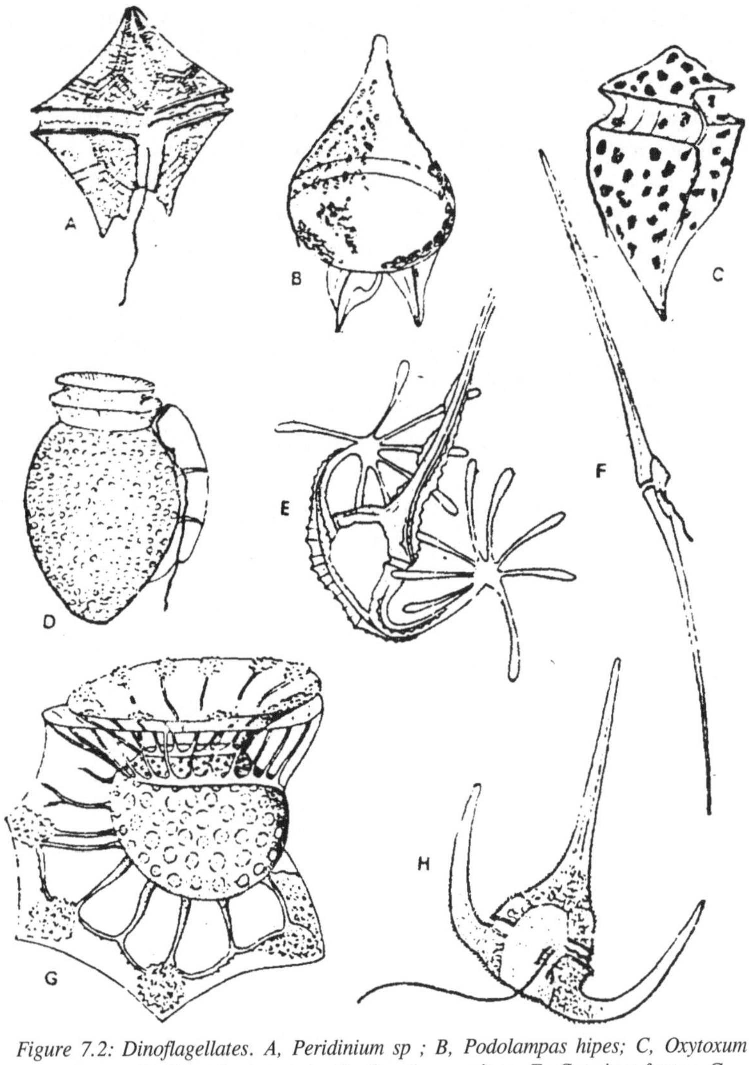

Figure 7.2: Dinoflagellates. A, Peridinium sp ; B, Podolampas hipes; C, Oxytoxum tessalutum: D, Dinophysis aeerta; E, Ceratium ranipes; F, Ceratium fusum; G, Ornitbocereus steinii; H, Ceratium tripos.

photosynthetic bodies. Forms of *photosynthetic* species (*zooxanthellae*) are symbiotic in diverse invertebrates and in the open ocean occur in various radiolarians. There are also *heterotrophic* forms, which are able to absorb and process dissolved organic substances as a source of energy. Some species even ingest minute *particles* of food.

Many dinoflagellates are *luminescent*. The light is produced in cellular organelles known as scintillons, which flash more frequently by night than by day. Whenever luminescence in the sea looks uniform from a distance and is without large blobs of light, the display is most likely to come from *dinoflagellates*.

At times '*brilliant*, short-lived bursts of light may dart across the sea surface and the crets of rolling waves glow as the *dinoflagellates* activated into emission through water disturbances create an *aquatic* version of *aurora borealis*. *Diatoms* form *transparent* but rather thick cell walls of hydrated, amorphous silica.

Just inside the cell wall is a thin layer of cytoplasm that holds the greenish or *brownish photosynthetic* bodies (*chloroplasts*). Actually the cell wall is formed in two halves, part of one fitting closely inside a corresponding part of the other. When the cell divides in two, each new cell is enclosed in one half of the old cell wall.

A new cell wall is then formed inside the *old half*. Thus as one vegetative division follows another diatoms gradually decrease in volume. The *shrinkage* is not indefinite but *stops* at a fixed cell size that varies from species to species. There is now an *auxospore stage* when the vegetative cells form male and female cells.

In certain species it seems that the male cells, which have flagella, swim into a cell containing eggs and *fertilize* them. The fertilized egg cells, which are next extruded through the opening that admitted the male cell, enlarge to full size and form the normal *siliceous* cell wall.

The cell divisions of the *vegetative* stage now begin once more. During unfavourable times, the diatoms of coastal waters also forms resting spores, which settle on the bottom and *germinate* when conditions improve. In the open ocean this kind of *renewal* is clearly impossible, but if buoyant resting spores are produced, as some *suggest*, they have yet to be discovered.

There are two main groups of diatoms. The pennate forms (*Pennales*) are bilaterally symmetrical; the centric forms (*Centtrales*) are radially *symmetrical*. Pennate species, some of which are mobile, live on the sea floor or attached to seaweeds, grasses and ice. The planktonic species are *centric* forms of diveres appearance: hair-like. needle-like, pill-box-like, *lamellate*, *stellate bracelet*—like, chain-like and so forth. Sizes range from 1 to 2,000 microns.

Sources of silicon may be in short supply in the sea, but there is another group of planktonic plants with siliceous cell walls, the *Silicoflagellara*. These forms, which bear two flagella and vary in size from 10 to 150 microns, play a *minor role* in marine productivity.

All the foregoing members of the phytoplankton are eucaryotes, organisms with their genetic material concentrated in a definite nucleus. Procaryotes which have their genetic material dispersed through the cell and not an in a nucleus are represented in the phytoplankton by the blue-green algae (*Cyanophyta*) and bacteria.

In blue-green algae the photosynthetic pigments are held by elaborate internal membranes. The well-known tropical species, *Trichodesmium erythraeum*, is a filamentous form that is often associated in loose bundles. Blooms of this *species*, which give the sea a rusty appearance and, indeed, gave the Red Sea its name, may at times cover great srretches of the *tropical ocean*.

It seems that *Trichodesmum* and certain other blue-green algae, fix molecular nitrogen and thus able to flourish in waters deficient in nitrates and other nutrient salts. Bacteria abound in the *euphotic zone*, including the *neustonic* layer dealt with earlier but decline markedly in the underlying waters, especially at levels below 1,000 metres. Many are attached to organic and *inorganic* particles and to *organisms*, both living and dead.

Though there are photosynthetic species, planktonic bacteria seem to play a minor role in oceanic productivity '...but in association with detritus they may from an *appreciable* organic *reserve* during times of low phytoplankton density'.

More significantly, bacteria and other heterotrophic organisms, such as yeasts and moulds, are the decomposers in ecosystems. Recent work by Azam and Hodson (1977) strongly suggests that most of the microbial heterotrophic activity in the ocean is due to bacteria that ore *unattached* to larger organic particles.

By transforming dead life into nutrient salts and accessory food substances, the decomposers provide the means of new life to the plant producers of the epipelagic ecosystem.

GENERAL FEATURES OF DISTRIBUTION

Phytoplankton communities flourish in the surface waters of the entire ocean. In any given area there is continual and sometimes rapid change in the composition of a community. In a litre of **sea** water the number of species may vary from less than 10 to greater than 250.

Each species waxes and wanes in relative abundance and the cycle is presumably shaped by a complex of physical and biological factors. As we shall see, supplies of nutrient salts are often limited, and as fast

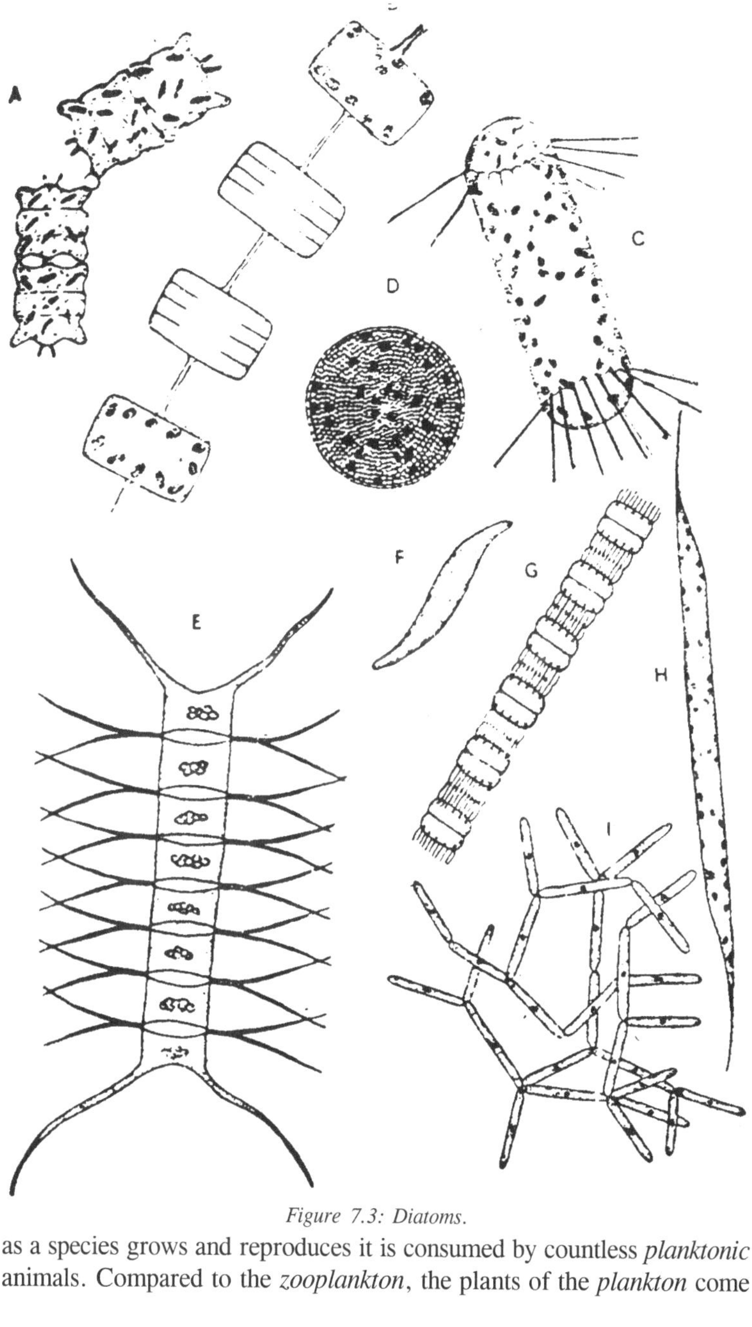

Figure 7.3: Diatoms.

as a species grows and reproduces it is consumed by countless *planktonic* animals. Compared to the *zooplankton*, the plants of the *plankton* come and go rather quickly. Even so, numerous phytoplankton species, like their animal counterparts, have spread over most of the ocean.

In a detailed study of certain species from oceanwide samples, Hasler (1976) found that she could divide them into cosmopolitan species. The latter could be subdivided into bipolar species northern hemisphere species and southern hemisphere species. But our present concern is largely with certain contrasting features in the *distribution* of the main groups of *phytoplankton*.

Diatoms are dominant in cool or cold waters. They flourish in polar seas, not only as planktonic species, but also as attached (pennate) forms on the underside of sea ice. Diatoms bloom in profusion during the long summer days in antarctic waters.

South of the *Antarctic Convergence*, where primary productivity is high, diatom ooze (and mud) accumulates on the deep-sea floor. Productivity is lower in the waters north of the *convergence* and here carbonate oozes are formed. *Diatomaceous* muds are also formed below the *diatom-rich* waters of the *subarctic* water mass in the *North Pacific*.

In middle latitudes diatoms flourish in the cool, nutrientrich waters that rise to the surface in upwelling regions off the coasts of *California*, Peru and southwest Africa. *Species* of *diatoms* are also *prominent* in *temperate* regions but in the *subtropical* and *tropical* waters they are generally much less evident and the individuals of most species tend to have thin siliceous walls.

An *outstanding* exception is in the eastern equatorial Pacific, where the remains so diatoms are common in the oozes under the divergence between the equatorial current and countercurrent. As will be seen the divergence draws up putrient salts to the surface where the diatoms can flourish. *Calcareous flagellates*, dinoflagellates and blue-green algae are often the most prevalent forms in warm oceanic waters.

But all three groups are represented in temperate and cold waters. Unlike many diatoms, members of these groups are able to subsist in waters of very low nutrient *concentrations*. On moving from coastal to oceanic waters there is usually a marked decrease in the size range of species in phytoplankton communities and also a decrease in the *minimum requirements* for nutrient. There may well be *parallel* changes in *oceanic* waters on moving from temperate to tropical regions.

The Euphotic Zone

Like their *land-based relatives*, oceanic plants synthesize energy-rich compounds, such as *glucose* and *adenosine triphosphate* (ATP), from the low-energy compounds, water and *carbon dioxide*. The *energy* for this process comes from sunlight absorbed by plant pigment (photosynthesis). In the ocean the main producers are the microscopic algae of the phytoplankton, which contain light-absorbing chlorophyll and accessory pigments in chromatophores.

The overall photosynthetic process may be represented as

$$nCO_2 + 2nH_2O\text{—visible light} \rightarrow n(CH_2O)\text{—}nO_2 + nH_2O$$

Wavelengths absorbed range from 400 to 700 nm (blue to red) and the relative light absorption over this *spectrum* varies some what among the groups of *phytoplankton*. There is also the differential absorption of light rays by the sea: thus, though chlorophyll can *absorb* red light, there is *virtually* none below a depth of 10 metres, where the blue-green part of the *spectrum* (400 to 600 nm) provides most of the energy for *photosynthesis*.

The euphotic zone of the ocean, where sunlight is strong enough for *photosynthesis*, extends from the surface to a depth of about 150 metres. *Photosynthesis* must be contained to the hours of *daylight* but *respiratory* processes, which consume the *energy-rich* substances formed during photosynthesis, go on all the time.

In culture media the respiration of phytoplankton seems to be about 10 per cent of the maximum gross photosynthesis but under certain conditions the respiration rate of some species increases by 2 to 3 times in the light.

If *dinoflagellates* are abundant in samples, respiration rates may be 35 to 60 per cent of the maximum gross photosynthesis and such high rates are though to be related to the *mobility* of the dinoflagenates; Whatever the relative levels of *photosynthesis* and *respiration*, the difference between the two processes over the life cycle of a species must be *sufficient* overall to provide for *growth* and *reproduction*.

At any given time, the rate of photosynthesis, which can be expressed as the carbon assimilated in milligrams per milligram of *chlorophyll* per hour, depends on the level of light intensity. *Experiments* show that there is a light saturation level above which the rate of *photosynthesis* is not increased, or may even be decreased, by further increment of light intensity. Below this level the rate of photosynthesis falls with decreasing light intensity.

Thus, in the exphotic zone the amount of carbon assimilated must fall with increasing depth until a level is reached (the compensation depth) where the amount gained during photosynthesis balances the amount lost during respiration. If the respiration of phytoplankton is taken as 10 per cent of the maximum photosynthesis graphs of photosynthetic rate against light intensity show that light values at the compensation depth are about 1 per cent of the surface radiation. The more *transparent* the sea, the greater is the *compensation* depth, which in the open ocean reaches a maximum level of about 150 metres. Clearly, a *phytoplankton community* will only maintain its identity if the populations of the member species are *adequately* represented at levels above the compensation depth.

As planktonic plants drift in wind-driven circulation they follow the turbulent motions of their medium. Turbulence, which increases with the wind and may be lively for long periods, will mix the phytoplankton below the euphotic zone. Some cells will be mixed back into this zone but many may never *return*, or *stay* so long in the *twilight* that most of their food reserves are consumed by *respiration*.

Furthermore, poorly nourished cells may become less buoyant and sink into the dark. Turbulent waters are not productive. In the northern North Atlantic, for instance, the spring outburst of phytoplankton follows closely the warming of a stable water column, when the 'seasonal' thermocline returns.

Turbulent mixing is unable to penetrate the marked density gradient of a thermocline. In tropical and subtropical waters, where the '*seasonal' thermocline* is more or less permanent, *phytoplankton production* continues throughout the year. On the other hand. the thermocline bars the upward transfer of nutrient salts and so limits primary production.

At already implied, staying in the euphotic zone depends on the buoyancy of the phytoplankton. Planktonic diatoms, which have cell walls of dense silica and no powers of movement, would seem to be ill *equipped* for *flotation*. Yet when diatoms actively growing in sea water are examined through a horizontal microscope they can be seen *poised*, *quite motionless*, *in midwater*, or they may move slowly up and down, carried by small *convection current*.

Diatoms thus appear to be perfectly buoyant and the reason seems clear. From time to time the protoplasm of the diatom flows together to form a round resting spore: at the same time, the cell loses the watery sap that forms at least *three-quarters* of its volume. The resting spore enclosed within the *siliceous* valves of the mother cell sinks in sea water, and so does the spore by itself.

Evidently the buoyancy of the diatom must reside in the cell sap, which would have a lighter salt complex than sea water if the cell tended to exclude the heavy *divalent ions*. An increase in the cell's lipid content would also increase buoyancy. The ionic mechanism is considered more important, especially in cells with large vacuoles. For instance, in the large diatom, *Ethmodiscux rex,* the total ionic content of living cells is about two-thirds of the content in dead cells and sea water,

But there are other *considerations*. It has been argued that in very nutrient-starved conditions, sinking is an active process for phytoplankton, enabling them to enrich their metabolism. Consider a plant cell motionless with respect to the water. Under these conditions there is the possibility of the cell soaking up the nutrients in its immediate vicinity and thus building up a shadow of low nutrient water around the cell.

The shadow effect would be overcome by sinking, since the medium surrounding the plant is being constantly changed. Effects of phytoplankton sinking can be observed in the vertical distributions of chlorophyll. Where nutrients are low in the surface water and the density of the water is also low, maximum *concentrations* of *chlorophyll* are found in the lower limit of the euphotic zone.

It has also been noted that these maxima occur where there is an increase in nutrients, *Sinking experiments* conducted by various workers have indicated that the buoyancy of the phytoplankton is somehow directly related to the physiological conditions of the cell.

Hence a healthy cell, which is one enriched with nutrients, is more buoyant than a cell that is nutrient-starved. In contrast, when the stability of the water column is low and vertical mixing is active, maximum growth and concentration of *chlorophyll* is near the surface. Experiments on living phytoplankton show that the sinking rate (in metres per day) ranges from zero to 30.

Larger and denser organisms sink faster than smaller and less dense ones of the same form (the smaller the organism the greater its relative surface area and frictional resistance to sinking). Relatively large '*bladder-like*' *diatoms*, such as *Ethmodiscus rel,* evidently depend on their very low density to maintain low sinking rates. Besides the relatively high surface area, inherent in their *smallness*, diatoms have also increased such area through the evolution of *spines*, *setae*, *gelatinous threads*, *wing-like projections* and so forth.

Apart from bacteria, the smallest members of the phytoplankton are the *micro-flagellates*, which are motlie and bounded by *fragile cell* walls. These forms should easily maintain their level, but the *calcareous flagellates* and *armoured dinoflagellates* carry substantial *ballast*. If both forms tend to swim towards the light, they will rise in the water column, but their calcareous or *cellulose* armour may well cause them to sink when they are inactive.

Certainly, the coccoliths or platelets of *numerous* species bear projections of diverse from which, as in diatoms, will increase their surface area and *retard* their rate of sinking. Large *dinoflagellates* swim at speeds from about 2 to 20 metres per day, and certain *species*, at least, change their position in the water column during the day. For instance, *Gonyaulax polyedra* displays a diet migration in which it absorbs *nutrients* from 10 to 15 m during the night and swims to the surface during the day, where light is available for photosynthesis and growth, but where nutrients are much lower than at 10 to 15 m.

In some tropical areas dinoflagellates make daily migrations between near surface waters and those of greater nutrient content below the euphotic zone. If this kind of adaptive response is common in the flagellated members of the *phytoplankton*. It may well go far to account for their success in the nutrient-poor waters of the subtropical and tropical zones.

In such *surroundings*, the *immobile centric diatoms*, which are much more tied to the '*shadow zone*' of nutrient depletion around them, would seem to be at a disadvantage.

Patterns of Primary Productivity

Primary production is the rate at which high-energy organic compounds are formed by photosynthesis from the common *inorganic substances*, carbon dioxide and water (or some other *hydrogen donor*). The alternative is needed because *photosynthetic bacteria* use other hydrogen donors.

Since *photosynthetic* organisms make their own foods, they are called autotrophic, a term that also fits *chemosynthetic bacteria*. But the main primary producers of the ocean are the algae of the, phytoplankton.

Primary production may be estimated by *measuring* the amount of carbon *assimilated* or oxygen produced over a given period. The first method, which was introduced in 1952 by E. Steeman Nielsen. involves adding a known amount of radioactive carbon (C^{14}) in the form of sodium bicarbonate ($NaHC^{14}O_3$) to bottles of sea water with the natural content of *phytoplankton* and other organisms.

The bottles may be left in the light or suspended in the euphotic zone. After suitable preparation, the amount of C^{14} assimilated by the *phytoplankton* can be estimated through counts with a *Geiger-Muller* tube. Oxygen evolved may be measured by using an *oxygen electrode* or the Winkler titration technique. The C^{14} technique, which is considerably more sensitive than the *oxygen* method in regions of low productivity, is the one generally used in the open ocean.

Primary productivity is usually expressed in milligrams of carbon assimilated under a square meter of sea surface per day. It will already be evident that primary production depends on a number of factors : the intensity and quality of light, the stability of the water column and the supply of nutrients. *Productivity* also falls with temperature.

Thus the *photosynthetic* rate of arctic and antarctic phytoplankton per unit of chlorophyll is less than that of phytoplanton in temperature or tropical waters. *Salinity* and *hydrogen* ion concentration (pH) may also be involved. Under nutrients are not only included the essential phosphates and nitrates but also accessory growth substances such as vitamins, notably vitamin B_{12}.

Vigorous phytoplankton growth also requires quantities of iron and manganese, needed for the formation of cholorophyll. Diatoms require silicates enough to make their cell walls. Measurements of *primary* production have now revealed the main patterns of ocean *productivity*. Differences in *productivity* controlling factors, but how are these to be unravelled?

The way was shown in 1840 by the *German chemist* Liebig in his book on the application of chemistry to agriculture and physiology. His statement that the 'growth of a plant is dependent on the minimum amount of food stuff presented' became known as Liebig's law of the minimum.

In 1899 another German chemist, Karl Brandt, thought that Liebig's law might also apply to the ocean; that plants might from time to time be limited in their growth and reproduction by lack of nutrient salts, such as phosphates and nitrates, which occur in small quantities in the sea.

Later research has amply proved the usefulness of Brandt's suggestion. By measuring the distribution of nitrates and phosphates in the ocean and the cycles in the rate of supply. of these salts to the euphonic zone, one may go far towards *understanding* the productivity of the ocean in space and time.

The subtropical and tropical belts of the ocean, where deep-sea animals are most diverse, will be considered first. In these regions the *intensity* of light and the stability of the water column are adequate for the growth and *reproduction* of *phytoplankton* in all seasons. Indeed, as already stated, primary production is more or less continuous throughout

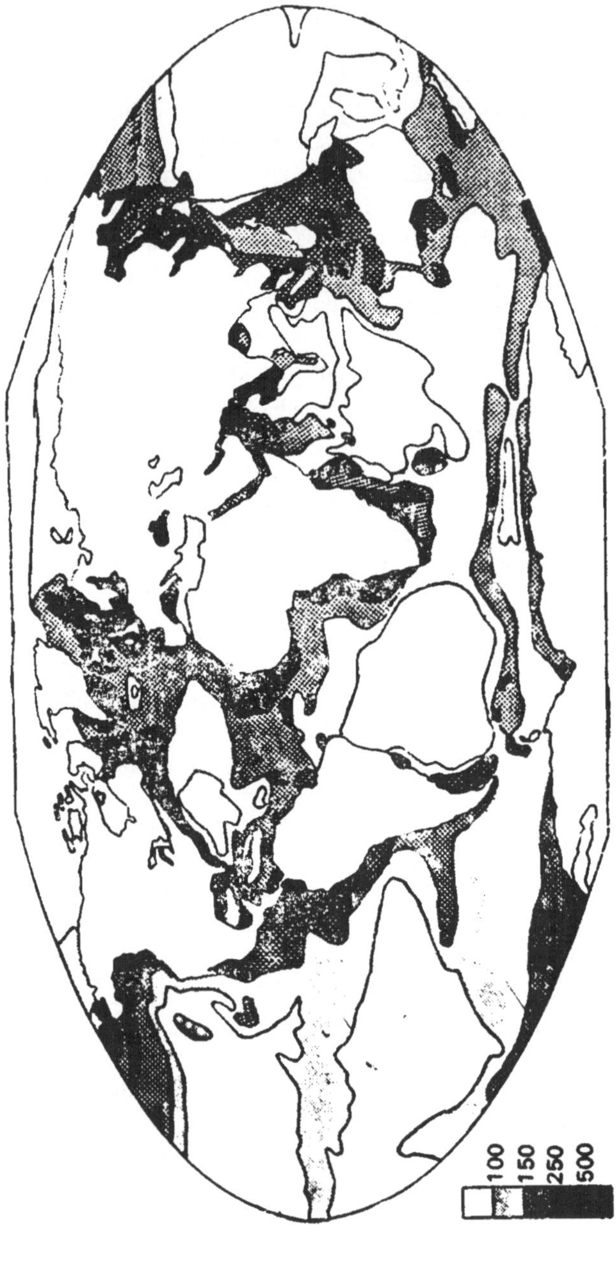

Figure 7.4: The distribution of primary productivity throughout the ocean, as estimated with the radiocarbon method in mg carbon per meter per day.

the year. But supplies of *phosphates* and *nitrated* in the *euphonic* zone are meagre, which may be seen in contrast to conditions in the entire water column.

In general, the *vertical* distribution of phosphate and nitrate concentrations (μg atoms per litre) is layered in a *characteristic* way. The surface layer with ins very low and rather uniform concentrations overlies a layer marked in depth by *increasing* concentrations, which in turn leads to a layer of maximum concentration, usually between depths of 500 and 1,500 metres.

Below this is a deep layer in which nutrient salt concentrations show relatively little change with depth. This stratification of nutrients is bound to life and death in the euphonic zone. The *proportions* of carbon, nitrogen and phosphorus in the protoplasm of planknonic plants is about 100 C : 15 N : 1 P (by atoms), and during growth these elements are drawn from the sea in *approximately* these ratios.

If the uptake of nutrients continues to the point where the most limiting nutrient is reduced below ins minimal level, growth of the *phytoplankton* will cease. And *nutrients* continually leave the euphonic zone. The plants tend to sink more *quickly* after death, when processes of decomposition eventually renew the supply of *nutrient* salts. At a depth of about 200 metres all plants material has been oxidized back into mineral form.

Animals of the euphotic zone also sink and decay after death. Moreover, potential nutrient-yielding material leaves the euphonic zone each day as food in vertically migrating animals. In one way or another, nutrients salts *accumulate* below the *euphonic zone*. If there is no updraft of nutrient salts into the euphonic zone, the phytoplankton must depend on the local *recycling* of nutrients by *decomposition* and the excretion of *nutrient-yielding* materials by the local animals.

The euphonic zone in subtropical regions overlies the central water masses, which are circumscribed by the great oceanic gyres. In these waters a virtually permanent '*seasonal*' *thermocline* underlies a stable, well-lit water column. Evidently the upward turbulent transfer of nutrient salts is so restricted that subtropical waters are the least productive of the major oceanic regions.

The waters are so clear and contain so little *particulate* matter in the form of phytoplankton and other microscopic organisms that there is little to interfere with the blue light *scattered* by the water *molecules*. Subtropical waters are a deep blue.

Deep blue waters have been called the deserts of the ocean but they are not uniformly deserted. Surveys in the eastern Pacific have shown that productivity may be enhanced where the *thermocline* is closest to the surface. In such regions the thermocline may be eroded if wind-induced turbulence is sufficient to *plough* the sea and bring *nutrient* salts to the surface waters.

A thermal front across the Sargasso Sea separates a *cooler* and more productive northern region from a warmer and less productive southern region. North and south of the front there is a difference in stability of the water column.

The upper part of the water column in the southern Sargasso Seas is well stratified during all months of the year, while that of the north is only well stratified from about May to October. These contrasting conditions are related to paralled contrasts in the abundance and distribution of *mesopelagic* fishes.

There is a wider range of primary production in equatorial waters, regions of which are several times more productive than are subtropical waters. North and south of the equator the trade winds drive the west-flowing equatorial currents which under the influence *inherent* in the earth's rotation, tend to diverge from the *equatorial countercurrent*.

Upwelling occurs along the *divergences*, and is particularly well marked over the eastern half of the *equatorial Pacific*. Here, the refreshing of the surface waters with upwelled nutrients leads to high *productivity* and good standing stocks of *zooplankton*, which support, inter alia, profitable fisheries for tuna and *billfishes*.

In the Indian Ocean the North Equatorial Current and the Equatorial Countercurrent are in full flow and divergence from November to March, the time of the *Northeast Monsoon*, *Shcherbinin's* (1971) studies of the geostrophic circulation even indicate that the direction of the North Equatorial Current undergoes no radical seasonal changes.

Russian surveys also show that the waters about the equatorial divergence (0-10°S) are rich in nutrient salts and high in primary productivity. But the northwestern Indian Ocean, particularly the Arabian Sea, is richer still in nutrients and plankton.

Evidently there is extensive upwelling of nutrientrich water northwards across the Equator to replace surface water flowing southwards and away from the Arabian Sea. In the Atlantic Ocean, the Equatorial Countercurrents is developed only over the eastern half, and it eventually flows into the Gulf of Gunea. Upwelling and zones of enhanced productivity are evident in unstable and sluggish waters between the above current system and the South Equatorial Current.

In *temperate* and *subpolar* waters the winter-cooled surface waters sink and form *convection* currents, the rising parts of which renew the supplies of nutrient salts in the euphotic zone. When spring returns the timing of the outburst of *phytoplankton* depends on the development of a stable water column and *adequate* levels of light.

Growth and *reproduction* are mainly in the spring but continue at lesser rates during the summer. Populations and communities decline during autumn as the thermocline *breaks* down and the days shorten. The surface layer in the antarctic is well supplied with nutrients salts by the waters that more up to replace the surface waters that sink at the Convergence.

During the long well-lit days of December and January, when the retreat of the ice has opened great expanses of the sea, and melt-water stabilizes the euphotic zone, production of the phytoplankton is at its height. Productivity declines during *autumn* as the ice *reappears* and the days shorten. Both *north* and *south* of the *Antarctic Convergence* parts of the Southern Ocean are among the most productive in the world.

During the productive season teeming stocks of plant and animal plankton support, inter alia, the great whales and millions of seals penguins and fishes. *Primary productivity* is high over great stretches of the continental shelves throughout the world, where nutrient salts and organic material from the land may contribute greatly to plant growth.

But some of the most productive near-shore are related to desert lands. Off northwest and southwest Africa in the eastern Atlantic, *Somaliland* and *Arabia* in the northwest *Indian Ocean*, and *Peru* and *California* in the *eastern Pacific*, seasonal or variable winds blow the surface waters away from the shore, and to take their place nutrient-rich waters well up from deeper levels.

The biology of these coastal upwelling regions is not our present concern, though there is evidence that the upwellings may enrich *neighbouring oceanic waters*: Off southwest *Africa* and *Peru* there is a cyclonic gyre such that the *Benguela* and *Peru Currents* leave the coast and flow into the open ocean in a northwesterly direction. Presumably the offshore transport of nutrient-rich water contrihutes to the high productivity of both gyres.

During the monsoons, particularly the southwest, upwelled water off the Arabian and Somali coasts may make some contribution to the high productivity of the open Arabian sea. Lastly, enhanced patches of productivity in the broad oceanic pattern may arise near islands. Oceanic currents *rounding islands* may generate large *eddies* and *upwelling* on the *leeward* side of the flow sufficient enough to lead to increased productivity. Prominent changes in under-water *topography* may also *interrupt* the flow of surface currents enough to cause turbulence and upward transport of *nutrient*—rich water.

On a smaller scale sea mounts may also cause upwelling. This survey of the patterns of oceanic productivity is all too brief, but the main object is to provide a *background* for later considerations. There we shall endeavour to see how far differences in productivity in space and time are related to the *diversity*, *distribution* and the *lifeforms* of deep-sea animals.

ANIMAL LIFE IN THE DEEP SEA

The evolutionary radiations of animals have penetrated all depths of the ocean. In the deep sea, as in neritic waters, bottom-dwelling species (the benthos) outnumber the *species* of *oceanic* space. The deep and shallow seas also alike in that animal life is most *diverse* in the *subtropical* and *tropical* belts.

There is also a *broad taxonomic similarity* and *community* between neritic and deep-sea faunas. Thus, while selection pressures in the deep sea have evoked *remarkable adaptations* in the *biota*, even the most modified forms do not seem excessively changed.

Pelagic deep-sea animals are represented from surface to near-bottom levels of the ocean. Beside the *permanent* residents in the depths, diverse species rise up each day to feed in the *productive* surface waters and/or use these waters as *nursery* grounds for their young.

As we shall see, if not altogether clearly, the fruits of primary production are adequately partitioned, though not evenly, among the many animal species of the pelagic realm. It is certainly easier to see how enough lifesustaining oxygen is *circulated* in the water masses to all parts of the ocean. And, like the water *masses*, *pelagic life* remains *recognizably stratified* throughout the water column.

Benthic deep-sea animals live at all depths from the threshold of the continental slope to the bottom of the deepest trenches. As on the *continental shelves*, an *epifauna* living on the sea floor may be distinguished from an *infauna* living in the sediments.

Again, in continuity with shallow seas, there is a *meiobenthic* fauna of small *invertebrates*, which form part of the infauna. Though benthic life is very *sparse* in the ocean *basins* below regions of low primary production, conditions are such that life is *sustainable* over virtually all of the *deep-sea* floor.

The present intention is not only to review the main groups of *deep-sea* animals but to see how they are *organized*, both structurally and *functionally*, for life in the main *divisions* of the deep sea. Such *consideration* will serve to *introduce* later parts of this book.

8

The Sea Shore Environment

The *seashore* of Britain is some seven thousand miles in length, but in area it is a very limited habitat as it extends only from the topmost sea-washed point of the beach down to the lowest point uncovered by the tide, a region amounting to approximately 0 75% of the land area of the *British Isles*.

Nevertheless, life is very abundant on the seashore and this intertidal region is one of the most exciting *habitats* to explore for it supports such a great variety of organisms. Here are to be found representatives from nearly all the invertebrate groups of animals (a selection that cannot be found in any one *land habitat*), though fish are the only truly intertidal vertebrates and the plants are limited to *seaweeds*.

All these *varying* forms of life have to tolerate ever-changing conditions and of these the tide is the *prime factor*. Its rise and fall twice a day means that at one time the surrounding medium is water and at another air ; as all the shore *inhabitants* have migrated from the sea, this poses the *problem* of resistance to *desiccation* during the period of *exposure*.

This, in turn, is affected by climatic conditions, as is the force with which the waves break on the shore. *Geographical* position and geological structure of the shore also govern the *populations*. Although we speak generally of the *seashore* it is not just one *habitat* but several, depending on the type of substratum *rocky* shore, *shingle* shore, *sandy* shore, *muddy* shore, because each supports its own particular communities The

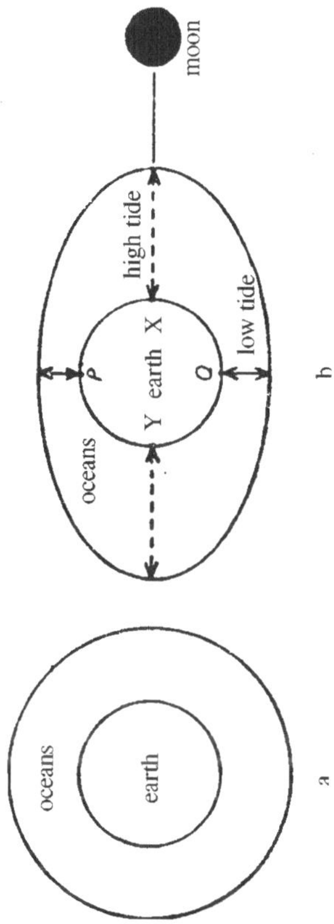

Figure 8.1: (a) No gravitational effect, (b) moon overhead at X gravitationally attracts oceans and earth to give high tides at X and Y, and low tides at P and Q.

various factors which control these *communities* will now be dealt with in detail.

Tides

If we could imagine the world without gravity, the oceans would be spread evenly around the earth's surface as shown in (a) of the following diagram. However, Our planet comes under the influence of the gravitational effect of the moon, and when the moon is overhead at X its gravitational attraction on the oceans causes a pile up of the waters; high tide occurs at X as shown in (b).

The moon also attracts the earth but, as the earth is a solid mass, it is not so strongly affected as the freely moving oceans and is pulled only slightly away from the water on the opposite side at Y, thus causing high tide here at the same time as at X. Simultaneously, low tide occurs at the regions from which the water has been withdrawn, that is halfway between X and Y, at P and Q, as shown in (b).

This *gravitational* attraction of the oceans occurs at every point on the earth when the moon is overhead. Therefore, as the earth rotates on its axis once in twenty-four hours, high tide occurs *twice* in every twenty-four hours; once when the moon is overhead and once when overhead on the *opposite* side of the earth. However, the *interval* between high water is not exactly twelve hours because the moon *circles* the earth.

The interval is approximately 12 hours 25 minutes ; if high water is at 11'00 a.m., the next high water occurs at 11.25 p.m. and the following at 11.50 a.m. the next day. The extent to which the tide rises and falls varies giving, *spring* tides and *neap* tides. The use of the word *spring* has nothing to do with the season, but is derived from a Norse word meaning to *swell*, and *neap* from a Norse word meaning *scarcity*.

At *spring* tides the sea reaches the farthest point up the beach at high water and the lowest point down the beach at low water. For the spring tides of greatest range these points are known as *Extreme HIM Water Springs,* EHWS, and *Extreme Low Water Springs.* ELWS.

At *neap* tides the sea flows to the lowest point up the beach for any high tide and ebbs to the highest point down the beach for any low tide. For the neap tides of least range these points are known as *Extreme High Water Neaps,* EHWN, and *Extreme Law Water Neaps,* ELWN. The whole intertidal area exposed between EHWS and EMS is called the *littoral* region.

However, as extreme spring tides and neap tides occur only occasionally, that is at the time of an equinox, it is more convenient to refer to the *Mean High Water Springs,* MHWS, *Mean Low Water Springs,* MLWS, *Mean High Water Neaps,* MHWN and *Mean Low Water Neaps,* MLWN. These are the average of all HWS, LWS, HWN, and LWN, respectively.

Two spring *tides* occur each *lunar* month, once a day or two after new moon and the other after full moon. Similarly neap tides occur twice each month, a day or two after the first and last quarter of the moon. Between *spring* and *neap* tides there is a *gradual* day-to-day variation in the ebb and flow between these limits. The *greatest* area of the shore exposed and *submerged* occurs at spring tides and the least at neap tides, as shown below.

This variation in the height of the tide is the result of the gravitational attraction of the moon and the sun. At full and new moon, the moon and sun exert gravitational pulls along the same *diameter*, but at the first and last quarter of the moon the *gravitational* pulls oppose each other.

As the movements of the sun, earth and moon are known, it is possible to predict the time and height of the high tide at any given place on the surface of the earth. This information is *compiled* for each year and *published* in the form of tide tables.

If tide tables are studied, it is found that MHWS ccurs in any particular region at about the same time of day. On the south-west coast of Devon MHWS occurs at approximately 6 00 a.m. and 6.00 p.m. G.M.T., and MLWS falls at *midday* and *midnight*. This means that the shore is uncovered during the hottest and coldest periods in the twenty-four hours, so the shore *populations* have to tolerate *extreme* conditions of *exposure*.

In contrast, on the south-east coast of Britain, between Dover and Harwich, MHWS occurs about 12.00 a.m. and 12.00 p.m. G.M.T., and MLWS at 6.00 a.m. and 6.00 p.m., so that here the exposure temperatures are comparatively *moderate*. Obviously the time of day at which the shore is uncovered plays a *considerable* part in determining

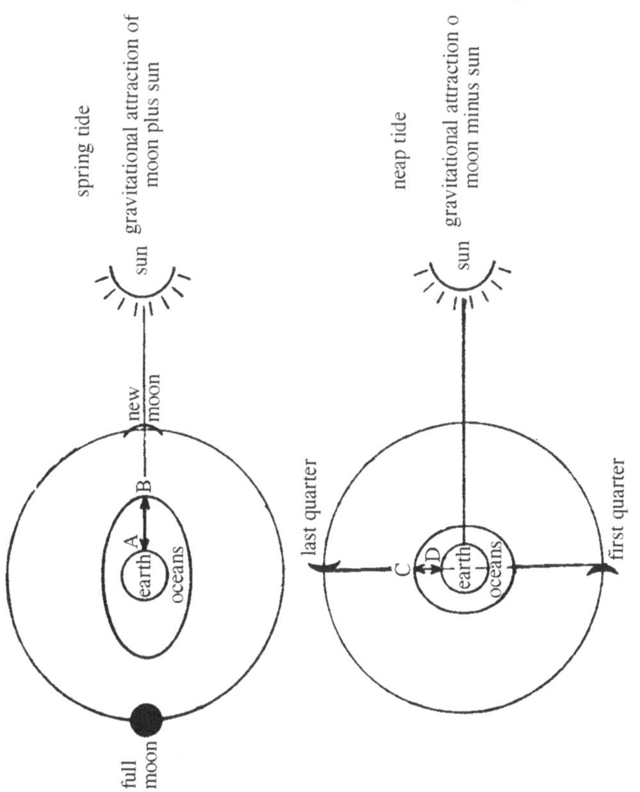

Figure 8.2: Position of moon and sun at spring and neap tides.

the *inhabitants*. The height to which the tide rises is not the same at every point along the coast but varies according to the geological structure of the coastline.

In the *Bristol Channel*, the rise and fall varies from 6 metres near the entrance at *Milford* Haven to 12 metres in the upper regions at *Avonmouth* and *Bristol*, whereas on the east coast, at Lowestoft, the rise and fall in only 2.1 metres.

The rate of *ebb* and *flow* of the tide is not constant throughout the whole six-hour period, a fact apparent to anyone waiting for the tide to go out. It seems a long time before it starts to fall then suddenly races away down the *beach*! This is because the rate of ebb is very slow in the first hour, speeds up a little during the *second hour* and *reaches* a maximum in the third and *fourth hours*, when half the overall fall occurs in just two hours.

The rate then *slows* down again in the fifth and sixth hours. Another fact which also affects the height of the tide is the wind. If there is an onshore wind the sea flows much *farther* up the beach than *anticipated* at high water—a fact *familiar* to people who live near the coast when, during winter *gales*, *promenades* are *flooded* and *damaged*.

On the other hand, if the wind is offshore, then the tide does not rise as high as indicated in the tide tables. Within the region of the littoral zone the period of *exposure varies*, so that the *inhabitants* near MHWS mark are normally exposed to the *atmosphere* except at high water spring tide, while those near MLWS mark are normally *submerged* except at low water spring tide; this accounts for the very different living *conditions* in these two areas.

Between these two extremes variations occur down the ·bore, and it is possible to divide the *littoral* area into zones or regions of similar conditions. *Beginning* at the top, the area above EHWS mark, although not *normally* covered by the tide, receives spray from the sea so is called the SPLASH ZONE. From EHWS to MEAN High Water (average of the high water levels ranging from springs to neaps) the shore is exposed for *long periods* and is covered only when the tide is higher than the Mean, and is referred to as the UPPER SHORE.

The MIDDLE SHORE ranges from MHW to MLW (average of the low water levels from spring to neap tides) where 90° % of the area is exposed and submerged daily. The LOWER SHORE extends from MLW down to ELWS, a region which is exposed only when the tide falls below the Mean. This is shown in the following diagram.

The *flora* and *fauna* of the LOWER SHORE are exposed for such short periods during a few days of each month only that they vary little from the sub-littoral forms, and there is no real dividing line between the two. On the other hand, the species of the UPPER SHORE have undergone considerable modifications to adapt themselves to the long periods of exposure. The small periwinkle. ***Littorina nerioldes***, which lives in rock crevices in the SPLASH ZONE, has the gill chamber modified for airbreathing, whereas the edible periwinkle, *L.* ***littorea,*** which lives on the MIDDLE SHORE, has the normal gill structure enabling it to absorb oxygen from the water in which it is submerged for some 50% of its life.

Desiccation

All plants and animals of the sea shore have to face the hazard of desiccation when exposed to the atmosphere by the ebbing tide. Water is all important to living organisms, ourselves included. We feel the effect of desiccation, or dehydration, on extremely hot summer days when so much water is lost from our bodies in the form of sweat that we seem to be continually thirsty. All living tissue, or *protoplasm,* consists of at least 70% water, so even the slightest loss upsets the delicate balance.

Wind and sun are responsible for this 'drying out' effect, so most of the shore animals hide in crevices, under rocks and seaweeds or bury themselves when the tide re-codes. As seaweeds cannot take this evasive action they wilt, becoming almost brittle if exposed for long, dry periods, though usually they regain their normal turgor once the tide returns. The brown wracks of the upper shore survive these conditions quite happily, but the more delicate red seaweeds would succumb and these are found inhabiting the lower regions of the shore.

Besides taking evasive action, many shore animals have, through the ages, become modified in some way to combat water loss. The periwinkle, the snail of the shore, is a good example. When the tide ebbs it retreats within its shell, closing the entrance behind it with a special horny disc attached to the rear portion of its body, thereby reducing water loss by evaporation to a minimum.

Temperature

As all the animals of the shore are *coldblooded,* even small changes in temperature affect their activities and, if sudden, may prove fatal. The sea temperature varies very little in comparison with the air, so this factor is another hazard facing the littoral fauna during the period of low water. However, the animals cope with the situation quite

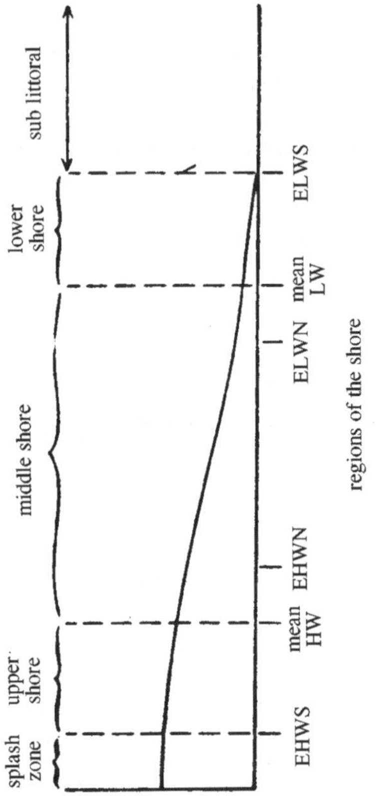

Figure 2.3.

effectively by reducing their activities to a minimum and, if mobile, *retreating* into *sheltered* positions under rocks and stones or below the sand. Gradual changes of temperature do hot seem to affect the animals, but when a sudden rise or fall occurs many may die.

The young, or larvae, are even more sensitive to changes, so a high fatality rate at this stage affects the size of future populations. The extreme *temperatures* of a hard winter or very hot summer take their toll. For instance, before the hard winter of 1963 one could drag a net over the rocks along the bottom of *Torquay breakwater* and be certain of bringing up many velvet swimming *crabs*, but for several seasons after that time ho crabs were to be found.

These crabs did not begin to *recolonize* the area for three years, and it was not until 1968 that their *numbers* were *comparable* to those of the years before 1963. Temperature also has a definite *controlling* effect oh the *geographical* distribution of shore populations and this explains why some *Mediterranean* species are found in the extreme south-west of Britain but nowhere else around our shores. Each species can endure a certain minimum and maximum temperature so an animal, such as the *edible periwinkle*, found on all coasts, is living within the centre of its range; it is a creature of temperate seas.

As the largest of the *acorn barnacles*, *Balanus perforatus,* is confined to the southwestern peninsula, this is evidently the northerly limit of its temperature range or, in other words, its minimum survival temperature. On the other sand, another acorn barnacle, *Balanus balanoides,* inhabits most coastal regions, but not *t*he *southernmost* tip of *Cornwall*, so sere, presumably, the southenly limit for the 'species has been reached, that is its maximum *survival temperature*.

It is worth noting that the temperature of the sea around the British Isles is higher than would be anticipated in such latitudes. The reason for this is that warm waters from the Gulf of *Mexico* are carried to our coasts by the North Atlantic Drift (the Stream).

Substratum

There are two principal types of substratum *stable* rocks or *unstable,* movable particles of shingle, sand or mud. Of the two, the stable environment supports the greater variety of flora and fauna as it is only sere that seaweeds and sedentary animals find suitable surfaces for attachment.

The nature of the rocks varies greatly from the chalk cliffs of Dover to the rugged granite of Land's End, but the mineral content has little effect oh the colonizers as they are interested in the rocks only as a medium for attachment.

However, the texture of the surface is most important. If it is very smooth, or readily crumbles, few *organisms* settle but, in contrast, a rugs surface with *numerous* cracks and *crevices* supports large populations. To some animals, such as the *piddocks*, *hardness* is the controlling factor because these *bivalves* bore into the rock and then remain within for the rest of their lives.

Hardness also determines the degree of erosion caused by the continual battering action of the waves; the softer the rocks the more readily they become eroded and deposited on the shore as single or sand. The unstable habitat of a single beach supports very little life owing to the continual friction between the pebbles, but a sandy beach contains hidden populations buried below its surface.

Burrowing animals also inhabit muddy beaches, although the variety of species is limited by the fineness of the particles which would block the gills of many sand-dwellers.

Wave Action

Most of us, through first-hand experience or the medium of the press, are fully aware of the devastating effect the force of waves, whipped up by *onshore gales*, has on our coasts: breaches in sea walls with *consequent flooding*, *damaged promenades*, cliff falls due to *undercutting* of the lower layers, etc.

This pounding action obviously affects shore populations, and oh the most *exposed rocky coasts* only truly tenacious *animals survive*. Examples are *sedentary* acorn *barnacles* and *limpets* which, though mobile, cling closely to the rocks with their powerful, muscular foot.

The *growth* of *seaweeds*, if any, in such positions is stunted and the modifications developed by some organisms to withstand these *unfavourable conditions* often *complicate identification*.

On sand and mud, the survival of fauna from wave action depends entirely on deep and rapid burrowing as the surface layers of the *substratum* become displaced, Even on *sheltered* shores the littoral *fauna* is subject to some wave action, but the way in which the animals *overcome* this problem will be considered in the sections on habitats.

The relative exposure of a coast depends on the *fetch* of the waves, that is the distance over which they travel before *breaking* on the shore. In the *British Isles* the west-facing coasts suffer the greatest exposure, for here the waves are swept across miles and miles of the *Atlantic Ocean* before reaching the *obstruction* of the land.

The *continual abrasive* action of waves wears away rock faces and changes the shore form, though the extent of erosion depends on rock hardness. On *unstable shores* rough seas churn up the sand and mud, and deposit it in different positions, thus altering the sites of *sand-banks*, *sand-bars* and *channels*.

Salinity

When rock pools are uncovered by the tide, heavy rainfall may dilute the water slightly ; not sun causes evaporation and increases the salt concentration, but normally these minor variations in salinity cause no hardship to the littoral plants and animals, although sub-littoral species could not tolerate such changes.

The same applies to the buried inhabitants of sand or mud, when rain percolates through to the lower layers. However, in estuaries, where fresh water mixes with sea water, the variation in salinity is sufficient to have a controlling effect on the populations.

Light

Many of the littoral animals are negatively phototropic, that is they move away from light and hide under stones or seaweeds, in cracks and crevices, or bury themselves below the surface. These reactions are the same as those *displayed* in *response* to other stimuli, but they are all inter-related and *concerned* with *survival* when the shore is *uncovered* by the tide.

Other animals are just the opposite and prefer well *illuminated* areas. To some, light is *necessary* for feeding because they seek their food by sight, while others track their food by touch or smell, and feed as efficiently in light or *darkness*.

The latter animals frequently confine their feeding to the hours of darkness in order to escape the notice of predators, and themselves remain hidden from their prey.

Seaweeds, as all green plants, require light for *photosynthesis,* the process by which plants manufacture *organic* compounds from simple substances.

The intensity of light is the important factor to most organisms. Each species prefers a certain amount of illumination and therefore attempts to remain within its *optimum* light intensity. We shall see an *interesting* effect of this on plankton in other section of this chapter.

All the factors mentioned in this section *influence* the lives of shore populations, and the balance between them determines the most beneficial *niche* for each species. A *zonation* of the fauna and flora of the littoral region therefore becomes *apparent*.

9

THE SEA SHORE AND THE SEA

Life on the shore cannot be considered in complete isolation from the sea for all the inhabitants have, through the ages, migrated from the sea. Some, such as channelled wrack and periwinkles, have become completely littoral in habit, but others such as Laminarians and rocklings, live both on shore and in shallow seas.

As in any other *habitat*, the animals of the shore are basically dependent on the plant life as a source of food and energy. Green plants are the only organisms with the ability to capture the *energy* of *sunlight* and use it to be bind together simple inorganic substances into complex organic compounds.

The green pigment *chlorophyll* absorbs the energy which is then used to combine chemically water and carbon dioxide into sugar, i.e. the energy is stored in the sugar molecules. This process is called *photosynthesis* and the waste product of the reaction is oxygen. With other nutrients absorbed from the *surroundings* some of the sugar molecules are converted into complex proteins.

Green plants are thus referred to as the PRODUCERS. Animals can only feed on organic matter so they are dependent directly or indirectly on plants. They are thus referred to as the CONSUMERS. The consumer which feeds directly on plants, a *herbivore*, is the *primary* consumer; the carnivore which feeds on the herbivore is the *secondary* consumer.

Thus plants are the source of energy as well as material r the build up and *maintenance* of animal *protoplasm*. The energy stored in food is made available to the organisms by respiration, an oxidation process in which carbon dioxide and water are the waste products. The sea contains the nutrients so important for plant growth; thus it is true to say that all shore populations depend on the sea for nutrition.

Seaweeds are the plants of the shore but, although some animals feed on them, the basic source of food for the majority is the floating life of the sea-the *plankton*.

The term *plankton* refers to all drifting and floating organisms whatever their size, but in most instances it is taken to mean the minute and microscopic plants and animals of surface waters.

Phytoplankton

The plants of the plankton, the *phytoplankton,* are mostly microscopic algae of two types, diatoms and dinoflagellates, both of which reproduce simply by dividing into two-an asexual method of reproduction called *binary fission*. When conditions are favourable the populations increase rapidly, particularly the diatoms, as they can divide three or four times a day. All phytoplankton are found in the surface waters where they can absorb the sunlight necessary for photosynthesis.

Although individual plants of the plankton cannot be seen with the naked eye, when massed in their millions they form a brown, red or green scum on the sea; occasionally some of this is left as a thin film on shore by the receding tide.

Phytoplankton are the principal producers in marine life, whether offshore, inshore or seashore.

Zooplankton

The animals of the plankton, the *zooplankton,* vary in size. Many are microscopic, but others, such as seagooseberries, are readily visible. Some of these *creatures* are *permanent* members of the plankton, such as the copepod crustacean *Calanus* which is the main food of the herring, while others are only temporary members.

These latter are the larval stages of marine animals, including many littoral species such as zoea larvae of shore crabs or veliger larvae of gastropods. These small animals of the *plankton* are capable of *swimming*, but their movements are not sufficiently powerful to transport them against water currents, so they just drift along.

However, they can swim up and down in a vertical migration. Research shows that zooplankton move upwards during the afternoon until dusk, *scatter randomly* throughout the hours of total *darkness*, rise again at dawn, then move downwards until midday. Why zooplankton move up and down in this way is not fully understood, but it is believed that each species prefers a certain light intensity and swims to keep within this optimum as its position varies was the rising and setting of the sun.

Many of these tiny creatures are *phosphorescent*, and on a quiet night their *myriad glowing* lights flicker over the surface when the water is *disturbed*.

FOOD CHAINS AND WEBS

Only a few animals feed on seaweeds and most of these are gastropods, such as *periwinkles*, *topshells* and *limpets*, so the phytoplankton are the principal producers. Many *zooplankton* feed on them directly and are thus primary *consumers*. However, some eat other zooplankton so are secondary or even tertiary consumers, or they may be *omnivorous* in their habits, feeding on phyto-or zooplankton, whichever is nearer.

Secondary consumers are any of the suspension feeders, either of the sea, such as the herring already mentioned, or of the littoral zone. Many seashore animals are sedentary and cannot forage for food, therefore they feed when the tide is in by filtering plankton from the sea. Various devices have been evolved for this purpose, as we shall see in the next section.

Tertiary consumers are the carnivores who eat the suspension feeders, and *quaternary* and later *consumers* are any other carnivores. This linkage is referred to as a *food chain* and below are a few examples.

Producer	*Primary Consumer*	*Secondary Consumer*	*Tertiary Consumer*
Seaweeds	Edible periwinkle	Man	
Seaweeds	Flat periwinkle	Fish	Man
Phytoplankton	Zooplankton	Barnacle	Blenny
"	"	Mussel	Starfish
"	"	Cockle	Man
"	"	Star sea-squirt	Cowrie
"	"	Breadcrumb sponge	Sea-lemon
"	"	Mysid	Pipefish

Many links in these food chains are interconnected and form a food web as shown in the following diagram.

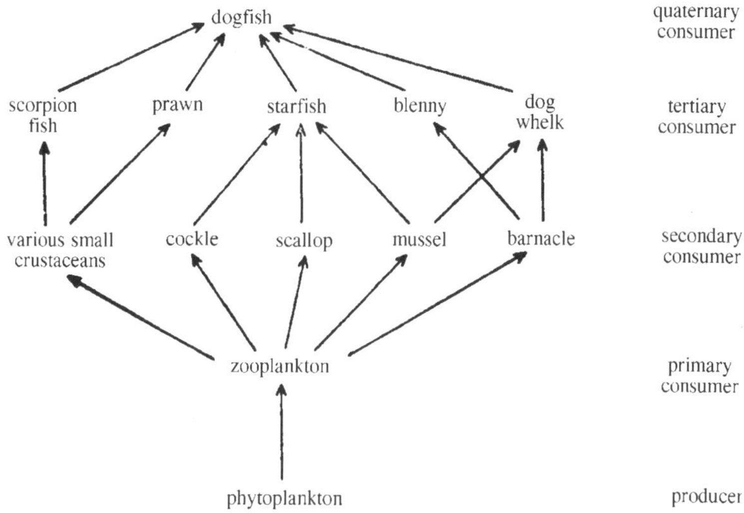

food web of the seashore

Figure 9.1.

The transfer of organic material in a *food chain* is far from efficient. At each link the loss in bulk is approximately 90%, so *enormous* numbers of *primary* consumers are necessary to support one tertiary consumer. For instance, *presuming* each *consumer* in the chain feeds on one type only, a blenny must eat 10 grammes of *barnacles* to increase its weight by 1 gramme.

These barnacles must consume 100 grammes of zooplankton and the latter 1000 grammes of phytoplankton. In other words, 1000 grammes of phytoplankton are necessary to support 1 gramme of blenny!

The primary consumers are *small* and *abundant compared* with the final predator, those in between being larger and *fewer* in number at each step. Such a *relationship* is referred to as the *pyramid of numbers*, and is shown opposite.

Organic Cycle

As on the land, bacteria are the decomposers of the sea. Dead plants and animals sink to the bottom and here the *various bacteria* break down the organic matter into soluble *inorganic* substances that replenish the *nutrients* of the sea. Again the principal salts formed are nitrates, followed by phosphates and *sulphates*, as these are all constituents of proteins. Thus the *organic cycle* of the sea is *comparable* with that on land.

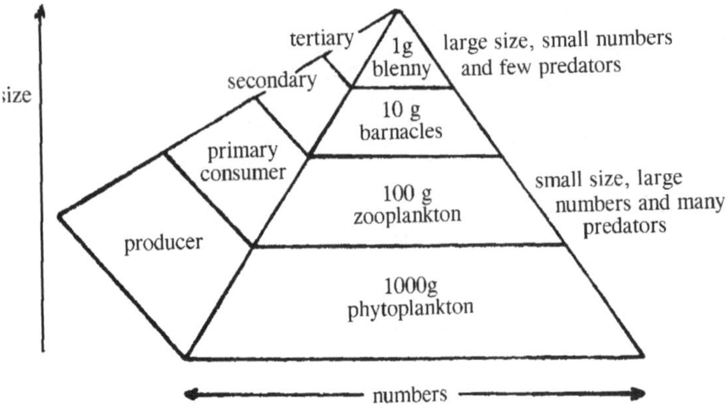

Figure 9.2: Pyramid of numbers.

Plankton Cycle

The abundance of plankton throughout the seasons is not constant. During the winter months it is at a minimum, but in early spring a sudden outburst of phytoplankton occurs, the *conditions* being at an *optimum* for *growth* and *reproduction*. After only a few weeks the numbers fall away *drastically* until another slight increase in the autumn, before falling to the winter minimum.

Fluctuations in zooplankton follow this pattern, though their numbers do not *decrease* so rapidly. In spring the rise in temperature and increase in light *intensity* give the favourable conditions for *phytoplankton* to utilize the *nutrients* of the sea for rapid growth and *reproduction*. About this time many of the creatures of the sea and shore are ready to spawn.

This produces a large influx of zooplakton which *voraciously* feed on the phytoplankton and greatly deplete the plant numbers. As summer approaches and the sun's intensity increases, the surface waters warm up and the *distinct* layers form, the warmer on top being separated from the colder below by a narrow zone through which the temperature drops rapidly.

This is called the *discontinuity* layer or *thermocline,* and once formed it prevents the mixing of the lower and upper waters ; nutrients released on the bottom by the decomposers cannot rise to the surface. Therefore, although sufficient sunlight is available, new generations of phytoplankton cannot be produced owing to lack of nutrients. This explains the summer *minimum*.

The thermocline forms during April or May, depending on the

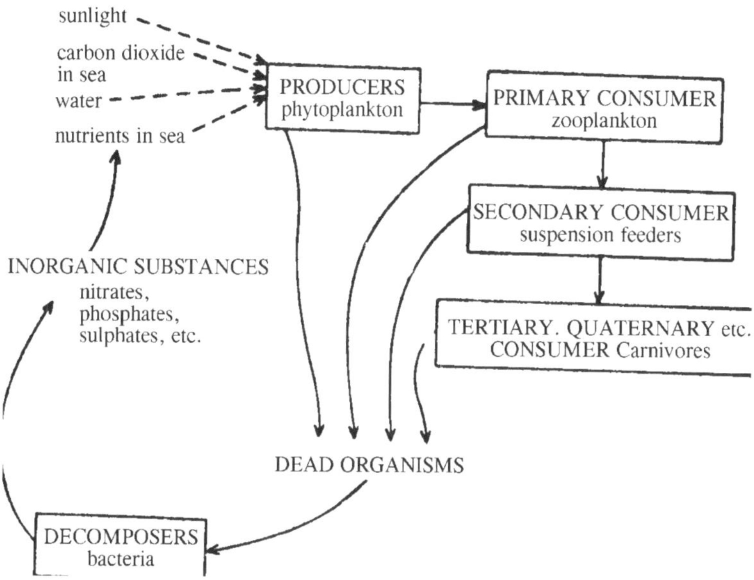

Figure 9.3: Organic cycle of the sea.

atmospheric temperature, and around our coasts it occurs at a depth of approximately 15 metres and forms a zone 2-3 metres deep.

During the autumn the surface waters begin to cool and the thermocline breaks some time in September or October. Mixing of the water follows, and with nutrients again present in the surface layers, phytoplankton increase in number. However, this is short lived because the temperature and light *intensity* soon fall too low and the plankton decrease to their winter minimum.

Throughout the cold months decomposition continues on the bottom and the released nutrients spread evenly throughout the sea, ready for the spring phytoplankton explosion.

Fertility of the Sea

As shown by the plankton cycle, the fertility of the sea varies with the seasons, but it also varies from area to area as on land. Fertility depends on the carbon dioxide, oxygen and *nutrient* content, light intensity, salinity and *temperature*. There is no shortage of nutrients in the oceans, but they are of use to *plants* only when present in the *illuminated* surface waters.

For a region to be fertile, water movements must occur for distribution of these nutrients from below to above. The high fertility of

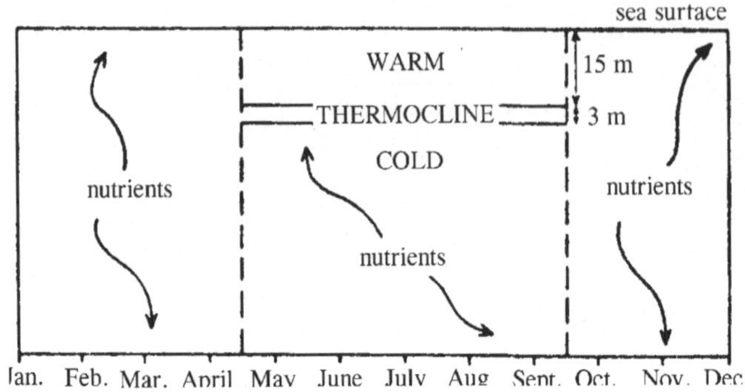

Figure 9.4: Distribution of nutrients throughout the seasons. Note the thermocline separating the warm and cold layers during the summer months.

British seas is mainly due to the mixing of the waters caused by the flow of the *Gulf Stream* around our *coasts*, *coupled* with the additional nutrients brought by it from the *Atlantic Ocean*.

Dispersal of Shore Animals

Many shore animals are also dependent on the sea for development of their young and *dispersal* of the *species*. The larvae are minute free-swimming *creatures* which form the *temporary plankton* of our seas. Here they feed, grow and drift with the currents until they are ready to take up adult life on the shore.

10

ROCKY SHORES

It is easily observed that plants and animals on tidal rocky shores *characteristically* occupy bands or zones parallel to the water's edge. It is widely held that the cause of this *zonation* is the regular *emersion* of the shore by the *tidal ebb*.

Those organisms intolerant of exposure to air remain low on the shore and those able to withstand desiccation often live higher on the shore. Surprisingly, perhaps, tides are not the principal cause of *zonation*. *Distribution* on the shore is primarily the result of a gradient of physical conditions on either side of an air/water interface. In non-tidal conditions there are still *recognizable*, if *compressed*, *patterns* of shore *zonation*.

Above the air/water *boundary* there will be evaporation at the surface giving graded vertical changes in air *moisture* content and on splashed marine shores a fine layer of salt may coat exposed rock surfaces.

Below this boundary, penetration of light decreases with depth and the amount of dissolved and *suspended* matter derived from the land decreases remote from the shore and at depth. The net result of these physical gradients is to create *supra* and *sublittoral* zones. Superimpose on this tideless shore the effect of wind-driven waves and this results in an in-between or *midlittoral zone*.

This is the situation which exists in the virtually tideless *Mediterranean* with a compressed midlittoral zone where changes in sea-level are controlled by changes in *barometric* pressure and wind force. An additional tidal rise and fall simply extends, and allows sub-division of, the *midlittoral* zone. Tides do not therefore initiate zoning but they do influence the pattern that the zones take.

PHYSICAL FACTORS INFLUENCING ROCKY SHORE ZONATION

Tidal Heights

The landward boundary of the intertidal area is extreme high water of spring tides (EHws) and the lower limit is *extreme* low water of spring tides (ELws). At spring tides more of the bottom of the shore is *exposed* at low water and more of the top covered at high water. Some organisms living at the top of the shore may be *wetted* only *twice* a month while others at the bottom of the shore may be exposed only briefly twice in a month.

The *neap* tide levels-mean high water neap tides (MHWN) and mean low water neap tides (MLWN)—are also important in *controlling* distribution because intertidal organisms between these levels on the shore will always be *submerged* again within 10 hours to 12 hours at most. Adaptations to combat this degree of *desiccation* are of a different order from those necessary to withstand *desiccation* for a fornight or longer.

However, predicted tidal level are often exceeded simply because onshore winds in combination with low barometric pressure may have the effect of raising *sealevel*, but calm, anticyclonic conditions with high *barometric* pressure tend to *depness* sea-level.

Temperature

The main feature that tides impose on the shore is the regular alternation of periods of immersion and then drying our during emersion. When the tide is in, organisms experience more or less uniform temperature governed by the *prevailing* temperature of the inshore water mass.

When the tide is out, however, air temperature, which is at once more variable and usually different from sea temperature may cause stress to certain stenothermic (tolerating only a narrow range of temperature) organisms and *restrict* their *distribution* to low on the shore. In summer, air temperature is often higher than the temperature of sea water with the *reverse applying* in winter.

Intertidal organisms of rocky shores need to be able to tolerate widely *fluctuating* temperatures at every ebb and flow of the tide. A low tide during the day in summer, exposidg *intertidal rocks* directly to the sun's rays, may cause rapid rises in body temperature in *organisms* attached to the surface.

The heating process is *enchanced* if the rock is a heat *absorbing*

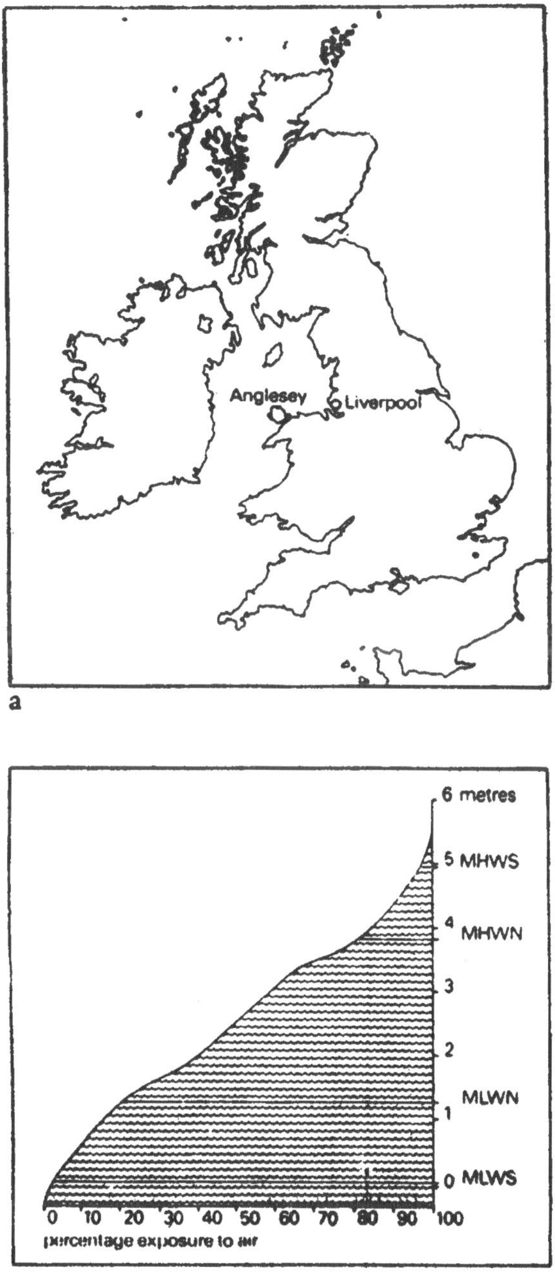

Figure 10.1: The percentage of time that various levels on the shore at Holyhead on anglesey in North wales are exposed to the air.

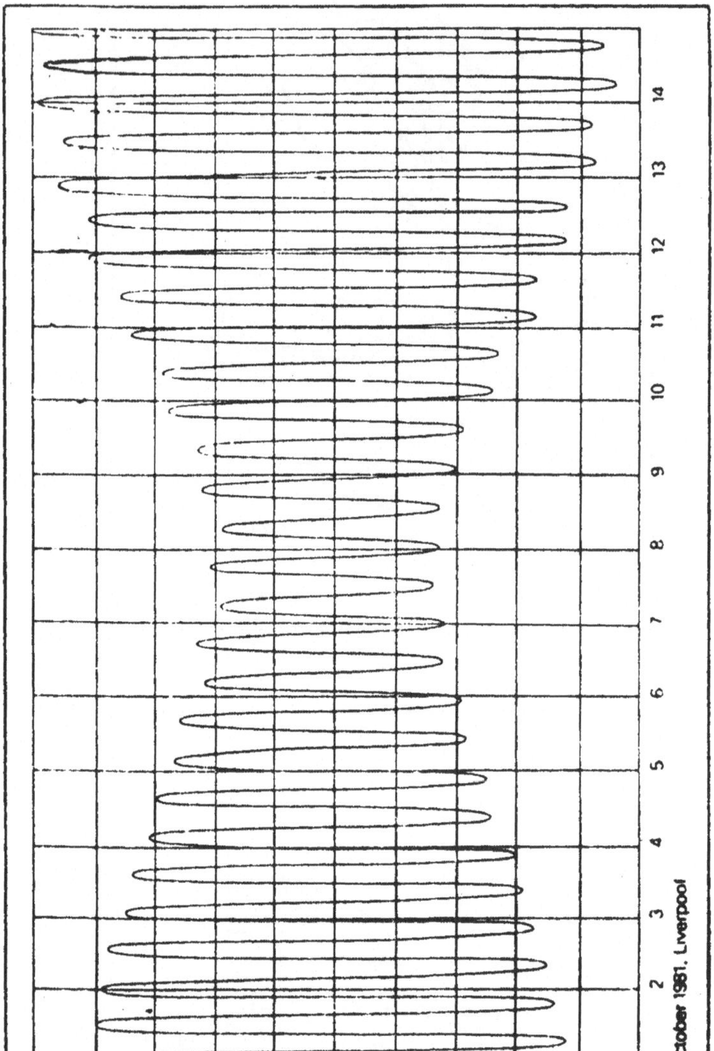

Figure 10.2: The spring/neep tidal cycle drawn from predictions.

dark colour. Conversely, at night at low water in the winter, organisms may be exposed to the risk of *frost*.

The level at which intertidal species live is not an infallible guide to their *temperature tolerance*. If the rocky shore is irregular, south and south west facing slopes (in the *northern hemisphere*) receive the full heating and drying effect of the sun, whereas nearby north facing *slopes* and areas of *overhang* are *shaded* and remain cooler.

The common European periwinkle *Littorina littorea is* able to withstand the potentially lethal heat of the summer sun, and body tissue temperatures may be only a degree or so lower than the 40°C recorded from the rock face. Heat death does not occur in this species until 46°C - at 30°C most other *shore molluscs* begin to show signs of distress-the sudden fall in *temperature* as the tide rises *stimulates* the animals to activity.

Desiccation

Dehydration causes stress in organisms and water loss is increased

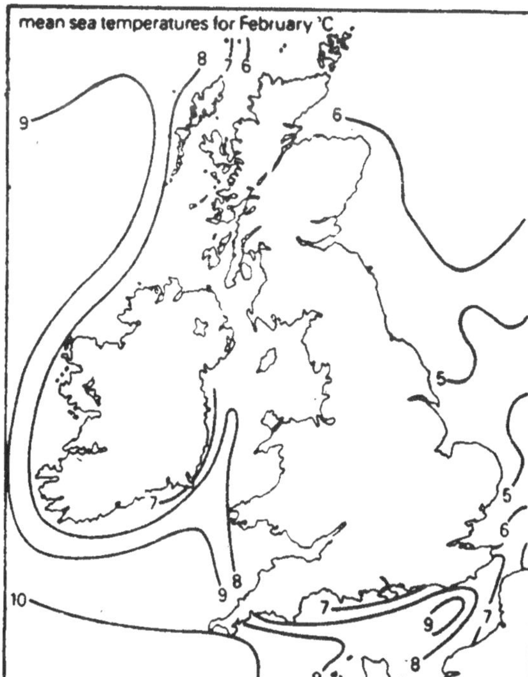

Figure 10.3: Mean sea surface temperatures (°C) around the British Isles in February.

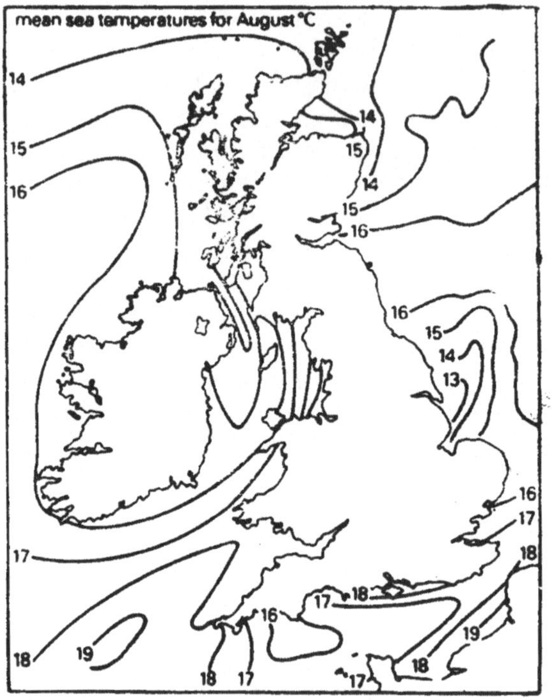

Figure 10.4: Mean sea surfae temperatures (°C) around the British Isles in August.

in bright sunlight and in windy conditions. Organisms at the top of the shore have adaptations to overcome this *problem*. These *adaptations* include a coating of *mucus* in the *beadlet anemone Acrini equina* and also the operculum in prosobranch molluscs.

The operculum in periwinkles consists of a horny plate impregnated with calcium and effectively closes off from the outside world those soft parts within the spiral shell. The limpet *Patella vulgata* homes in at low tide and remains stationary in a definite position on the rock. The foot muscle anchors the animal firmly with a pull of up to 3.5 *CM-2* .

The edges of the conical shell fit perfectly with small indentations in the rock. Water is retained in the mantle cavity just inside the shell and while firmly clamped to the rock the animal suffers little desiccation. Adult limpets living high on the shore have taller shells than those near low water mark or in rock pools. It seems likely that the tall shell with a narrow base is produced by long periods of clamping down tightly on the rock to prevent desiccation.

The mantle is responsible for new growth of the shell at its margin

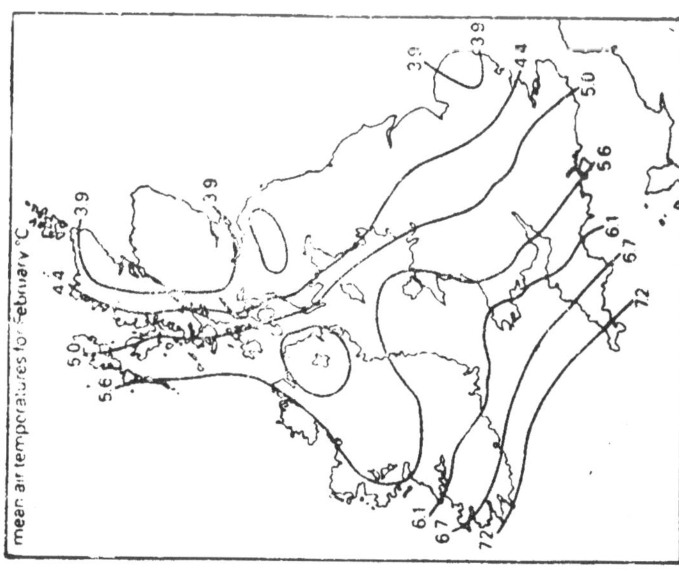

Figure 10.5: Mean air temperatures (°C) over the British Isles in February.

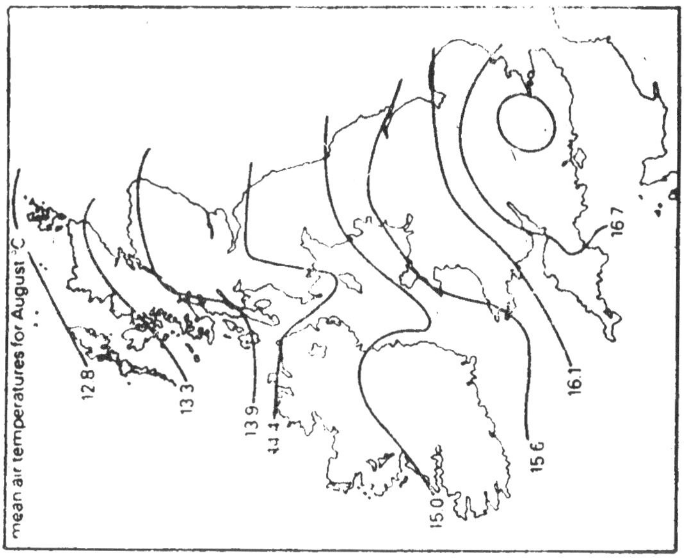

Figure 10.6: Mean air temperatures (°C) over the British Isles in August.

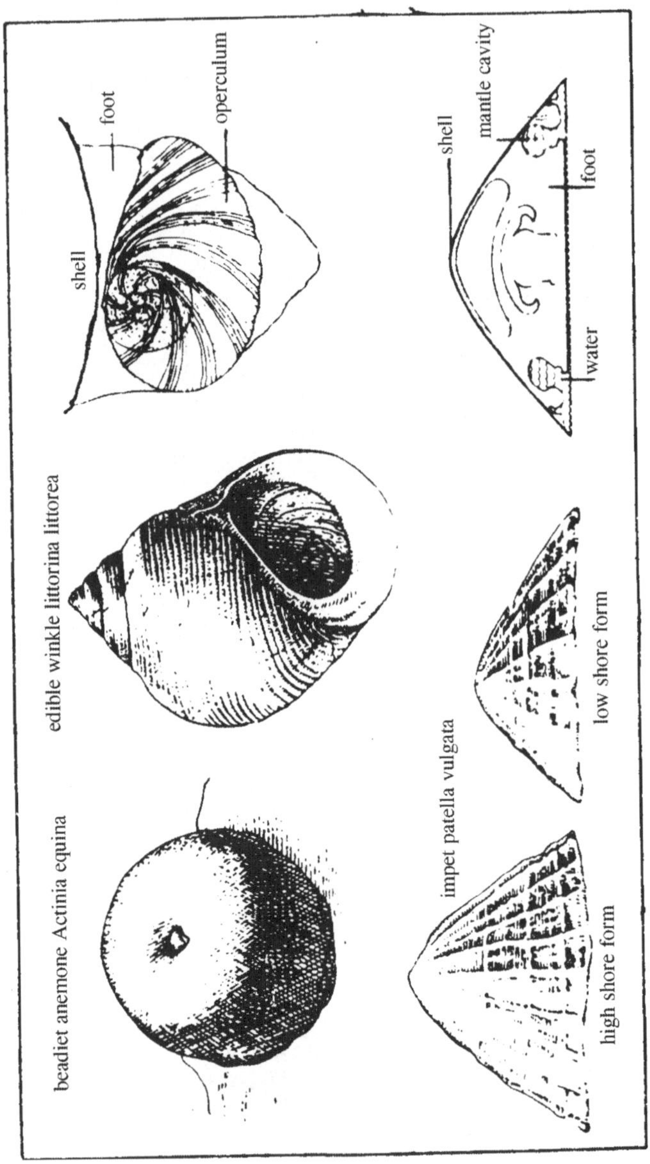

Figure 10.7: Some adaptation to withstand desiccation.

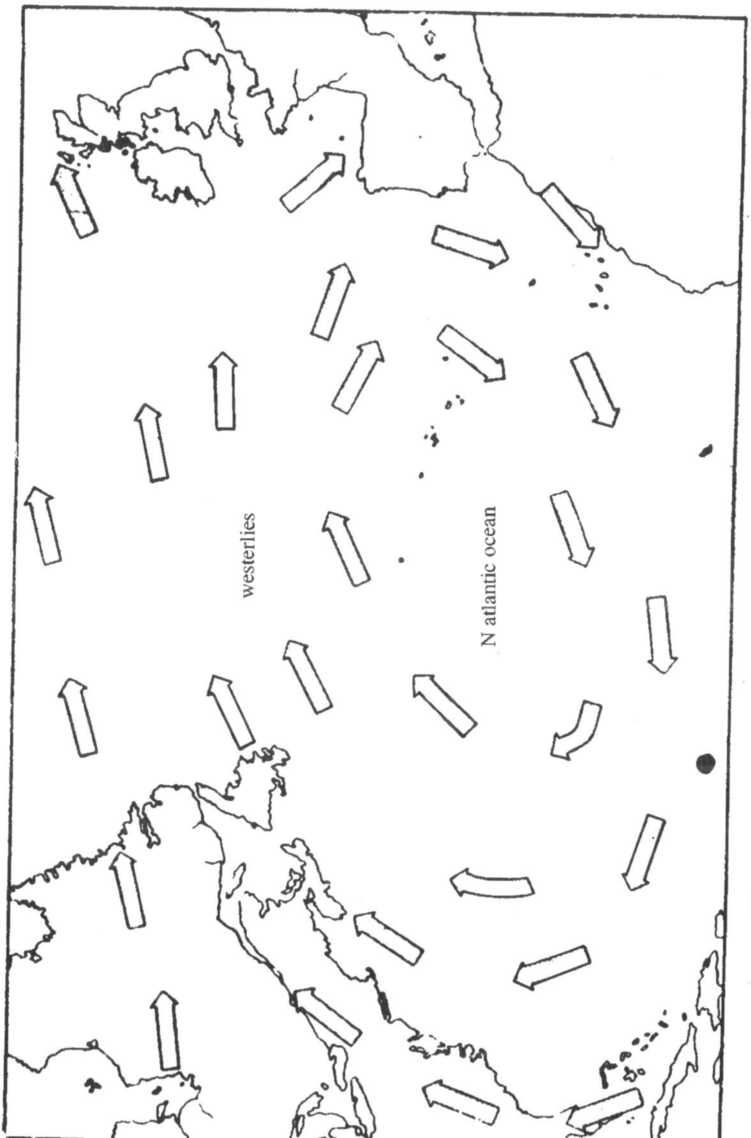

Figure 10.8: Prevailing westerlies blowing over the North Atlantic.

and the continual *downpull* of the foot muscle also has the effect of pulling in the mantle. Lower on the shore or in rock pools the shell muscles are relaxed for longer periods and the *mantle spreads* more widely, producing a *flatter shell*.

Exposure

The distance of open sea over which the wind may blow—the fetch—governs the degree of wave action to which a coast is '*exposed*'. The longer the *fetch*, the greater the wave action. Headlands, receiving the full brunt of the *prevailing* south *westerlies* across the North Atlantic such as those jutting out to sea in western *Ireland*, will suffer from greater *exposure* than the leeward side of an *island*.

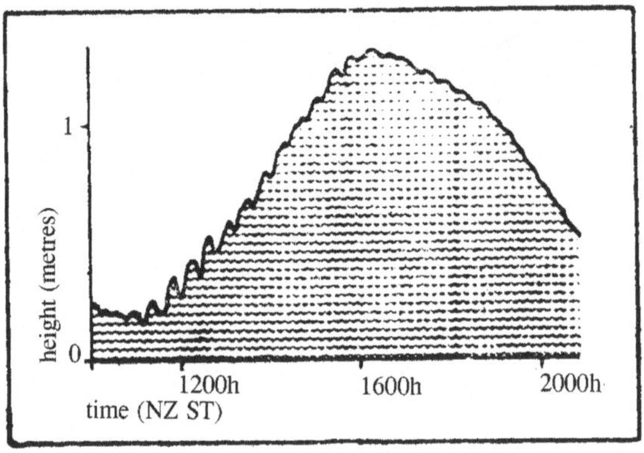

Figure 10.9: Record from automatic tide gauge in Wellington Harbour, New Zealand, showing 'slop' or seiche phenomenon.

Associated with large oceans are *oscillations* in water level that give rise to '*swell*' which may mask the effect of tidal rise and fall. In Wellington Harbour in New Zealand this non-tidal '*slop*' or seiche phenomenon may be picked out on *automatic tide gauge* recordings and is the result of a *pendulous* motion of water generated by storms or by earth tremors which have often taken place at great distance from the site where the effects are *observed*.

In general, slightly sloping, sheltered areas have a low exposure rating but open coasts with deep water close inshore and vertical cliff faces provide the most violent conditions with a high exposure rating.

It is possible to use the width of a *particular* zone, such as the black lichen *Verrucaria* at the top of the shore, to assess the degree of exposure. If it is a narrow band confined within tidal limits and lower on the shore there is a mass of the brown alga knotted wrack *Ascophyllum nodosum* (on *European coasts*), then in *combination*, these

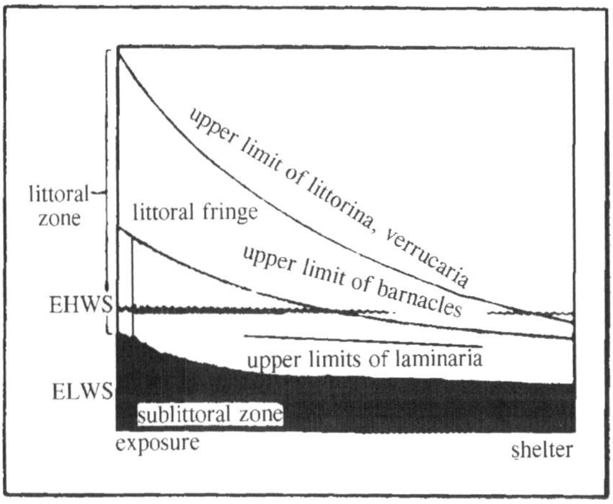

Figure 10.10: Generalised scheme of zonation on rocky shores of varying degrees of exposures.

suggest sheltered conditions. If there is a wide band of *Vorrucaria* lying above the normal tidal range and in the midshore region there is the mussel *Mytilus* and red algae, then these are good dications that the shore is exposed.

Barnacles do well on both kinds of shore especially various species of *Balanus,* but on the more exposed coasts *Chthamalus predominates*. There are some pitfalls in using zonation patterns to assess the degree of exposure. *Grazing herbivores* may keep the algae in check to such an extent that a shore may give the impression of more exposure than is really the case.

Moderate oil pollution through reduction or loss of certain species loads to an apparent shift towards greater exposure on *exposed* coasts and towards more *shelter* on *sheltered* shores. The position in the food web and factors affecting the distribution of some on the common *inhabitants* of *rocky shores* are examined below.

ALGAE: PRIMARY PRODUCERS

Green

Sea lettuce *Ulva lactuca* is found commonly on rocky shores, often in brackish (a mixture of sea and fresh water) conditions. This alga has a life cycle which includes two freeliving stages—*gametophyte* and sporophyte.

In cosmopolitan *Ulva* the two stages in this alternation of generations look alike, the green coloration of the plants resulting from the *pigment* chlorophyll contained in *chloroplasts*.

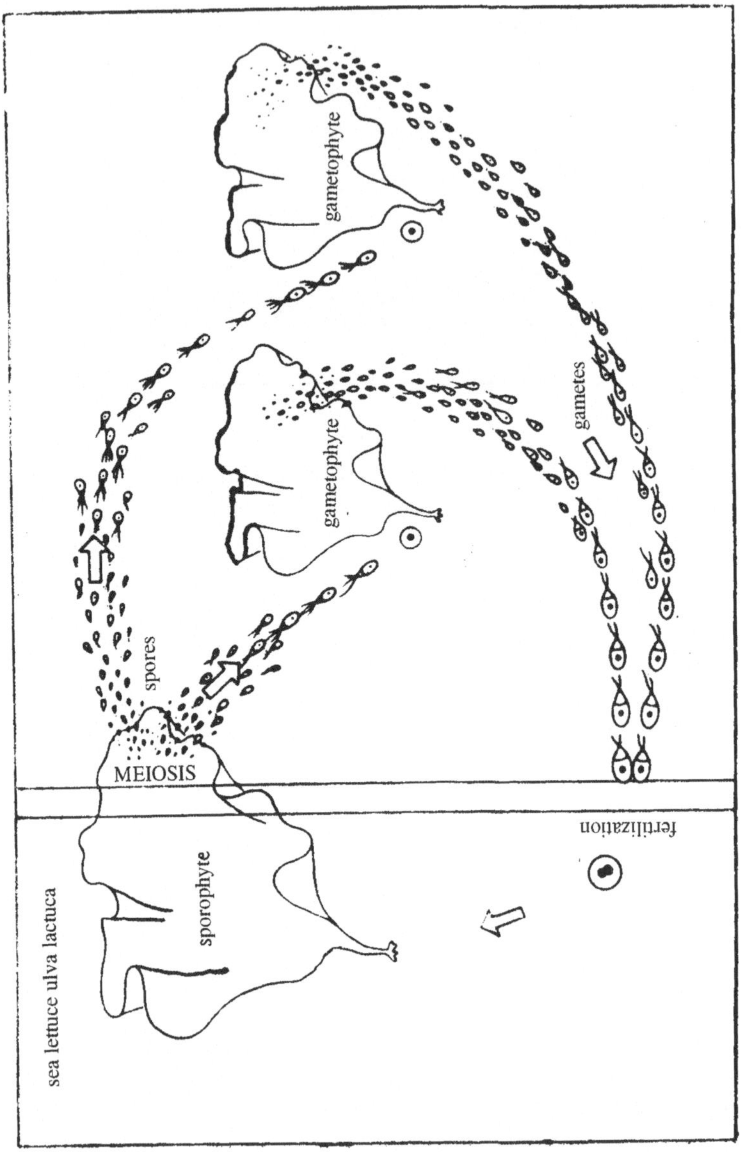

Figure 10.11: Life cycle of the green alga sea lettuce Ulva lactuca with an isomorphic alteration of generation which look alike.

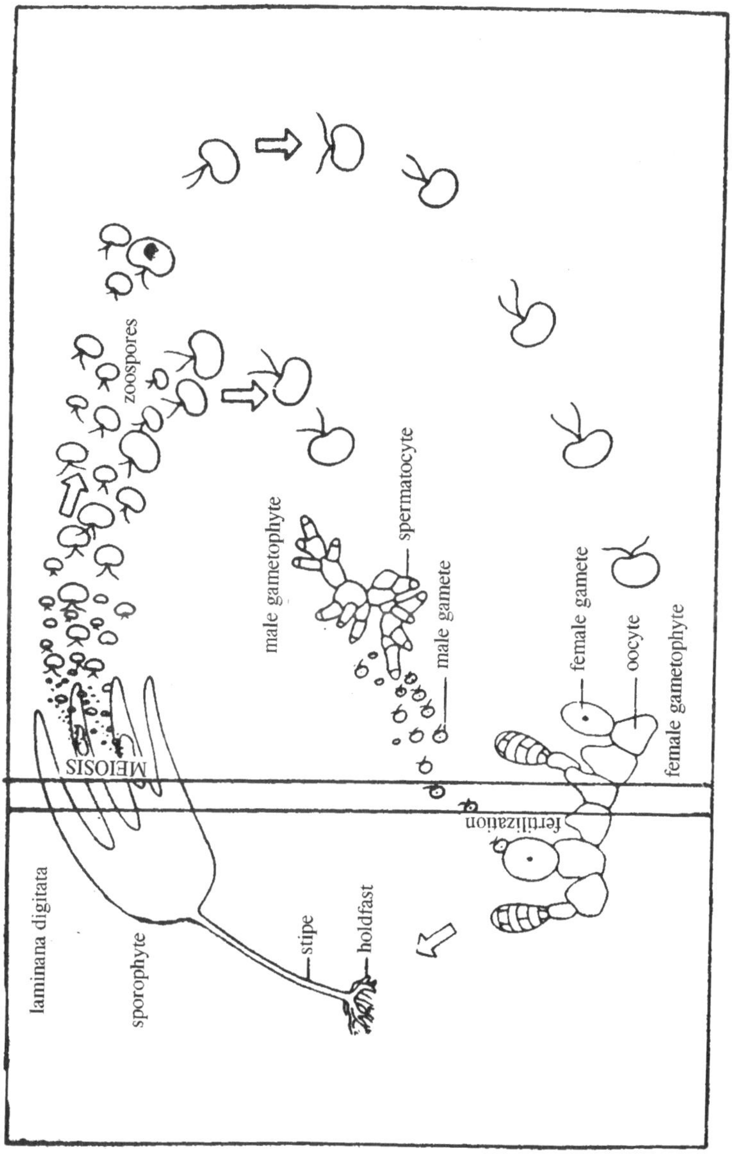

Figure 10.12: Life cycle of the brown alga oarweed Laminaria digitata in which there is a heteromorphic alternatio of generations, a small gametophyte and a large sporophyte.

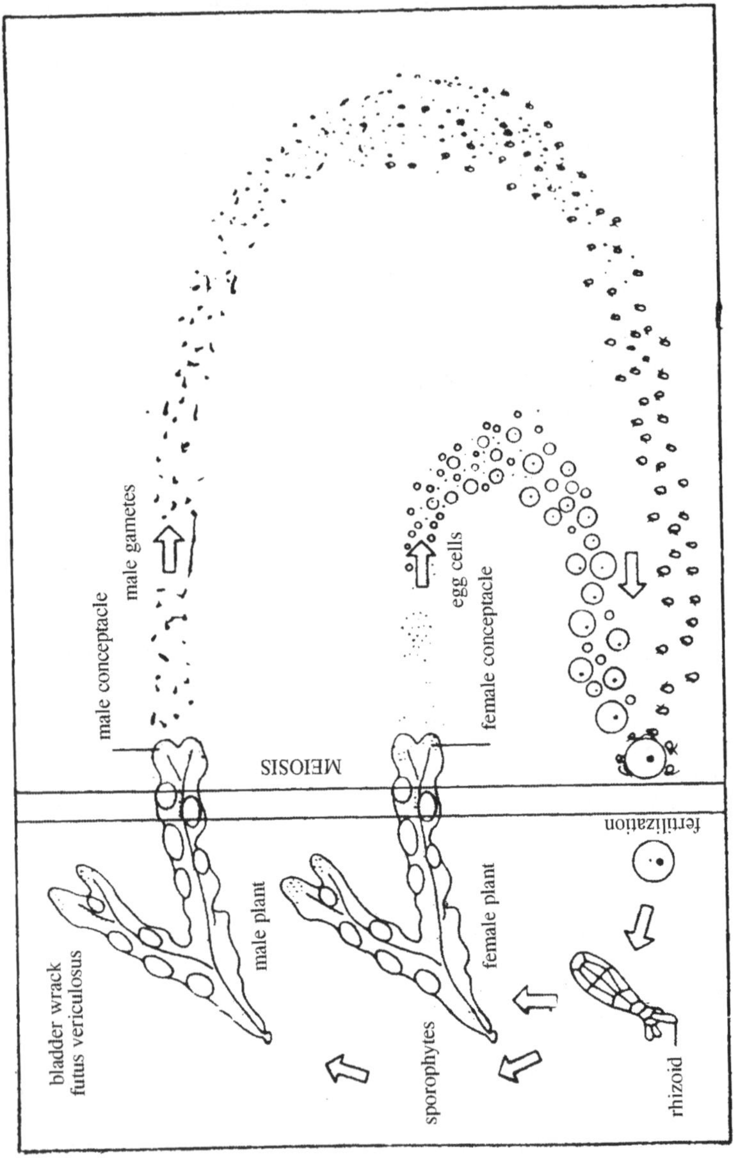

Figure 10.13: Life cycle of a fucoid brown alga bladder wrack Fucus vesiculasus with one free-living stage, the sporophyte.

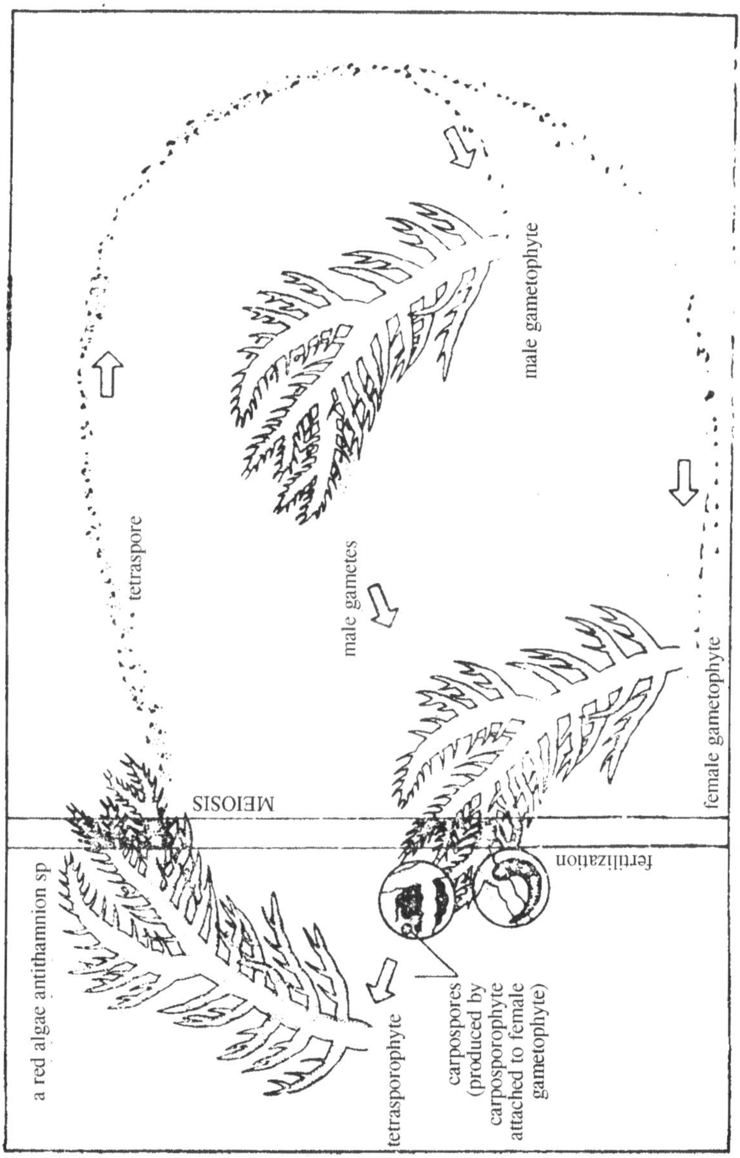

Figure 10.14: Life cycle of a red alga Antithamnion with a third generation—the carposporophyte.

Brown

Brown algae contain photosynthetic pigment which include fucoxanthin giving the characteristic brown colour to to the plants. Giant kelps such as *Macrocystis pyrifera* may reach 60 m or more in length and are harvested off the coasts of *California*, *South Africa* and the *Falkand Islands* for use in the *alginate* industry.

In Europe, the kelps, species of *Laminaria* attain lengths of only a few metres. These are the sporophyte generation but there is also a tiny filamentous gametophyte generation. Other brown algae such as Neptune's necklace *Hormosira banksii* which occurs in southern seas and, more common in the northern hemisphere, the *fucoids* such as bladder wrack *Fucus vesiculosus* have only one main stage (*sporophyte*) in their life cycle.

Relatively sheltered shores on either side of the Atlantic are dominated by the brown *seaweed* family *Fucaceae*. On European coasts a distinct pattern of zonation of the fucoids is apparent with channelled wrack *Pelvetia canaliculata* occurring just below the *Verrucaria* belt. Spiral wrack *Fucus spiralis, Fucus vesiculosus* and/or *Ascophyllum nodosum* occupy the upper and midlittoral zones respectively, with a band of serrated wrack *Fucus serratus* just above low water mark. Below this and extending into the sublittoral are the kelps such as *Laminaria saccharina,* the oarweed *Laminaria digitata* and *Laminaria hyperborea.*

Red

The red coloration of these algae is a result of the pigment phycoerythrin which bleaches quickly in strong sunlight. A blue pigment phycocyanin may also be present in these so-called '*red*' *algae*. They are characterized by a *complex life cycle* some are harvested for agar.

Molluscs

Many gastropods graze on algae *Planktonic* larvae of limpets settle about MLWN but *higher* on the shore in pools and damp shaded areas. During the first year of life an area of rock surface about 75 cm^2 CM -3 of limpet is required on which to browse. *Limpets* rasp away with the *radula* (a *horny tongue* with rows of teeth) at settling algal spores but larger algal plants of *Enteromorpha, Ascophyllum* and *Fucus* are eaten also during the course of their 60-cm zigzag feeding traverses at high tide.

The littorinid winkles of European shores such as the small periwinkle *Littorina neritoides,* the rough periwinkle *L. saxatilis,* the

Figure 10.15: Secondary consumers (not all drawn to the same scale)

flat periwinkle *L. littoralis* and the edible periwinkle *L. littorea* are zoned in that order from the top of the shore. The species *saxatilis* and *littoralis* continua to be re-classified by taxonomists. *L. neritoides* and *L. saxatilis* occur above EHWS especially in exposed regions with a marked splash zone.

In sheltered conditions they may extend no higher than MHW . *L. neritoides* prefers very exposed, steep, *creviced rock* faces whereas *L. saxatilis* generally prefers more shelter. This latter rough periwinkle extends down to ELWN. Both winkles tolerate considerable exposure to air and also lowered salinity caused by rain water; both feed mainly by rasping minute *algae* and *diatoms* from rock faces. *L. saxatilis* is viviparous, hatching live young.

The veliger larva feeds on albumen within the egg until finally the embryo rasps its way free with the radula and escapes from the egg membranes to live in the same rock crevices as the adults. *L. littoralis* has a shell with a *depressed* spire (hence the common name) and lives both on the east coast of North America and on the west coast of Europe.

It has many phenotypic variations in colour ranging from a citrina (yellow) form through aurantia (red-orange) to olivacea (dark green). In combination with zigzag banding and stripes in contrasting colours 12 varieties have been recognized. This species lives in association with the algae *Ascophyllum* and *Fucus* which providc both shelter and food.

Winkles show strong negative geotaxis both in and out of the water; desiccation reverses this, however, preventing them from rising too high on the shore. The edible winkle *L. littorea* ranges from MHWN to ELWS living on rocks and among gravel. Permanent clusters of up to 950 m^{-2} may be found at low tide when inactive.

They feed on micro-organisms and detritus from the surface of the substrate and are effective in controlling the settlement of algal spores by rasping with the radula. *L. littorea* was introduced into the United States of America from the British Isles and was recorded from the coast of Maine in 1868. By 1880 it had dominated the Massachusetts coast and is thought to have been responsible for eliminating the indigenous *L. palliata* from New England shores.

Top shells such as *Mondonta lineata are* also browsers but tend to prefer more shelter, having poor powers of adhesion if disturbed, *Gibbula cineraria* produces large quantities of sticky mucus perhaps to increase its grip.

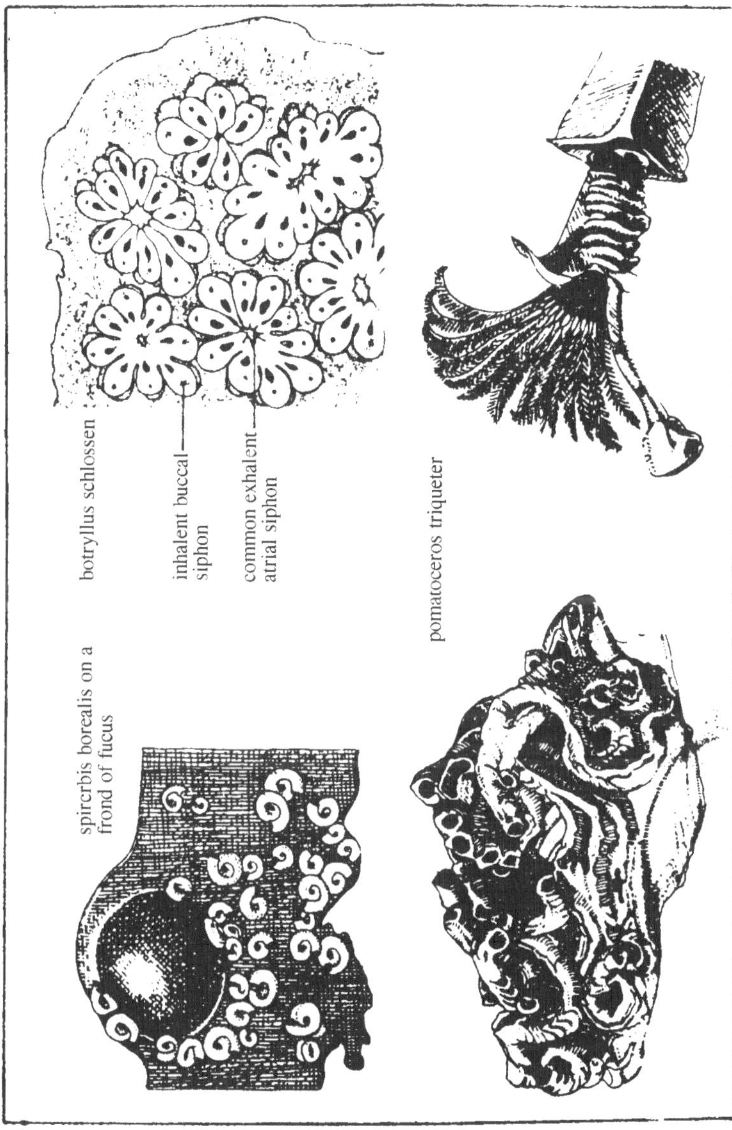

Figure 10.16: Filter and suspension feeders.

Echinoderms

The sea urchin *Echinus esculentus is* also a browser. It has a complex masticatory *apparatus* known as *Aristotle's lantern*. Twenty calcareous pieces are connected with muscles and ligaments to five *mobile* teeth. These rasp organisms such as algae and encrusting invertebrates.

This species lives just below tidal levels but may be uncovered at ELWS. In south west England they are confined to the sublittoral but further north appear on the lower shore and in pools. *Attachment* to the rock is by tube feet and the urchin's presence on *turbulent* coasts shows how effective these are in anchoring the urchin. Continuous removal of *Ecbinus* from *experimental* test sites leads rapidly to the growth of a dense algal sward.

Much the same effect was noted on certain Cornish beaches following the *reduction* of the browsing limpet population after the oil spill from the tanker *Torrey Canyon* and the use of toxic dispersants. Within two or three years the rocks were covered by a rich intertidal growth of algae ; the limpets took longer to recover.

SECONDARY CONSUMERS

Molluscs

The preferred diet of the dog whelk *Thais (=Nucella) lapillus* consists of barnacles *Balanus balanoides* and *Chthamalus stellatus* which effectively restricts its distribution to the middle shore. While it may take a whelk up to two days to bore into the shell of the mussel *Mytilus edulis* it takes much less time and effort to consume a *barnacle*. The whelk positions itself above the barnacle and simply forces open the valves and *anaesthetizes* the prey before *ingesting* the soft parts.

Decapod Crustaceans

Other secondary consumers include voracious shore crabs *Carcinus maenas* and the rock pool shrimp *Palaemon elegans* which preys anything that moves.

There is also a variety of filter and suspension ,feeders including the barnacles and tube worms such as *Spirorbis borealis* often found on fronds of *Fucus serratus low* on the shore and *Pomatoceros triqueter* encrusting rocks around low water mark.

Colonial ascidians such as *Botryllus schlosseri* encrust stones and other ascidians low on the shore, and filter feed. Minute inhalent and exhalent siphons lead to and from the pharyngeal filter that is lined with mucus to entrap food particles.

Universal Patterns of Zonation

The Stephensons pointed out in 1949 that zones on rocky shores, whilst applicable world-wide, could not be defined solely in terms of tidal levels but must be categorized in terms of the distribution of organisms. They concluded that there were five zones

1. Superalittoral zone or maritime belt lying above tide marks but subjected to fine spray in rough weather.
2. Superlittoral fringe extending from the upper limit of barnacles up to the lower limit of flowering plants.
3. Midlittoral zone extending from the upper limit of the barnacles down to, for example, the top of the kelp belt.
4. Infralittoral fringe extending from the top of the kelp belt to ELWS.
5. Intralittoral zone extending from ELWS to the lower limit or seaweed or even to the edge of the continental shelf.

That these zones are universally applicable (at least in cool temperature waters) may be shown by comparing typical patterns of zonation on exposed and sheltered British rocky shores with similar shores in New Zealand. Most of the individual species are different with the barnacle *Chamaesipbo* replacing the northern *Balanns.*

Brown fucoids are less in evidence in the New Zealand midlittotal, Neptune's necklace *Hormosira banksi* forming the replacement together with a more diverse green algal cover than is usually found on shores in the northern hemisphere.

But the delimiting upper level of barnacles and the upper limit of the low shore kelps are present with only minor variations on all cool temperate marine rocky shores (in polar regions these are no barnacles, in the tropics, no kelps).

Rock Pools

Those organisms particularly sensitive to desiccation are often able to extend their range upshore in shaded damp crevices. A permanent presence of water in rock pools might be expected to extend the range of those species to even higher levels on the shore. However, apart from a few red coralline algae such as *Corallina* and the limpet *Patella aspera* for which desiccation appears to be the limiting factor, this range extension rarely materializes.

Rock pools have their own physical characteristics unshaded shallow pool; will show marked changes in temperature, salinity, oxygen and pH levels. Special physiological adaptations may be necessary to cope

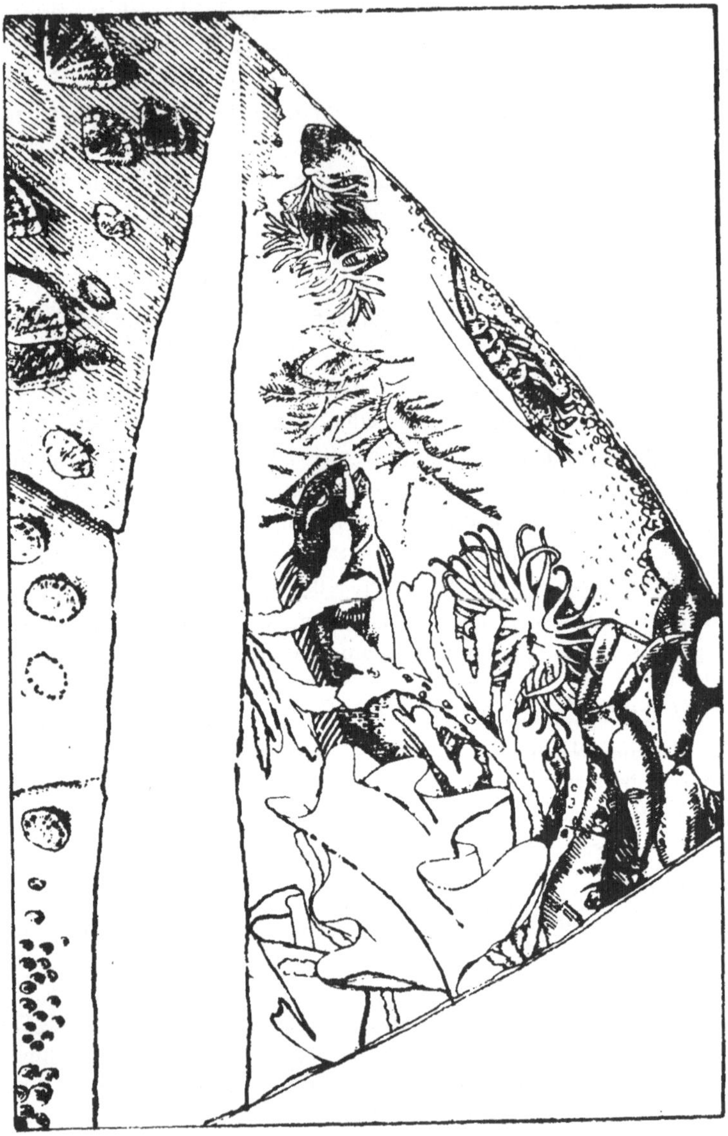

Figure 10.15: Midshore rock pool.

with such widely fluctuating changes as those that occur in a high-level pool that is exposed -to sunlight and/or rain for a fortnight and is then suddenly inundated by a high spring tide.

Nevertheless rock pools on the low and middle shore which experience a regular tidal change of water often contain a rich and varied selection of shore organisms, a feature explored for generations by the fossicking net and bucket brigade.

11

Plants of Rocky Shores

Of the several *seashore* habitats, rocky shores exhibit the greatest variety of *animal life* and are the only type to support large plant *populations*. The latter, of course, consist of the seaweeds.

The words rocky shore conjure up in the mind's eye a different picture for each of us depending on the particular region of the coast we have visited. If our *journeys* have taken us to the west coast of Cornwall where the shore and cliffs suffer the continual *onslaught* of Atlantic milers, the picture *presented* is *bleak*, with barren areas of rock only sparsely clothed with *vegetation*.

On the other hand, if we are familiar with some of the sheltered bays of *South Devon* the picture envisaged is of rocky expanses covered with luxuriant growths of *sea-weeds* varying in colour from bright green. through *greenbrowns* to red. First of all, why do *seaweeds* grow in such *profusion* on *rocky shores*?

The answer is quite simple; rocks are stable and form a suitable base for attachment. Unlike *terrestrial* plants, seaweeds do not need a root system because they absorb nutrients directly from the sea, but they do possess a '*rootlike*' structure, called the holdjast, for anchorage. This *holdfast* grows into *rock cracks* and *crevices*, thus gaining a firm enough grip to prevent dislodgement by the pounding action of waves.

Seaweeds belong to the *non-flowering* class of plants called ALGAE and all contain chlorophyll, though its presence is sometimes masked by other pigments, as is the case in the brown and red *seaweeds*. Ail photosyhthesize and therefore require *plenty* of sunlight. For this reason seaweeds are confined to shores and *shallow seas*.

Seaweeds are the producers in certain *marine* food chains but, although they are the staple diet of some shore *dwellers*, many animals depend on them, principally for protection from *desiccation* when exposed by the ebbing tide and for shelter from wave action when the sea returns. Numerous creatures take advantage of this *amenable* habitat, but before studying them we must first give our attention to the seaweeds themselv es.

Classification As already mentioned, there are seaweeds of varying colours, and for classification purposes they are divided into

CHLOROPHYCEAE-greens
PHAEOPHYCEAE -browns
RHOUOPHYCEAE -reds

The Chloruphyceae are usually bright green and very easy to recognize, but in the *Phaeophyceae* and *Rhodophyceae* there is often colour variation brought about by the bleaching action of the sun so that a red weed, such as *carragheen* or *Irish moss*, *Chondrus crispus*, may appear dull green, or even a yellowish white if exposed for a sufficient length of time.

This *bleaching* is particularly prevalent with detached seaweeds thrown up on the shore and can cause considerable confusion in identification. Brown seaweeds are not typically brown but vary from olive brown to dark green.

Structure

In *comparison* with the familiar plants of the garden the physical structure of seaweeds is very simple, and the whole plant is called the *thallus*. The *thallus* is anchored by the holdfast, from which arises the stem or stipe, and at the tip this develops into a *flattened* or easy, serves the useful purpose during exposure of trapping moisture in the channel formed between the frond and rock surface.

The *fronds* branch in a very definite manner, termed *dichotomous* branching. One frond divides into two; each of these in turn divides twice, and so on to the tips. This form of *branching* is typical of most *wracks*.

During neap tides some areas of the upper shore remain exposed for several days and at these *periods*, particularly in the hot dry months, the normally olive-brown fronds become *shrivelled* and almost *black*, though they quickly regain their usual *turgor* when next *submerged*.

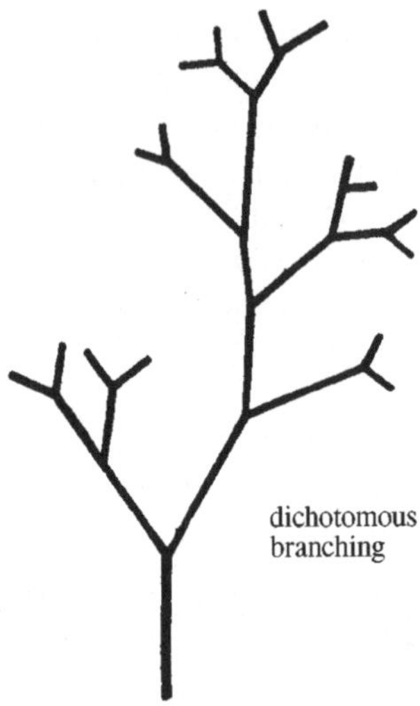

Figure 10.1: Dichotomous branching.

Pelvetia may survive in the splash zone, but here growth is very stunted.

The reproductive structures, the *receptacles,*, develop at the tips of the fronds and when ripe appear yellowish orange. They contain both male and female gametes ; that is *Pelvetia* is a hermaphrodite.

Flat or spiral wrack, *Fucus spiralis,* occupies the next belt down the beach, overlapping the lower edges of the upper shore and the upper region of the middle shore. The flat *cylindrical* frond, whose size, shape and texture varies from species to species.

When the tide is in the complete plant is *submerged*, and at this time the exchange of gases and other substance occurs by diffusion over the whole surface of the *thallus*.

Reproduction

There are no flowers, but most seaweeds reproduce sexually. The minute male and female gametes are usually released into the sea, where fertilization occurs, and the *zygote* so formed may be dispersed some distance by the water currents before it deposits on the bottom and develops into a new plant.

Even though zygotes may be carried to other regions of the shore, only those that deposit on the correct zone develop to *maturity*. *Vegetative reproduction* occurs in many *seaweeds*, but the actual method varies with the different types. In some simple *forms*, such as the sea-lettuce, the frond just divides into two or more and each part *continues* to glow, while in the large oarweeds new growth occurs at the tip of the stripe, and when the new frond is well developed the old one is broken *off* by the force of the waves.

Some seaweeds also *reproduce* asexually by means of spores, which appear as slight swellings on some part of the found, and when *released* germinate into new plants.

As there are several hundred different species of seaweeds, it is possible for us to consider only the most common forms found around the costs of *Britain*.

Brown Seaweeds and Zonation

The greatest amount of cover is given by the tougher types of brown seaweeds, called the *wracks,* and, as each can withstand certain periods of exposure only, their positions down the beach are zoned.

Starting at the top of the shore, the first brown seaweed encountered is channelled wrack, *Pelvetia canaliculata,* with fronds terminating in divided tips 5-15 cm long, *hanging* from the rocks in dense *clusters*. The edges of the fronds are inrolled, a feature which, besides making identification fronds, up to 12 mm in width, have a smooth edge, a midrib, divide at the tips and are generally between 12 and 20 cm long, although they may reach 35 cm in length.

The ripe receptacles are very distinctive oval, orange-brown swellings at the tips of the fronds and, like *Pelvetia*, contain both male and female gametes. The middle region of the shore supports two wracks bearing air bladders for buoying their fronds up near the surface when the tide is in.

These are bladder wrack, *Fucus vesiculosus,* and knotted wrack, *Ascophyllum nodosum* and both are confined to this region because their bladders could not withstand the increased pressure at greater depths of water. Sometimes they live side by side, but more frequently one species is present on a particular shore.

F. vesiculosus has a frond from similar to *F. spiralis*, but with a wavy margin and small bladders on either side of the midrib, arranged in pairs, and the fronds may be from 30120 cm long. The receptacles are again at the tips of the Bonds, but they contain only gametes of one sex, the female receptacles appearing yellow and the male bright orange when ripe.

In winter months it is not always easy to identify bladder wrack because the fronds become badly damaged du in-storms. Ofter only the midrib survives above the holdfast, bearing just a few torn shreds of

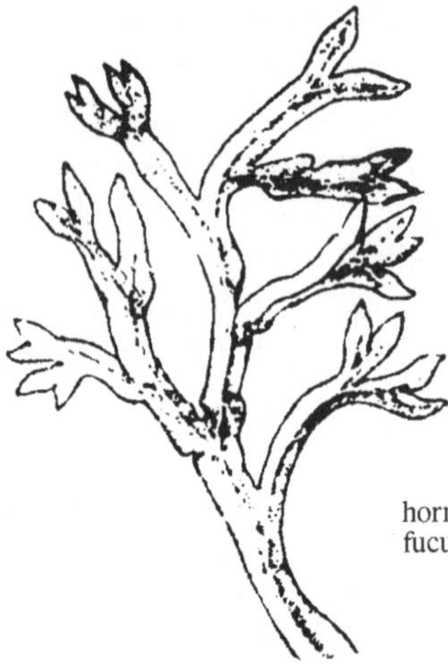

Figure 11.2: Horned wrack. Fucus ceranoides.

fronds with no signs of air bladders. *F. vesiculosus* is capable of colonizing many varied environments and in adapting itself becomes so modified that it is difficult to recognize, particularly as air bladders may be absent. This is one of the tricks of nature which leads the methodical man a marry dance!

Ascophyllum nodoosum is very different. The frond is narrow, like a thick flattened cord, with no midrib, but containing large egg-shaped air bladders arranged singly down the centre at intervals of around 7-10 cm, depending on the size of the plant.

A. nodosum, unlike the other wracks, branches irregularly and grows to a great length, maybe to 3 metres in its most favourable situation-a well-sheltered shore. On exposed shores it gives way to *F. vesiculosus.* which is a much hardier plant.

The reproductive bodies of *A. nodosum* are borne at the tips of special short side branches arising along the length of the fronds, and when ripe these *receptacles* are bright yellow in the male plants and yellow olive in the *females*.

Quite frequently, knotted wrack is camouflaged by a tufted covering of the red seaweed, *Polysiphonia*. When looked at through a hand-lens, *Polysiphonia is* seen to consist of a latticework of fine branches arising in a tuft from the *holdfast*, which is firmly attached to the *Ascophyllum* frond. A plant which attaches itself to another plant, but absorbs *no nourishment* from it, is called an *epiphyte ;* many seaweeds exhibit this *epiphytic habit*.

Horned wrack, *Fucus ceranoides*, is another inhabitant of the middle shore, but only where *fresh water* is present. Obviously we shall find this seaweed is a common member of estuarine flora. The fronds have a definite *midrib*, divide *dichotomously* and bear narrow, pointed *receptacles* at their tips.

Intermingled with *F. vesiculosus* on the lower regions of the middle shore the last of the fucoids, serrated wrack, *F. serratus*, appears as a flat matlike covering to the rocks. The fronds are distinctly flat with a midrib, but the margins are serrated or toothed, hence the common names of serrated or saw wrack.

The receptacles do not form swollen bulbous structures as in the other wracks, but extend as a flattened, blistered area over the terminal 2-4 cm of the frond, those of the male plant appearing bright orange when ripe. Sometimes sterile structures in the form of small, fine, white hairs are dispersed over the fronds.

F. serratus is one of the commonest British seaweeds and clothes a wide belt of rocks, extending down on to the lower shore where it is exposed only for brief periods during the low water spring tides. Its preference for this position indicates that *F. serratus* is not so well modified to resist desiccation as the other wracks.

The fucoids are perennials, though they probably survive no more than three seasons owing to battering by the waves, but *Ascophyllum,* in its sheltered situations, has a slower rate of growth and a longer length of life.

Two epiphytes commonly found on *Fucus* are the filamentous brown seaweeds *Ectocarpus* and *Sphaecelaria.* In each the hairlike fronds branch into fine threads, but in *Ectocarpus* they may be up to 25 cm in length and hang in a matted mass, wheareas in *Sphaecelaria* they form dense tufts about 2.5 cm long.

Now we have reached the zone which is little different from the sub-littoral region and here are found the largest and toughest of the brown seaweeds. These are the oarweeds whose extensive holdfasts harbour a multitude of small organisms.

These holdfasts are very tenacious, but on occasions they are attached to insecure rocks so that in rough seas the rock, holdfast and oarweed are carried up the shore, thus giving the interested beachcomber an opportunity to study the wealth of life sheltering within the confines of the holdfast.

These oarweeds are rarely completely exposed; more frequently the stipes stand out of the water, but bend over so that the frond droops into the water. If there are deep pools in the lower regions of the middle shore these oarweeds may grow in profusion around the edges, trailing their fronds below the surface.

Tangle, *Laminaria digitata,* has a very thick, smooth, cylindrical stipe that is flexible enough to allow the large leathery fronds to sway with the moving currents as the tide ebbs and flows. In a young plant the frond is entire, but as it grows it divides into many straplike sections and somewhat resembles a hand.

The number of straps varies according to the environmental conditions, the more sheltered the area the less the number of divisions. Sometimes this species is replaced by cuvie, *L. hyperborea,* which has the same type of frond, but the stipe is hard with a rough surface and stands upright for 60-90 cm when exposed.

Sea belt, *L. saccharina,* has a much narrower, shorter stipe *L. digitata* and the frond, rather more yellowish in colour, extends into a

Figure 11.3: Dabberlocks, Alaria esculenta.

long, narrow, wavy belt, about 10-15 cm in width, but extending in length to 1½ metres or more.

When exposed the fronds drape *horizontally* along the rocks, but when partially submerged float outstretched, moving gracefully to the motion of the tide. This *oarweed* is also found in *deep* pools on the lower middle shore and its specific name is derived from the sweet-tasting substance which *exudes* from the dry fronds.

It is this seaweed which children love to take home for a weather guide, the belief being that rain is about when the *frond* is moist and limp, and sunny weather when it is *firm* and *dry*.

Another oarweed somewhat similar to *L. saccharin,* but found only on very exposed coasts, is dabberlocks, *Alaria esculenta*, which is recognized by its prominent midrib.

Very low on the shore a few isolated furbelows, *Saccorhiza polyschides,* may be exposed and this species is identified by its large bulbous holdfast from which arises a tough, flattened stipe, very twisted and frilled at first, but widening into a massive frond divided like *L. digitata,* though much larger.

This shows a gradation in size down the shore with the smallest seaweeds inhabiting the upper regions and the largest the lower and sub-littoral regions. In other words, those with the smallest surface area survive the longest periods of exposure; they are the adapted to withstand desiccation.

The large weeds on the lower shore are uncovered for so short a time that desiccation is no problem, but when the tide is in their fronds are well below the surface so the light received is of reduced intensity ; thus they are specially adapted to contend with this problem.

Rock Pool Vegetation

Rock pools vary in size, depth and situation, and each type supports its own special community.

Deep Pools

As already mentioned, deep pools of the middle shore may be bordered by the oarweeds, *Laminaria saccharin* and *L. digitata.* Another tough, leathery brown seaweed, in the form of long, narrow, flat straps, floats outwards from the edge of pools where it arises from green-brown button-like structures. This is thongweed, *Himanthalia elongata,* and the unique feature of this species is that these long, dichotomously branched straps are the *reproductive structures*, equivalent to the small receptacles at the tips of *fucoid fronds*.

Figure 11.4: Pod-weed, Halidrys siliquosa.

The thongs range from 1 to 2+ metres in length and when ripe appear blotched. Thongweed may also be found low on the shore where it must not be mistaken for the round, *unbranched bootlace weed, Chorda filum,* whose fronds are *slimy*, reaching up to 6 or 7 metres, though they often appear as coiled masses owing to the tendency of the fronds to *twist* together.

On the south and west coasts of Britain, from the walls of pools from the middle shore downwards, the yellowish olive dichotomously branched fronds of *Bifucaria rotunda* float outwards in masses, always remaining covered with water.

Near by the submerged fronds of the bushy *Cystoseira tamariscifolia* may appear bright blue, but as soon as this seaweed is removed from the water its beauty is lost. The pod-weed, *Halidrys siliquosa,* may abound in the same pool. This is another brown seaweed, much branched and quickly recognized by the pod-shaped air *bladders*. It also inhabits the lower *shore* and it is often found among the debris of the driftline.

The most attractive of our brown seaweeds, popularly called peacock's tail, *Padina pavonia,* lives on the verges of these middle shore pools. The fronds are flat, firm, fan-shaped, concentrically marked and rise stiffly from the holdfast to a height of only 2-5 cm, through they can grow to a maximum of 15 cm. Many species of *Padina* flourish in the warmer seas of the would, but *P. pavonia* is the only one capable of surviving our temperate climate and is found only along our southern coasts.

Outstanding against the dull olive-brown seaweed are the clusters of dark green, cylindrical, dichotomously branched fronds of *Codium,* growing to a length of approximately 30 cm. The characteristic feature of this green seaweed is the velvety surface of the fronds.

Shallow Pools

The shallow pools have a particular beauty of their own often enhanced by the pinkish mauve coloration of the sides and bottom. Anyone could be forgiven for attributing this attractive shading to the structure of the rock surfaces but, even though of inanimate appearance,

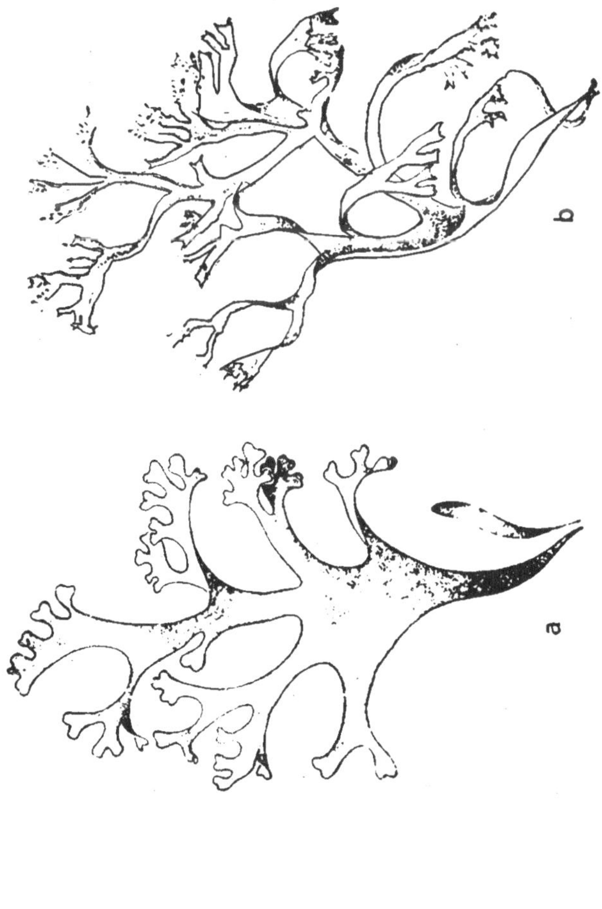

Figure 11.5: (a) Irish moss or carragheen, Chondrus crispus with dichotomously branching flat fronds, (b) Gigartina stellata with dichotomously branching channelled fronds.

the area is covered with vegetation-the encrusting red seaweeds, *Lithophyllum* and *Lithothamnion.*

The hard limy structure of the thallus is formed from absorbed calcium and magnesium and the pinkish mauve colour is the resultant effect of the lime on the normal red pigments of the plants. On death this colour is lost, first fading to tones of grey and then to white. The two forms are very similar, but the thallus of *Lithothamnion* has moue flured edges.

Corallina officinalis is another calcareous red seaweed commonly bordering pools, but this has a normal thallus and grows in tufts ranging in colour from deep mauve, pinkish mauve, yellowish pink to white, depending on exposure.

The branched fronds, usually 2-7 cm long, though they may reach a maximum of 12 cm, grow in stiff tufts from a small calcified encrusting holdfast up to 1 cm in diameter, and the limy skeleton is segmented, a feature which makes identification simple. The tufts often appear edged in a lighter colour because fading first occurs at the tips of the fronds. *Corallina* is to be found on most rocky shores of Britain, from the middle shore downwards.

Purple tinted founds of *Chondrus crispus* may glisten just below the surface, but this iridescent beauty is lost once the plant is lifted clear of the water. This red seaweed in not entirely confined to pools and may be found over a wide area from the middle shore down to the edge of the sub-littoral zone.

The flat fronds, about 1 cm wide, branch and termiante in short dichotomous divisions with rounded tips giving a characteristic form 7-15 cm in length. However, difficulties in identification do arise because this species has several variable forms; for instance, in exposed positions the fronds are narrow and appear nearly cylindrical.

Normally *Chondrus crispus* is dark red, but it can be pinkish red and turns green at the tips when exposed for long periods in hot sun, finally bleaching to yellowish white. The important feature to remember is that the fronds are flat and their edges *never* inroll; this distinguishes *Chondrus* from *Gigartina stellata C. crispus* was, and still is, collected for use in the manufacture of jellies and blancmanges, and as the main source was the rocky coast of Ireland it acquired the popular name of Irish moss or carragheen.

The small brown seaweed *Dictyota dichotoma* grows at the edges of shallow pools and its delicate dichotomously branched, olive-brown fronds, about 14 or 5 mm wide, with no midrib, often intermingle with *Corallina.* It may also be found on rocks of the middle shore and lower. This species is abundant on south and west coasts of Britain, but becomes sparser towards the north and east.

An unusual brown seaweed, *Leathesia difformis,* epiphytic on other weeds, but floating on the surface of shallow pools, has the fronds blown out into hollow lobed spheres up to 4 cm in diameter.

Some of the green seaweeds are found in the around the pools and sea-lettuce, *Ulva lactuca,* with its typically broad but thin fronds, is fairly common. However, it is not confined to pools and when uncovered by the tide the fronds lay limply over rock surfaces.

Cladophora, a darker green in colour, hangs from the sides of pools in tufts of branched threads. Under water it has a delicate traccry, but when exposed or handled the threads form an indistinct mass about 7 cm long.

Enteromorpha is the bright green seaweed which forms a slippery covering over the rock surfaces in all regions and also extends into some pools, where it is attached to stones or other seaweeds such as *Corallina,* or even to slow-moving animal inhabitants such as the limpet. *Enteromorpha* is most conspicuous in late winter and early spring when it may carpet large expanses of rock, particularly where fresh water mingles with sea water. These grass green seaweeds are annuals and by the end of the summer the dying fronds become bleachcd.

Red Seaweeds

It is obvious that the brown wracks and oarweeds form the greatest bulk of the seaweed population, but for the greatest variety of species we must look to the red seaweeds. More generally the *Rhodophyceae* are located lower down the shore, many in rock pools, indicating they are not very tolerant of *exposure.*

This is understandable because they do not have the tough, leathery structure exhibited by the wracks and many obtain shelter beneath the fronds of *Fucus serratus.*

On the middle and lower zones *Gigartina stellata* may be abundant. It is very similar in size and structure to *Chondrus crispus,* but *Gigartina* has channelled fronds formed by the inrolling of the edges and it also may bear short, knoblike outgrowths over the surface and edges ; these are the reproductive structures.

In the same area, quite large expanses of rock may be covered with *Laurencia pinnatifida* whose branched fronds, although only 7-10 cm long, terminate in small spearheads. Normally dark red, this weed turns *yellowish green* in sunny situations and in the higher regions of the

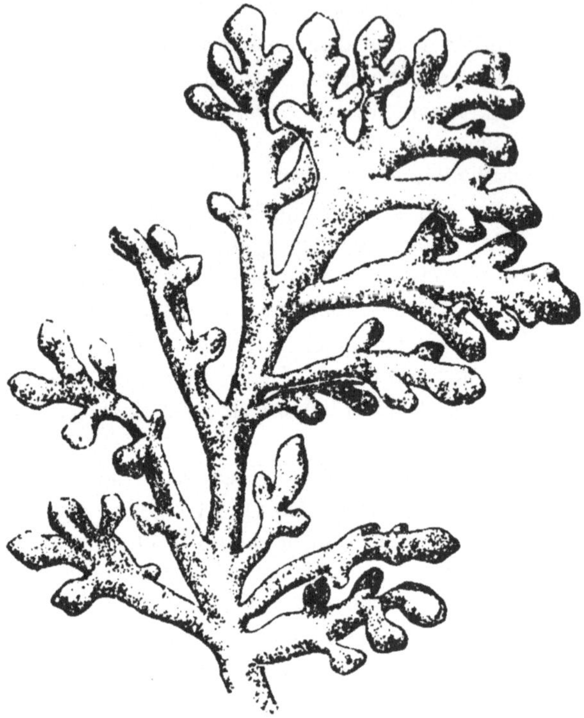

Figure 11.6: Laurencia pinnatifida, close-up showing spearhead tips to fronds.

middle shore the plants are much shorter and form a close covering to the rocks.

Lomentaria articulata is a pale pinkish red weed, unmistakable because of the beadlike structure of its branched fronds. It grows in tufts on the lower shore, often as an *epiphyte*, and, besides being *constricted*, the fronds are shiny and delicate.

Plumaria elegans is often found alongside *Lomentaria*. hanging in lank, dark red tufts, some 5-10 cm long from sheltered rock overhangs; perhaps with purse sponges attached to it. *Plumaria* branches *irregularly* and when *floating* in water the fronds have a feathery appearance.

Ceramium rubrum is a very common species inhabiting all levels of the shore either attached to rocks or to other seaweeds.

Its pinkish red fronds, marked with darger bands, are fine and terminate in divided tips facing inwards like a pair of forceps. The fronds, 7-30 cm long, grow in tufts and very in colour from dark red, bright pink to yellow-white when bleached by the sun.

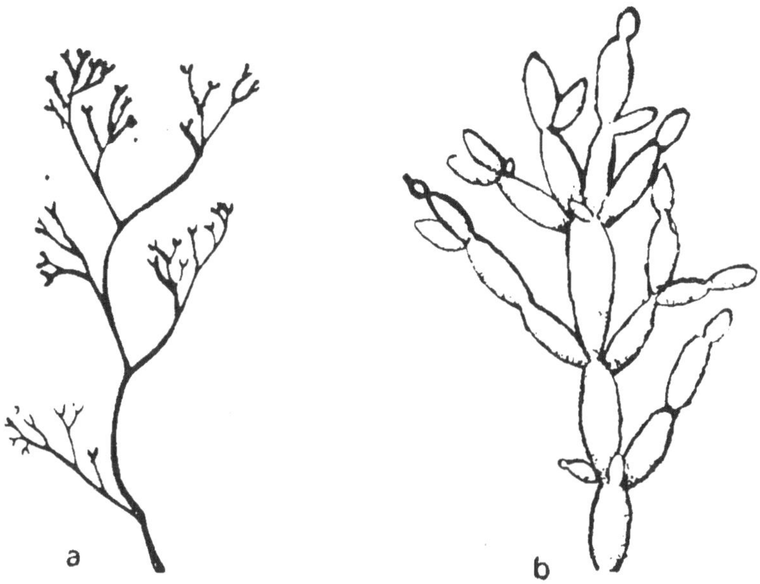

Figure 11.7: Ceramium rubrum, with forcipate tips to fronds, (b) Lomentaria, articulata close-up showing constrictions of fronds.

Occasionally, after rough seas have ripped the plants from the rocks, their fronds are washed ashore in masses to form an unusually colourful display.

Dulse, *Rhodymenia palmata,* another common red weed, grows in clusters on the lower shore either attached to rocks or to oarweeds and wracks. The flat fronds, arising from a very short stipe, gradually increase in width in the shape of a V, then divide either dichotomously or into several branches of equal size (palmate).

Often very small fronds grow outwards from the edges of the main fronds; the overall length of the plant may be as much as 30 cm. Two attractive inhabitants of the lowest regions are *Delessaria sanguinea* and *Phycodrys rubens* growing on rocks or epiphytically on *Laminaria.*

Both may reach a length of 25-28 cm and have a distinct midrib in the leaflike fronds. *Delessaria* fronds have a continuous edge whereas those of *Phycodrys* are indented and resemble oak leaves ; on this account the tatter is often called the sea oak.

The detached fronds of these two species become deposited higher on the shore and this is where they are most likely to be encountered. Laver, *Porphyra umbilicalis,* although a red seaweed, usually appears brownish in colour. It has a thin expanded flat frond, similar in form to *Ulva*, which clings closely to rock surfaces when exposed. It may be found at all levels, but more particularly in the upper zones and it is most prolific during the winter months. This is the edible seaweed called '*laverbread*'.

For anyone interested in testing their palate, prepare it in the following way. First wash thoroughly in fresh water and then boil until tender. It becomes a brownish-black glutinous mass which may be eaten, but it is much testier if fried with bacon.

In discussing the Rhodophyceae it is difficult to decide which species to consider for their numbers are so great; the foregoing are a small selection of some of the commonest, and further information may be obtained from specialist books.

Blue-Green Algae

A fourth group of algae, the Myxophyceae, although not strictly seaweeds, do have a few representatives on the shore. These blue-green algae are singlecelled though they' form colonies, some being filamentous, such as *Calothrix confervicola* which grows in minute tufts on other small algae.

Others form small gelatinous masses, such as *Rivularia atra* which grows in hemispherical jellylike black-green blobs up to 4 mm in diameter on rocks and stones. This is the most primitive group of algae; they have no sexual method of reporduction and contain a blue pigment which combines with chlorophyll to give the blue-green colour.

Litchens

Seaweeds are the main plant colonizers of rocky shores, but another form of vegetation also grows on some rocks-the *lichens*. Out of each of the tide, but within range of sea-spray, *Xanthoria porietina* adorns the rocks in bright yellow-orange foliaceous patches and on the upper shore the encrusting film of *Verrucaria maura* may be mistaken for black pathces of tar.

Lichina pygmaea, a larger commoner lichen, grows in black tufts of up to 2.5 cm high, over a wide area extending from the upper shore down to the mean tide level. It is fairly tolerant of wave action and therefore often grows in sufficient abundance to give a dense covering to the more exposed rocks.

The lichens, which are found in many varying habitats, are unique forms of plant life, consisting of two unrelated species growing together in close association. This partnership of mutual benefit is called *symbiosis*, and in the lichens the two partners are a fungus and an alga. The grey-green stiff tufts of *Ramalina* grow best when regularly sprayed with sea water and bridge the gap between the seaweeds of the intertidal zone and the flowering plants of the fringing cliffs.

FLOWERING PLANTS OF ROCKY COASTS

As a habitat, the cliffs of our rocky coast do not present a very hospitable *environment* because in such exposed positions the colonizers have to counted with both wind and weather. Even when out of direct reach of sea-spray the *atmosphere* is so heavily laden with salt, and the salinity of the soil so high, that special *modifications* in the structure of the plants are necessary for their survival.

Plants capable of absorbing water from such salty soil solutions are called *halophytes*. The slope of the cliffs and their aspect, and the nature of the rock strata are also controlling factors in this habitat.

On some rocky coasts the sea does lap the base of the cliffs and here we may find a few flowering plants growing on the rocks themselves though, of course, only in *crevices* and depressions where a little soil has collected.

Along the south and west coasts of Britain rock samphire *Crithmum maritumum,* adapts itself to this situation with its long, tough roots capable of penetrating deeply into the cracks and its succulent leaves which store water. It is a perennial with a stern of about 30 cm tall, but this tends to bend, spreading the branches outwards close to the rock surface.

The fleshy leaves are divided into narrow leaflets and the yellow flowers, in umbels, appear from July to September. Cliff spurrey, *Spergularia rupicola,* rock sea lavender, *Limonium, binervosum* and thrift, *Armeria maritima,* also survive on rocks where soil is at a minimum. All are perennials with long woody root systems capable of penetrating cracks and crevices.

Cliff spurrey, a very low-growing plant, with—trailing, slightly downy stems, bears small five-petalled pink flowers from June to September and is more commonly found in the south and west of Britain.

Rock sea lavender is similar to the common sea lavender of salt-marshes but the stems are shorter, the leaves smaller and narrower, and the deeper mauve flowers arranged more closely on the flower spikes. It is in bloom from July to September.

Thrift, or sea pink belongs to the same family as sea lavender, but the tubular, five-petalled, pink flowers are crowded together in clusters at the tips of leafless flower stalks. The leaves are rather fleshy and form a cushion-like mat on rock surfaces which feel springy underfoot. The flowering period extends from April to October.

Some cliffs are so sheer and the crevices so few that little vegetation can find a foothold. but others tumble away in gentler slopes with many ledges and sheltered dips that are colon'zed by plants. Here again the beautiful thrift may flourish as it is one of the commonest and most adaptable of our coastal flowers.

Sea campion, *Silene martima,* happily takes root on ledges where only small amounts of soil become deposited and its low form enables it to survive the force of the winds in such exposed positions. Sea campion is not confined to this habitat and a mass of its white flowers is a common sight on shingle beaches throughout the summer.

On many cliff tops the cultivated farmland extends within a short distance of the edge so the coastal plants are confined to a narrow belt. Mixed in with rough grass the flowers of sea pink, sea plantain and kidney-vetch make a colourful show.

Sea plantain, *Plantago maritima,* is a perennial belonging to the same family as the troublesome weed of our lawns. The flowers are in a spike and the yellow anthers appear first at the base; as these winter, those above ripen. All stages of the flower may be seen during June, July and August.

Inland plants which are found growing within reach of seaspray often exhibit minor modifications and in the kidneyvetch, *Arithyllis vulneraria,* the clustered, small pea-flowers range from the normal yellow to orange or bright red, while the leaves become more fleshy.

Two other members of pea family, sea clover, *Trifolium squamosum,* and hare's-foot clover, *T. arvense,* tolerate a salty atmosphere and the later may be found only a metre or two above high water level. Both are annuals and flower during midsummer.

Throughout the summer the cliff tops may be adorned with masses of the white daisy-like flowers of scentless mayweed, *Tripleurospermum (=Matricaria) maritimum.* This species, very tolerant of exposure, is found along the whole of the Atlantic seaboard, but only rarely along the east coast.

Wild carrot, *Daucus carota,* both subspecies *carota* and subspecies *gummifer,* frequent cliff tops, sometimes side by side. They have the common cow-parsley form of inflorescence, but often the central florets are a deep pink red when first opened, though they gradually fade and blend with the outer yellowish white florets.

The inland relative, fennel, *Foeniculum vulgare,* is sometimes found among the grasses of cliff tops. but only in situations well away form sea-spray. The compound leaves consist of fine, narrow leaflets which form a delicate tracery; the yellow flowers appear in July and August.

This species may grow to a height of 1 or 1½ metres, if in a reasonably sheltered position, and when cultivated its seeds are used for flavouring and its leaves for garnishing food.

A delightful flower which may enhance the beauty of the Atlantic seaboard is the spring squilla, *Sailla verna.* Its dainty blue flowers raise their heads only 5-10 cm above the surroundin; turf but, nevertheless, are a conspicuous and lovely sight when carpeting large patches of cliff-top.

Squilla grows from a bulb and has the long, narrow leaves with parallel veins typical of the lily family. It blooms in April and May. It is not possible to list even a small number of the flowers one *may* find on cliff tops simply because so many of the inland species survive here, provided they are not within direct reach of the sea-spray.

12

ANIMALS OF ROCKY SHORES

Exploring a rocky shore is one of the delights of many a town-bred boy or girl for here may he seen many fascinating and, to them, weird creatures, hut to the zoologist it is an unusual and happy *hunting* ground because rocky shore *populations* include representatives from nearly all the *phyla* or groups of *invertebrate* animals (animal without *backbones*).

This great diversity of *fauna* is due to the many micro-habitats within the one environment, for here animals live under rock overhangs, beneath boulders and stones, buried in sand or gravel below stones, among seaweed fronds, in rock pools, within rock crevices, in their own rock borings and on hare rock; hut whatever their habitat, all are adapted to survive the rigours of *periodic exposure* and *submergence*.

From topics discussed in the first section it is obvious that the variety of fauna differs from one rocky shore to another, hut if we follow the ebbing tide down a sheltered shore a fair selection of the *commonest* populations may he *encountered*.

As we clamber down from the cliff-topes 'the first animals to catch our eye are acorn barnacles, not single ones, hut large populations, together showing up as a white hand along vertical rock faces. The width of this hand varies, with the slope of the shore and species of barnacle. With the two commonest, *Chthamalus stellatus* and *Balanus balanoides,* the upper limit of this belt is approximately high water springs in the former, but mean high water in the latter and should both be present on one shore, *B. balanoides* is found below *C. stellatus*.

Closer study reveals that each barnacle is a small, *boxlike* structure, formed of several limy plates, with its base fixed to the rock, but *exhibiting* no signs of life. The animal, a *crustazean*, is tucked away inside and will not protrude its body until covered by the tide and then it simply flicks its legs in and out to trap plankton. Their cementing technique is so efficient that some *species* survive the constant onslaught of ocean breakers on the most exposed shores of out *coastline*.

Despite their protection, barnacles fall prey to other animals and one predator, the dog whelk, *Nucella lapillus,* can always be found crawling over and around them. It feeds by forcing its special toughened tongue, or radula, between the movable surface plates of the *barnacle* and then sucks up the juicy flesh from inside. The shell of dog- whelks feeding entirely on barnacles is a dirt)-white colour and as this blends with their prey, they may be somewhat difficult spot. During the spring, clusters of their yellow, vase-shaped egg capsules abundant in rock crevices.

Empty barnacle shells offer shelter to minute creatures and the small bivalve *Lasaea rubra* may be fund bidden here as well as among the lichen, *Lichina pygmea.* Its white, oval shell, only about 1·5 mm long, is tinged with red.

Above this barnacle belt, hidden away in rock cracks in the lichen area, tiny, grey black, smoothshelled small periwinkles, *Littorina neritiiodes,* may live. Thcsc small periwinkles are terrestrial in most of their habits, but remain dependent on the sea for dispersal, protection and development of their eggs, which are shed during the winter months when rough seas reach these splash zone rocks.

In some of the same crevices young rough periwinkles, *L. saxatilis,* may also be found; these are easily recognized by their grooved shells. Rough periwinkles may be white, cream, brown or grey and larger specimens abound on rocks and in shallow pools of the upper shore.

In some of the small rock hollows we may see a mass of blue-black valvet floating on the surface of the trapped sea water. This is a cluster of one of the few insects found on the beach, the springtall, *Anurida (=Lipura) maritima.*

The high water level is always marked by the deprise left behind by the receding tide and if we disturb a clump of decaying seaweeds our feet are enveloped in a host of small jumping creatures-the shore hoppers *Orchestia.* These crustaceans '*hop*' by flexing their tails.

Limpets dot the bate rocks and on soft sandstone deep circular grooves form where limpets constantly clamp down their shells on the same site each time the tide ebb. This habit prevents desiccation, and if we try to dislodge a limpet the tightness of its grip soon becomes apparent.

Limpets, like periwinkles, are univalves, but their shell is just simple cone, sometimes tall and at other times flat. It is believed that this *variation* in shape is related to an individual *limpets* home ground. For instance, if it lives on exposed rock, constantly buffeted by the waves, the shell is laid down in a *high cone*, but if in a sheltered pool, the shell is deposited in a more flattened form, the difference being controlled by the extent of contraction of the *lownward* pulling adductor muscles which alter the position of the *shell-secreting mantle*.

Rocks on which limpets have established themselves are usually bare as these molluscs browse on sea-weeds when submerged. Dark red or greenish-brown fleshy blobs under the edges of rocks, and in crevices, are closed beadlet anemones, *Actinia equina, but* in nearly shallow *Lithophyllum* encrusted pools, these coelenterates display their flowerlike beauty with spread tentacles, ready to catch any passing prey.

Some of the beadlets, usually those a little farther down the shore, have their crimson columns spotted green and these are known as '*strawberry*' anemones. The columns of beadlet anemones often harbour the seaspider *Pycnogonum, a* small, eight-legged, pale brown animal which may also be found among the debris at the top of the shore.

Wherever sea-anemones abound, the grey sea-slug, *Aeolidia papillosa,* is sure to be near by as it feeds solely on anemones. Its skin is extended into tubular papillae giving the appearance of a shaggy coat. On south and west coasts the toothed topshell, *Gibbula lineata,* crawls over rocks browsing on seaweeds around mean high water level, but does not venture much farther down the beach.

In the middle shore zone, in open, shallow, sunny pools. may be seen the gracefully waving tentacles of snakelocks anemones, *Anemonia sulcata*. Unlike beadlet anemones, the tentacles of snakelocks cannot be withdrawn and when uncovered by the ebbing tide hang limply from the column, their brown colour blending with the rocks.

Small snakelocks may be found in clusters in shallow crevices on the surface of rocks, and sometimes when the animals are in full sunlight the tentacles are apple green with mauve tips. Daisy anemones, *Cereus pedunculatus,* also live in shallow pools, but their namerous short tentacles soon withdraw and disappear below the surface when touched or when the pool dries out.

They are attached to rocks beneath the floor of the pool, so contraction of the column pulls them downwards. Another good place to search is under loose stones and rocks, especially those resting on other stones, for these give plenty of room for animals to crawl in and out, and provide excellent protection.

After looking beneath a rock *always* return it to its original position before dislodgement to ensure that all plants and animals are restored to their normal surroundings. If this is not done, many may die. One of the commonest of all rocky shore inhabitants, the common shore crab, *Carcinus maenas,* crawls away sideways to new cover when disturbed in its hideout below a stone.

Beware of the nippers, and if you want to pick up a crab, grasp its carapace between your thumb and first finger just behind the attachment of its chelae legs. In this way the nippers cannot reach your hand. If a female, she may be carrying eggs on her abdominal appendages, but look carefully to see they are eggs and *not* the sac-like structure of the parasitic barnacle, *Sacculina.*

Broad-clawed porcelain crabs, *Porcellana platycheles,* have a flattened body and chelae for adhering flush agains, the undersurface of rocks; when disturbed the) are relatively sluggish in their movements compared with shore crabs. They are hairy, and mud particles stick to them so that they appear a dirty brown in colour.

Long-clawed porcelain crabs, P. *longicornis,* have a typically smooth, round carapace. They have no hairs and long antennae, so they cannot be mistaken for the broad-clawed from.

Pirimela denticulata is a pretty little crab-found under and around stones on clean gravel. It is about 12 mm broad and the carapace may be green, brown purple or red, and may even be motled.

Gommaric locusta, a close relative of the shore hopper, is abundant under stones, but does not 'hop'. When disturbed it just wriggles away on its side with its tail tucked underneath.

When we dislodge certain stones an unpleasant occur may reach our nostrils, and the gravel or sand beneath is found to be blackened. This is caused by bacteria which rapidly develop wherever the oxygen content is low. A similar condition occurs a few centimetres below sand and mud, appearing as a black lyer when the sand is dug.

Turning over a stone on muddy gravel may display many actively coiling and twisting fine, yellowish-red threads. These are the tentacles of the burrowing polychaete worms commonly called redthreaes, *Audouinia* searching for food particles, but once exposed these are quickly withdrawn. Tentacles of enother burrowing polychaete, *Amphitrile,* may be uncovered, and if we scaleworm, *Harmothoe lunulata,* sharing the same burrow. This type of togetherness where one animal benefits from the association but in no way harms or helps the other is called *commensalism. H. lunulata* is happy to live in e similar way in the tubes of other burrowing animals, but it is also discovered on its own under rocks.

As another stone is turned en unattractive, slimy, coiled black mass may be laid bare end attempts to uncoil it will show it to be the very long body of the bootlace worm, *Lineus.* Although somewhat wormlike in appearance, this is no en annelid (true worm) because it is unsegmented; it is one of the nemertines (ribbon worms).

Chitons, or coat-of-mail shells as they ere sometimes celled, cling closely to the undersurface of stones with their large foot, but if irritated they bend bend their flexible bodies into bells, rather like woodlice. Chitons are molluscs, but their shells ere formed of eight overlapping plates.

Flatworms, flat-bodied creatures, some 2-3 cm long, may be seen gliding over upturned rocks, but they are not easy to detect as they blend well with the background. Some species also live amongst seaweeds, and if the placed in a bucketful of see water the flatworms emerge in their full glory, swimming gracefully by undulating body movements.

Squat lobster ere small crustaceans similar to lobsters, but with the abdomen tucked firmly under the body, more like crabs, though it can be flexed to jerk the animal backwards through the water. Two species may found under rocks, but the smaller one, *Gelathea squamifera,* with its inconspicuous brownish green is the commonest. *G. strigosa* with its colourful blue and red carapace, is larger, but found only occasionally very low on the shore.

Several echinoderms lodge themselves beneath rocks end the common starfish. *Asterias rubens,* probably needs no introduction. Globular, spiny creatures are see-urchins, *Psammechinus miliaris* being the commonest. Its green spines may be mauve tipped and are frequently cohered with small pebbles or pieces of shell, probably for camouflage, though few predators can relish a mouthful of their spines!

Sea urchins move slowly on these spines; they go in search of small encrusting animals which they dislodge by means of five strong teeth surrounding the mouth. Brittlestars have five long, thin arms radiating from e smell central disc so are easy to distinguish from starfish. *Ophiothrix fragilis* is the commonest species, but it is e very fragile creature and must be handled carefully as bits of its arms readily break off.

Seacucunrbers, *Cucumaria,* shelter under stones, but they are not easily recognized as relatives of starfish because the body is elongated end the mouth surrounded by a circlet of tentacles. One species, C *saxicola,* is commonly celled the seagherkin, so this gives some idea of the shape.

By now we have almost reached the water's edge and on turning loose stones a splashing end slithering means a shore fish is retreating in search of new cover. Common blennies, *Blennius pholis* are frequently found as they enjoy a period of exposure to the atmosphere.

If you watch them in en aquarium some are sure to be resting on their paired fins with the head well clear of the water. The butterfish or gunnel, *Pholis (=Centronotus) gunnellus,* is recognized by its elongated, sideways flattened body with about a dozen large, white. ridged dark sports on each side below the dorsal fin.

The bullhead or sea-scorpion, *Myxocephalus (= Cottus) scorpius,* is a ferocious-looking fish with its broad, flattened, spiny heed and

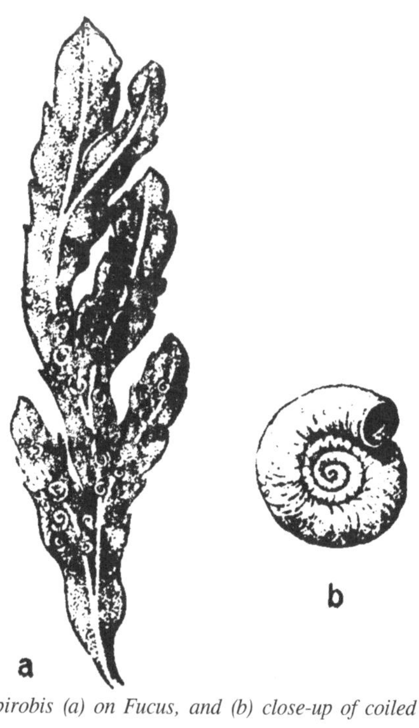

Figure 12.1: Spirobis (a) on Fucus, and (b) close-up of coiled limy tube.

Figure 12.2: Limy tubes of Pomatoceros triqueter.

spine-bearing operculum. Needless to say, unpleasant pricks can be received from these spines. Rock gobies, *Gobius paganellus,* are typically goggle-eyed with the caudal fin rounded, so are easily identified.

On turning a stone a small flattened, reddish fish, with two large black spots surrounded by yellow circle on its back just behind the eyes, remains steadfastly in the same position This is the pretty Cornish sucker, *Lepadogaster lepadogaster (=L. gouani),* which has its pelvic fins modified into a large sucker so that it can firmly grip the rocks. Or we may find the two-spotted sucker, *Diplecogaster (=Lepadogaster) bimaculata,* with its orange body marked with reddish V-shaped bands and a black spot behind each pectoral fin.

Occasionally the deep-water lumpsucker, *Cyclopterus lumpus,* is stranded at low spring tides in the spring when it comes ashore to spawn. It is a bulky fish without scales, but its body is covered with tubercles.

Our attention has been fixed on life beneath stones, so now we must return to the middle shore and work down again, this time looning for creatures on the rocks and sheltering among seaweed fronds.

Univalve molluscs are prolific on rocky shores. Some, such as the edible periwinkle, *Littorina littorea,* are immediately obvious as they remain on the bare rocks after the tide has fallen, their bodies being completely withdrawn to avoid desiccation.

However, some will we observed crawling along the bottom of shallow pools, over and amongst seaweed and wherever there is sufficient moisture to prevent dehydration. *L. littorea* overlaps the lower limit *of L. saxatilis,* but is abundant on the lower half of the middle swore where large populations congregate in rock crevices. The fourth periwinkle the species, *L. littoralis,* Inhabits approximately the same area though it extends a little farther into the lower shore zone where serrated wrack gives it sufficient cover.

This periwinkle exhibits a great colour range from white, yellow, orange, brown to back, has a flattened spire giving the shell a more oval shape and resides amongst the fronds of bladder and serrated wrack. On the former its shape gives some form of camouflage as its shell could be mistaken for an airbladder of the weed.

In spring its egg capsules form small, oval, closely adhering jelly masses on fucoid fronds, especially *Fucus serratus.* Some of the fronds of these wracks may be dotted with white limy circles about 2 mm in diameter; these are the homes of the tube-building polychaete worms *Spirorbis* and a close relative, *Pomatoceros,* builds its elongated, ridged tubes on rocks and stones in the same area.

Hydrodis fix themselves to fuciod weeds, seeming to form a plantlike tracery even through they are animal colonies related to sea-anemones. However, to admire their flowerlike beauty they must be viewed under water with a magnifying glass. *Obelia genticulata* and *Dynomean (= Sertularia) pumila* are two common species and these in turn may act as supports for other animals.

The small stalked barnacle, *Scalpellum scalpellum,* is one such *epizooic* animal (an organism which attaches itself to an animal, in the

Figure 12.3: Stalked barnacle Scalpellum scalpellum on hydroid Dynamena.

same way that an epiphyte attaches itself to a plant, instead of to rocks or stones).

Other univalve molluscs to be found on this middle region are the flat or purple topshell, *Gibbula umbiltcalis,* whose purplestriped, flattened cone can be seen over the whole area, and the grey topshell, *G. cineraria,* whose silver-grey conical shell is confined to the lower middle and lower shore.

Mussels, *Mytilus edulis,* attach themselves by strong threads to exposed rocks where they leisurely filter their food from indrawn sea water when covered by the tide. These are one of the few non-burrowing bivalves, and where mussels abound, dog-whelks and starfish are near at hand as both are partial to a mussel diet.

Dog-whelks feeding on mussels secrete a brown shell as opposed to the white shell as opposed to the white shell of barnacle feeders, but some have a brown and white banded shell, the results of periodic diet changes. Slipper limpets, *Crepidula fornicata,* will probably be on some mussel shells and on loose stones and empty shells in this zone.

They are filter feeders like the mussel and therefore compete for the same food. *Crepidula* is a pest on oyster-beds. During late spring the sub littoral sea-hare, *Aplysia punctata,* ventures on shore for the sole purpose of laying its eggs.

On exposed rocks the sea-hare curls up and looks like a dark brown or purple fleshy blob, but in a shallow pool it expands and raises its lateral fleshy lobes above its back in swimming. Crawling over rocks, but sheltered by seaweeds, we may find the bright green paddleworm, *Eulalia viridis,* but more conspicuous are its egg capsules, which hang from *Fucus* as bright green globes.

Rock overhangs give excellent shelter and as the tide ebbs from the lower regions of the middle shore a colourful array of encrusting animals gradually comes into sight, intermingled with some of the more delicate red seaweeds. The green or buff breadcrumb sponge, *Halichondria panicea* with its exhalent openings situated at the top of minute volcanoes, is easy to identify and alongside may be the beautiful orange *Hymeniacidon.*

These are both colonial sponges as is the urn sponge, *Sycon,* whose cylindrical from protrudes from the surface. Solitary forms such as the flattened purse sponge *Grantia compress,* hang downwards among the red seaweeds, sometimes attached to weeds instead of rocks.

Patches of deep red superimposed with cream stars are colonies of the compound star sea-squirt, *Botryllus schlosseri,* which also encrust fucoids alongside boxlike covering of the sea-mat, *Membranipora*

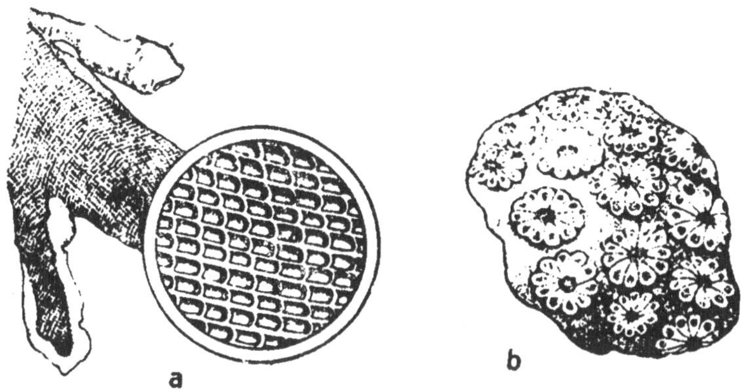

Figure 12.4: (a) Seaweed encrusted with a sea-mat and details of its boxlike form, (b) colonies of star sea-squirt. Botryllus schlosseri, with the common exhalent opening of the centre of each cluster.

membranacea. Other sea-squirts such as *Morchellium, Aplidium* and *Sidnyum* adorn the rocks with splashes of red, yellow and orange. The red gooseberry, *Dendrodoa grossularia,* looks very much like the fruit from which it takes its name, but if you touch one you will be rewarded by a jet of water splashing your face!

This explains the common name '*sea-squirt*' given to this group of animals. Less colourful are the solitary forms such as *Ciona,* but these larger species show off their internal organs through their transparent outer covering or test, as it is called.

Clavelina lepadiformis is a most attractive animal but must be searched for diligently as it is not so abundant as the other sea-squirts. Many small creatures, such as the queer-looking skeleton shrimp, *Caprella,* the two small British cowries, *Trivia arctica* and *T. monacha,* the common or painted topshell, *Calliostoma zizyphinium* and the long-legged spider crab, *Macropodia,* crawl over and hide in the crevices of these encrusted rocks.

Here also, plodding along on its large foot in search of the breadcrumb sponge, we may detect the sea-lemon, *Archidoris pseudoargus,* in its coat of yellow, specked with red. This gives splendid camouflage on H*alichondria,* its staple diet. White, coiled bands alongside are its egg ribbons. Another much smaller seaslug, *Goniodoris,* may be near by, feeding on sea-mats and seasquirts.

Fronds of some seaweeds may be so covered with colonies of the sea-mat *Flustrellidra (=Flustrella) hispida* that it is difficult to identify the plant beneath, and another colonial polyzoan, *Eugula,* hangs freely emulating many of the hydroids.

On south and west coasts the small, short-armed starfish, the cushion star, *Asterina gibbosa,* may be located on these lower rocks, but its dull greenish-red colour makes it *inconspicuous* on its rocky background. Near by we may be lucky enough to find one of the most dainty and attractive echinoderms, the feather-star, *Antedon bifida.*

Below rock overhangs in gullies and crevices, particularly where there is some sand, the dahlia anemone, *Telia felina* spreads its tentacles in a wide circle close to the surface as its column is short though very broad. Plumose anemones, *Metridium senile,* are occasionally encountered on the lowest rocks, but these are only small specimens as this is a sub-littoral species.

Only rarely the parasitic anemone, *Calliacus parasitica,* is found on rocks far it normally lives in deeper water on the back of edible whelk shells occupied by hermit crabs.

Small clumps of the yellowish-white soft coral, dead men's fingers, *Alcyoninum digitatum,* may be exposed at lowest spring tides only, as this is a sub-littoral species. It looks most ununattractive, but when placed in sea water it becomes transformed into something of beauty as the tiny polyps emerge.

When hunting around the rocks of the lower middle shore look out for the ferocious velvet swimming-crab, *Macropipus (=Portunus) puber,* in its handsome armour. If it is irritated, it poises itself with chelae outstretched in a most menacing manner.

Low on the shore the small hairy crab, *Pilumnus hirtellus,* may be discovered and easily recognized by its covering of hairs. Here, too, a stranded spiny spider crab, *Maja (==Mafia) squinado,* may be found sheltering in a rocky crevice. Another decapod crustacean, *Athanas nitescens,* only about 2 cm long, lobster like in shape, but red in colour with a longitudinal white stripe, may be found sheltering amongst seaweeds of the lower shore.

Small saddle oysters, *Anomia ephippium,* live on rocks and stones low on the shore. Like mussels these attach themselves by threads, but their valves are flattened and circular growing close to the rock surface.

On south-west coasts a lucky find on stones of the lower shore is the dainty Chinaman's hat, *Calyptraea chinensis.* It belongs to the same family as the slipper limpet and, like it, is a filter feeder-an unusual method for gastropods. The shell is a circular, rising to a point at the centre, hence its common name.

Stipes of some laminarians exposed on the lower shore may be pock-marked with deep gouges in the tissue. These indicate that the pretty blue-rayed limpet. *Patina pellucida,* has been having a meal, and search will soon disclose the culprit. In young specimens the rays are bright electric blue, but with age they lose their brilliance.

Laminarian holdfast offer ample shelter to many small animals, and if a laminarian complete with holdfast has been ripped free from the rocks, place it in a bucket of sea water and watch for the creatures to emerge.

The banded chink shell, *Lacuna,* is another gastropod found on laminarian stipes, though it also browses on fucoids of the lower shore. Now let us turn our attention to rock pools and discover what variety of creatures lurk among the seaweeds lining the walls.

Of course, many animals we have already encountered take refuge in pools and in this way are able to survive higher up the shore than usual. Some species are found only on shore in pools, thus indicating that they are incapable of withstanding the hazards of exposure to the atmosphere.

However, even in pools, conditions are not as constant as in shallow seas. In hot sun evaporation of water alters the salinity, the rate of photosynthesis increases making the water more alkaline as carbon dioxide is absorbed and oxygen evolved, and the temperature rises. Heavy rainfall also affects salinity and if there is no sunshine the water will be less alkaline.

If low water springs is at night, then the carbon dioxide released during respiration of both seaweed and animal inhabitants increases the acidity of pools (carbon dioxide dissolved in water forms carbonic acid). All these changes occur gradually as the tide ebbs, but when it rises the inflowing water soon floods the pools and conditions quickly revert to that of the sea.

In deep pools these fluctuations are not so great, and those very low on shore are not exposed for a sufficient length of time for the inhabitants to suffer hardship, but in the shallower pools, uncovered for several hours, the inhabitants must be able to withstand these wide variations or succumb.

The shallow pools encrusted with *Lithophyllum* and *Lithothamion* (Plate 1) are usually scattered with beadlet anemones, and from crevices daisy anemones may be seen showing their heads. Winklets, topshells and dog-whelks abound in pools of their particular zone and, of course, limpets often with a little green seaweed such as *Enteromorpha* growing from their shell.

Univalves are typical of rocky shores, but bivalves are not. (except mussels) although in pools with a sandy or gravel bottom carpet shells, *Venerupis spp. may* sometimes be found.

In shallow pools some of the winklets, topshells and dogwhelks may seem to make jerky movements instead of their usual slow steady crawl and on a closer look we soon see why; the shells are occupied by small hermit crabs. These animals are shy and quickly withdraw into their borrowed homes when touched.

They are the young of the large hermits which live in edible whelk shells in waters offshore, and as they grow they move house to a larger shell. It is entertaining to watch a hermit crab in an aquarium select and move into a new abode. First of all he rolls a shell over to expose the aperture, then gingerly explores it with his large claw to see if it is empty and test it for size.

This is an elaborate process, but when he is satisfied it is suitable, he moves it so that the aperture is next to that of his own shell. He then draws out his abdomen and rapidly inserts it into the fresh shell and takes a grip of the columella with his modified abdominal appendages. Finally he jerkily turns the shell over and continues on his way.

The hermit crab takes all this care because without a shell he is vulnerable to predators and would not survive for long. Occasionally two hermits choose the same shell for their new home and then a clashing of claws ensues until the vanquished moves off leaving the conqueror to move in.

Just to be contrary, the victor may change over to the new shell and then decide that the original was more suitable and move back again, leaving the object of the fight empty! Ordinary shore crabs occasionally scuttle across the bottom of the pool when disturbed, and among the seaweed fronds long-legged spider crabs hide, often camouflaged with growths of seaweed which the crab itself places in position.

These live in the deeper pools. To find them, gently pull a fairly finemeshed net through the edging weeds and scrutinize the catch carefully, because out of water these crabs tend to fold up their extensive legs.

Crustaceans specifically found in pools are the swimming forms seen shooting through the water as we move some or the seaweed. These are the prawns, *Palaernon (=Leander) squilla* being the commonest; it is similar to the common or edible prawn, but considerably smaller. These fast-moving creatures need to be caught with a net and along with them may be trapped the small, prettily coloured chameleon prawn,

Hippolyte varians, with its back bent typically at a right angle, and also *Athanas nitescens* already mentioned.

Cast skeletons of all these crustaceans will also be picked up in the net. Common prawns, *Palaemon (=Leander) seratus,* are encountered only in the deeper pools very low on the shore, for their normal habitat is around the rocks just below low water mark. These arc the edible prawns on sale at the fishmongers, but they are not bright pink when in their natural habitat.

Their greyish, transparent bodies blend with the rocky background to help keep them out of sight hungry fish swimming by. As prawns are a favourite diet of many sea fish they are used by fishermen as bait. To catch prawns the fishermen often use a special circular drop net. This has a mesh of approximately 1 cm and is held open to a diameter of about 60 cm by a metal frame; frequently an old bicycle rim minus the spokes is used.

Three ropes, equally spaced around the edge of the frame, attach the net to the main rope. A piece of heavy string is fastened to the frame so that it stretches across the diameter and to this are fixed fleshy fish bones or other suitable bait. The net is then submerged at

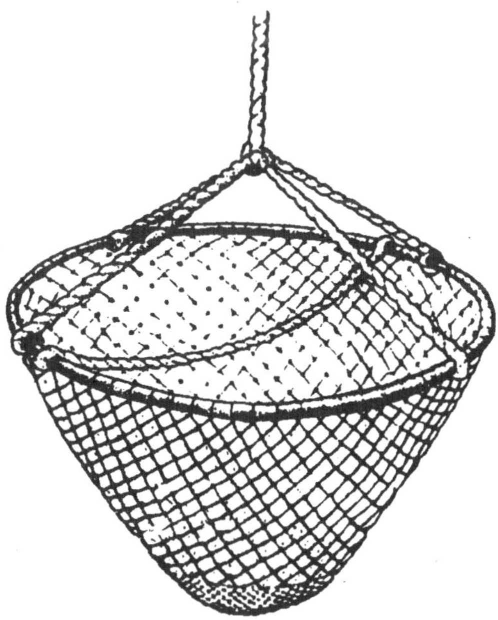

Figure 12.5: Drop net for catching prawns, the bait is attaches to the cross string.

the edge of a rock pool, or over the edge of a breakwater, so that it hangs beside the rocks with the frame horizontal.

It is left in this position for about ten minutes then drawn out carefully, keeping the frame horizontal; as it leaves the water any prawns feeding on the bait fall into the bottom of the net. Prawns are fascinating to watch in an aquarium because they are so meticulous about cleanliness.

The first two pairs of legs, which terminate in fine nippers, are forever moving over the body to remove any particles or growth on their carapace and they can bend the long second pair around to scratch their backs! Berried females can be seen moving their abdominal appendages back and forth to aerate thoroughly the developing eggs.

Internal organs show up through the transparent exoskeleton and if a prawn has just fed, the food can be seen in its alimentary canal. Movement of the gills in the branchial chamber may be observed, and in an infected prawn the parasitic isopod, *Bopyrus,* is visible within this cavity.

Rare finds in deep pools are small lobsters, *Homarus gammarus (=H. vulgaris),* and crawfish, *Palinurus elephas (=P. vulgaris),* for these are sub-littoral species. The lobster is bright blue with very large nippers and the crawfish brown, spiny and with small nippers. The latter inhabits only south and west coasts. An even more unusual find is an octopus.

The fish we discovered under rocks and stones also inhabit the pools, and in deeper pools other species may be encountered such as sticklebacks, rocklings, wrasse, pipefish and the yound of deep-water fish. Most shore fish have the habit of protecting their developing eggs, which are laid in relatively small numbers compared with deep sea fish.

The latter discharge large quantities of eggs but only one or two may survive the rigours of life in the open waters and reach maturity. Pipefish have long narrow bodies, as their name implies, with an

Figure 12.6: Worm pipefish Nerophis lumbriciformis.

Figure 12.7: Fifteen-spined stickteback, Spinachia spinachia.

elongated snout adapted for sucking in their food—a most unusual habit.

The mile fosters the eggs in a special cavity below the abdomen formed by folds of skin; even after release, the young remain around the male and occasionally reenter the cavity for protection. The commonest species to be found on shore is the worm pipefish, *Nerophis lumbriciformis,* as all others live around sub-littoral rocks.

Wrasse found in pools are the young of the several species inhabiting shallow seas and some are exceedingly pretty in gay colours of green, blue, red, orange and yellow. The adults venture shorewards in the breeding season to make simple nests of seaweed in intertidal rock crevices.

The fifteen-spined stickleback also makes a nest, but it is the male who carries out the hard work and when it is completed he entices a female within to lay her eggs; then it is he who stands guard over them until they hatch. In the case of blennies, again it is the male who protects the eggs which are laid under rocks without the shelter of a nest.

Now to the animals which gain the greatest protection—those living deep within rock crevices. RockWorms, relatives of ragworms, extend only their heads from their hideouts when covered by water, and rocks must be split open to find them. The two commonest are *Eunice harassi* and *Marphysa sanguinea.*

Pollydora are small annelids which bore U-shaped tubes into rocks and shells. The only signs of the live worms we are likely to see are their small, fine tentacles extending from the mouth of their tubes in the bottom of a *Lithophyllum* encrusted pool.

On our shore we have one most unexpected rock borer and that is the sponge *Cliona celata.* It lives on the lower shore,. peppering limestone with hundreds of tiny holes. It also bores into bivalve shells and this is where evidence of its work is prominent.

Bivalve molluscs are the most prolific rock-borers of our shores and *Hiatella* is probably the commonest. It burrows into soft rock, mainly limestone but sometimes sandstone, low on the shore and in shallow seas. The largest rock borer is the common piddock, *Pholas dactylus,* but it is found only in the south-west, which is the northernmost limit of this Mediterranean species.

There are several smaller piddocks living in the same area, but they are all difficult to locate as they inhabit the very lowest regions of the shore and abound in greater numbers in shallow seas. After storms the empty valves may be washed ashore, but as these are very delicate and brittle, the chance of finding a complete undamaged pair is unlikely.

13

Life on Sandy Shores

At first glance a sandy shore appears very *barren*—just An extensive mass of sand, perhaps slightly rippled by wave action, but with no signs of plant or *animal life*—a very *different* sight from the rocky shore clothed in *seaweeds*.

However, on walking down the beach a shell or two embedded in the surface sand catches the eye, indicating that perhaps, after all, a living creature is somewhere near at band. A closer look at the sand shows that the surface is not *absolutely smooth* but is perforated by small holes. This is the answer-the animals live buried *beneath* the sand.

A sandy shore is devoid of seaweeds for the simple reason that there is no solid surface (available for attachment of their holdfasts. As *no* seaweeds/grow here, protection against wave action, *desiccation* and *predators* is lacking, so to *survive*, the animal life resorts to living within the *sand*.

Some animals always remain below in their burrows, but others become active when the tide rises and venture away from their hideouts. Hundreds of microscopic animals, called the *interstitial* fauna, live between the sand *particles*, but as these cannot be readily observed they do not come within the scope of this book.

At low water springs and old fisherman may be seen walking backwards along the water's edge, every now and then extending what appears to be a stick or thin rod into the sand. Investigation shows that the stick is a metal rod, perhaps 5 or 6 mm in diameter, with the tip ground into a spearhead, which the fisherman inserts into an appropriate hole, twists around and eventually pulls out with a razorshell impaled on the end.

It looks very easy when observing an expert, but a novice is lucky to spear even one creature in a couple of hours! The razorshell is a bivalve mollusc with long, narrow valves so that in shape it is somewhat like a large pea pod. The common large razorshell which the fisherman seeks for bait, or even a tasty meal, is the pod razor, *Ensis siliqua,* in which the two valves are straight.

It lives just below the surface and has two short siphons, one for the intake and one for the removal of water via the hole in the surface sand. As soon as the razorshell feels a vibration on the surface it discharges a jet of water and rapidly burrows deeper by means of its foot. The rate at which it can move down through the sand is quite surprising and the explanation for our empty appear.

The fisherman's footfalls disturb the razorshell, so by walking backwards he is able to observe the water ejected and note the correct hole down which to probe for his victim. If a live razorshell is laid on the sand the movement of its foot can be observed. First the foot extends fully, pushing downwards, and then the tip swells as body fluids are pumped into it.

This bulbous tip acts as an anchor, so that on contraction of the muscles connecting the foot and shell the animal is drawn into the sand. This process of foot extension, followed by anchorage aid muscle contraction, is repeated until the animal is completely below the surface and the siphon hole is the only indication of its presence.

A visitor after dark may find a razorshell protruding a few centimetres above the surface and, if stealthy and quick, succeed in withdrawing it just by grasping and pulling. Another method of obtaining specimens is by placing salt over the hole; this usually brings the razorshell to the surface and the projecting shell can be grasped and extracted as above.

The salt acts as an irritant, causing this response in the animal. However, the more useful way of collecting razorshells is by digging, but it is no easy matter to obtain an animal intact because they are so sensitive to the slightest of vibrations.

The siphons of the razorshell are short, and it is a suspension feeder, filtering food particles from the indrawn sea water. Normally it remains buried, but in rough weather the scouring action of the sea

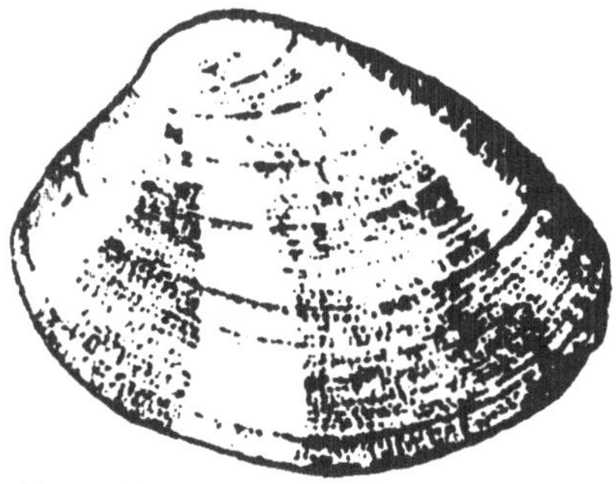

Figure 13.1: Striped venus. Venus stratula.

may bulldoze it out of the sand and carry it shorewards to rest finally amongst the pile of debris at the top of the beach.

The sword razor, *Ensis ensis,* has thinner, curved valves and is smaller than E. *siliqua,* so it does not fall victim to the fisherman's spear even though it inhabits the same area.

Many other bivalves inhabit the sandy shore, especially the various members of the trough shell family, *Mactridae*, whose empty valves are an easy find for the shell collector. Very occasionally what appears to be a small bump on the sand turns out to be a trough-shell with siphons and valve edges exposed.

These animals are also suspcnsion fccdcrs, as arc the venus shells which live in the same habitat. The striped versus, *Venus striatula,* is the commonest.

The edible cockle, *Cardium edule,* lives just below the surface on the middle and lower shores, but as it also inhabits muddy sand, we shall leave consideration of this species until life on muddy shores is discussed.

Two other bivalves frequently found are the wedge shell, *Donax vittatus* and the tellin shell. *Tellina tenuis,* both with long siphons for deposit feeding. The latter has a very thin, glossy shell which may be white, pale pink, rose or salmon.

No one can resist picking up and admiring attractive empty bivalves scattered on the sand, but sometimes we are disappointed to find that an apparently perfect shell is pierced by a small round hole. The culprit is another member of the molluscs, but this time a univalve, the necklace shell, *Natica alderi.*

This animal has a special gland which secretes a chemical substance capable of dissolving the limy shell of its prey. As soon as the shell is perforated, *Natica* inserts its proboscis to feed on the juicy contents. This carnivore burrows in the sand out of sight, but sometimes a sluggish movement in shallow water indicates a specimen pushing its way along on its enormous foot.

The netted dog-whelk, *Nassarius reticulatus* is a univalve which bulldozes its way through the sand with only its siphon above to indicate its presence. As in all whelks, this siphon allows clear water to be inhaled even while *Nassarius is* scavenging in the sand for fleshy food particles.

As we wander down shore towards the receding tide we may find the level surface is interrupted by tube like structures, with fringed edges, protruding more or less upright to a height of 2 and 3 cm. These are the upper ends of the homes of sandmasons, *Lanice conchilega.*

Each tube is uniquely formed by the worm itself; when covered by the tide it collects small particles of sand and shell with its extended tentacles and wafts them into its mouth. Here they are subsequently coated with a mucous secretion which sticks them together to form a protective tube. Keen fishermen are down on the shore at low tide digging for another favourite bait, ibis time the lugworm, *Arenicola marina* whose presence is obvious from the coiled casts of sand and nearby depressions.

The lugworm lives in a U-shaped tube with two openings, one above its head and the other above its tail, but it does not form this tube from particles as the sandmason does. Instead, the lugworm burrows into the sand and secretes a mucus which holds the walls in position.

The food of the lugworm consists of small particles of detritus and to obtain this it swallows large amounts of sand. The organic material is digested as the sand passes along the worm's alimentary canal, and the unwanted particles are egested through the anus and deposited on the surface above in the form of the familiar coiled worm-cast.

Survival of the lugworm is dependent on an ample supply of oxygen for respiration and this is ensured when the tide returns. A continuous current of water flows into the burrow from the rear end, forward over the gills and out through the head opening, the worm itself maintaining this current by alternate contraction and relaxation of its body muscles.

Because of the upward force of water at the head entrance, the particles of sand remain loosely packed and readily subside to form a depression as the worm ingests the lower layers-hence the coiled cast *and* the accompanying depression. The lugworm does not often venture from the safety of its burrow as it is such inviting prey for any carnivorous neighbours. However, as the casts high on the beach are much smaller than those nearer the low water mark, the lugworm must periodically, as it increases in size, leave the safety of its tube and swim seawards before burrowing out a new home.

Several other worms live within the sand, one of the commonest being the white-or cat-worm, *Nephthys hombergi.* This species is a very active swimmer and, unlike the lugworm, does not have a permanent burrow. It is carnivorous and continuously hunts prey such as very small or young crustaceans, burrowing into the sand only when the tide recedes.

The flattened, segmented, whitish body has a dark line running along the centre of the back, which makes identification easy. *Nephthys is* found 8 to 10 cm below the surface. *Glycera convoluta,* often dug up with *Nephthys,* is recognized by the round body segments, many in number, narrowing to a point at both ends ; when exposed this worm tends to coil.

The ragworm, *Nereis diversicolor,* may be found in sand, but it is much more common in mud its inclusion in the chapter on muddy shores is more appropriate. On digging down into the sand we find the colour does not remain uniform, but that a black layer shows up a little way below the surface.

This indicates poor aeration and the consequent presence of bacterial colonies since these are the only organisms capable of living in situations with such a reduced oxygen content. The position of this black layer varies according to the substratum; the more permeable the sand, the lower the layer.

Of the sand-burrowing echinoderms the sea-potato, *Echinocardium cordatum,* is the most abundant. Unlike other seaurchins it is not round, but heart-shaped, and has specially modified spines on the undersurface for digging down into the sand. The only visible sign of this animal is a star-shaped depression in the sand on middle and lower shores, which is the opening of the shaft leading up from its burrow some 20 cm below.

This urchin moves sluggishly and it is therefore quite easy to dig up a specimen. After rough seas, empty tests (skeletons) of *Echinocardium* may scatter the beach, but care must be taken in handling them as they are extremely brittle. The burrowing starfish, *Astropecten irregularis,* normally lives offshore, but occasionally a specimen may be found low on the beach.

It digs itself straight down by means of its modified tube-feet and spines, and leaves *no* telltale hole on the surface. However, movement of the marginal spines ensures that a water current passes over the animal for respiratory purposes and this disturbance may leave a faint trace on the sand indicating its presence when the tide recedes.

Two burrowing sea-cucumbers, *Leptosynapta inhaerens* and *Lapidoplax digitata,* may possibly be found in the same area as *Echinocardium.* They differ from rocky shore specimens in having an elongated, wormlike body and no tube-feet. Both species also inhabit muddy shores, but *Lapidoplax* is confined to south-west and west coasts. Frequently the commensal scaleworm, *Harmothoe,* shares their burrows.

Searching for the hidden sand-dwellers is far more rewarding at night, as some of them venture above the surface when darkness hides them from predators, and desiccation from the hot sun is no longer a hazard.

In the beam of a powerful torch, or preferably a paraffin vapour lamp, an empty depression about 4 cm in diameter may be seen, with a parallel but winding track leading away, perhaps as far as a metre, to what appears to be a blob of sand.

Closer inspection shows this to be the only true sand-burrowing crab in Britain, *Corystes cassivelaunus.* Its common name is '*masked*' carb and the reason for this is obvious once the sand has been cleaned off its carapace.

The antennae of masked crabs are especially long and bear two rows of stiff hairs which interlock to form a tube when the two are held together. This special adaptation allows the crab to remain completely buried, with only the tips of the antennae level with the surface of the sand.

In this position clear water is drawn down the tube, passed back over the gills for oxygen absorption and finally expelled from the underedge of the carapace. This flow is in the opposite direction to normal when the crab is above ground.

The masked crab inhabits, only areas of *clean* sand because the meshwork of antennal hairs would not prevent the entry of very fine mud particles which, if present, would rapidly clog the gills.

The sexes are distinct, the chelae of the male being much longer than in the female. Occasionally a pair of these crabs may be seen with the male fiercely gripping the female in one of his chelae and h.- may even move around still holding her.

The significance of this action is a mystery at presets, although it may well be concerned in the mating habits of the species. *Corystes* is found very low on the shore at spring tides, during a few months of the year only, as it is really a sub littoral species. In the south-west it can be found inshore from April to July, but is most abundant during May.

Further hunting after dark may reveal the tentacles of the daisy anemone, *Cereus pedunculatus,* spread flush with the surface, but with the slightest disturbance the tentacles close and disappear below the sand. Small hermit crabs scuttle around in the shallows and here too a dab can be detected hurriedly covering itself with sand as the torch beam picks it out.

An interesting and successful way of collecting some of the inhabitants very low on the shore is by pushing through the shallows a special type of long-band led net, designed by shrimpers of old. This shrinipers' trawl is a long bag of fine net held open by a straight edge of wood or metal at the base, and a half hoop above to which the handle is attached.

The straight edge is pushed through the upper 4 or 5 cm of sand to disturb any buried creatures and, by the forward movement, force them into the bag. On emptying out the net the most prolific animal of the catch is sure to be the common shrimp, *Crangon crangon (=C. vulgaris),* the most familiar crustacean to be found on any sandy shore.

During daylight hours it usually remains buried, but even when on the surface detection is difficult, the body colour blending with the sand. The shrimp needs this camouflage for it is a favourite food of many a fish and it also helps when stalking prey, for the shrimp is an omnivorous feeder.

The contents of the net will include many other interesting animals, perhaps the little cuttlefish, *Sepiola atlantica,* which so attractively flashes on and off its bright lights, like a neon sign. This luminescence is a feature of cephalopods.

The lesser weever, *Trachinus vipera,* may be in the trawl as this fish buries itself with only the top of its head protruding so that, unobserved, it can keep a watchful eye for its main diet, the shrimp. Care must be taken in handling this fish because it can inflict a painful sting owing to the presence of poison glands at the base of its dorsal fin and opercular spines.

On this account it has acquired the local name '*sting-fish*'. The lesser -and eel, *Ammodytes tobianus,* may be in the catch. This fish his an elongated body with no pelvic fins, thus giving it an eel-like appearance. It is not a true sanddweller like the lesser weever, as it swims in shoals and feeds on young sprats and crustaceans, resorting to the sand only when predators are near at hand.

It then burrows by means of its spoon-shaped lower jaw which projects beyond the upper jaws. The greater sand eel, *Hyperoplus (=Ammodytes) lanceolatus,* is not such a common species, though it may be caught *in* the same manner.

The sand goby, *Pomatoschistus (=Gobius) minutus,* also falls victim to the trawl as it lives in the same area as shrimps. Young of the various flatfish are likely to be in the net, ranging in size from a couple of centimetres upwards and, should it be a very low spring tide, even a specimen large enough for the fishmongers's slab may be taken in this way.

The shrimpers' trawl may force out of the sand some stems and leaves of the *one* flowering plant found on the shore, eelgrass, *Zostera.* This plant was prolific on British coasts until the 1930s when it was attacked by an unknown disease which depleted the *Zostera* beds. The leaves are bright green, long and narrow, forming an underwater forest when supported by the water.

At last eel-grass is becoming re-established, and at low water springs a few small clumps may be exposed. On returning up the beach the *driftline* or *strandline* is well worth studying though, of course, most of the creatures found here are dead or dying. However, one crustacean inhabits this region, the sandhopper, *Talitrus saltator.*

This amphipod burrows into the sand below the debris during daylight hours and surfaces at night to feed on any available plant or animal material. The sandhopper always remains above high tide mark on account of its inability to survive submergence. Like all amphipods its body is laterally compressed and it appears to 'hop'.

The strandline reflects the inhabitants below the sand in both littoral and sub-littoral regions. In winter, shells of the '*red-nosed*' cockles are prolific and after an onshore gale whole live specimens may appear, each extending its long red foot in an attempt to roll into a position where it can burrow. This is the same type of movement as in the edible cockle.

The debris may be dotted with bodies of the sea-mouse, *Aphrodite aculeato*, a deep water annelid (segmented worm), though this is not immediately apparent from its dorsal surface, because the back of its oval-shaped body is covered with a thick mat of long grey bristles When seen in a shaft of sunlight these bristles become iridescent, transforming the dull animal into a creature of beauty.

Several of the offshore crabs become victims of winter storms Examples are the masked crab, *Corystes,* already mentioned, *Portumnus*

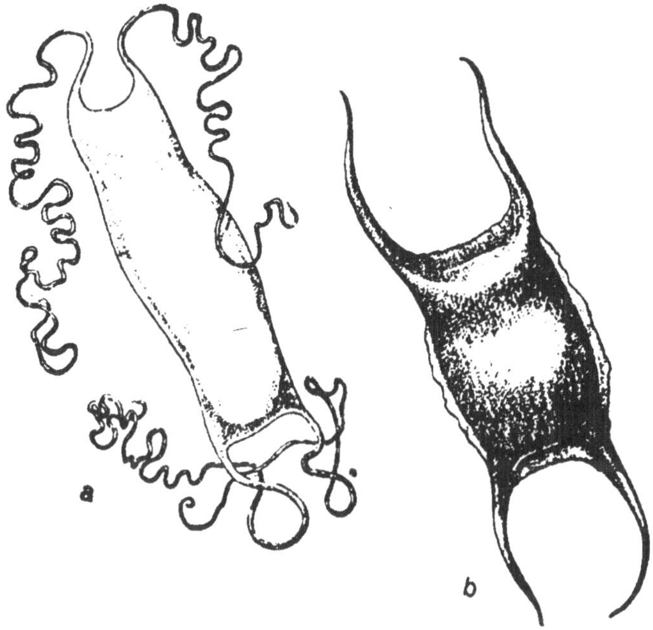

Figure 13.2: Egg-cases (a) dogfish and (b) skate.

latipes another sand-burrower but also active swimmer, shown by the paddle-like fifth pair of legs, the common swimming-crab, *Macropipus (=Portunus) depurator,* and the angular crab, *Goneplax rhomboides (= G. angulata),* readily recognized by the rectangular carapace, twice as broad as it is long.

Goneplax has its eyes on long stalks which can be setracted into grooves along the anterior edge of the *carapace* and, like *Corystes,* the male is distinguished by its first pair of legs which are three times as long as the width of its carapace.

Sometimes the edible whelk, *Buccimum undatum*, is washed ashore, but more frequently clusters of its egg-cases litter the strandline and from a distance look' rather like bath sponges. When bright yellow the cases contain developing eggs, and well-formed embryos can be seen moving within when studied with a hand-lens.

When we turn over some whelk shells in the debris, we find they contain the hermit crab, *Pagurus (=Eupagurus) bernhardus.* Live specimens of the razorshell and other sand-burrowing bivalves may occur along the strandline as well as their empty shells, together with a few live necklace shells. Fish, too, may be *amongst* the stranded and also the empty egg-cases of skate and *dogfish*.

Wood washed ashore comes in all shapes and sizes: branches and tree trunks fallen from cliff faces many miles away; planks of wood washed overboard from timber-carrying vessels; broken timber from boats and ships lost at sea. Some may be pieces of wood worn away from nearby piers or gtoynes which are riddled with small holes and tunnels.

This is the work of the gribble, *Limmoria lignorum, a* small crustacean which attacks wooden piers near low water level. This isopod burrows just below and parallel to the surface of the wood, making a tunnel about 5 mm in diameter, with minute borings through the roof. These holes, which allow a water current to flow along the tunnel, indicate the presence of the animal below.

Continuous burrowing in the wood by many generations eventually causes weakening and the outer layers break away ; the gribble then penetrates the newly exposed layers and, over the years, gradually reduces the diameter of the pier until it collapses.

Occasionally a piece of timber drifts ashore burrowed with tunnels two or three times the diameter of those of the gribble. These have been formed by the shipworm, *Teredo*. This animal is not a worm but a bivalve that grinds its way through the wood, making a perfectly circular burrow which is its home for life.

It is interesting to note that none of the burrows crosses another. There are many species of *Teredo,* but only three are found in British seas. Goose barnacles, *Lepas anatifera,* are stalked barnacles which attach themselves to floating timber so they are not found unless flotsam bearing them has drifted ashore.

They are easily recognized by the stalked attachment and white plates from between which, when below water, the appendages rapidly protrued and withdraw to trap plankton ; thus the feeding mechanism is the same as that of the acorn barnacles found on rocky shores.

These creatures are just a few of the possible 'finds', so in summer or winter a study of the standline can be most rewarding for the enthusiastic beachcomber.

The fauna of a sandy shore is governed by the several factors discussed elsewhere in this chapter, but exposure is of particular importance. When the wind is blowing on to a wide, open sandy shore the tops of the waves start to break long before they reach the beach, and when they do arrive at the shallows they break with such violence that the turbulence caused results in the transport of the coarser particles up the beach.

In this way separation of the different grades of sand occurs with the coarser material high on the shore and the finer near low water mark. Breakwaters are erected on such beaches to counteract this action.

This deposition, however, is in no way permanent as is obvious if one beach is visited regularly over the years. The positions of pools vary and the height of the sand up certain indicators such as breakwaters, groynes or hondrails, shows how the sea plays havoc with the sand particles, piling them perhaps a metre or so high at a certain spot and in a few weeks or may be days, with the change of wind and current, clears them to another section of the beach.

This instability of the habitat is quite a hazzed for its inhabitants. Particle size determines the retentivity and porosity of the sand, the coarser grades drying out more rapidly as the tide recedes. During neap tides the surface sand high on the beach dries out completely and is readily blown by the wind.

As has been seen, this is *nor* the region the animals inhabit ; they choose to borrow in the area from high water neap tides seawards. Burrowing in this region, they protect themselves from desiccation in hot dry weather as the evaporation of water cools the surface layers and a few centimetres down the sand remains damp and at a fairly constant temperature, so once buricd an animal has few worries.

Zonation

Zonation on sandy shores is not so evident as on rocky shores. However, it can easily be shown by simple investigations similar to those suggested in Section 6. For instance, stations may be set up down the shore, and at each a quadrat dug to a predetermined depth. The numbers of each different organism found can be recorded, this information later being transferred to a suitable chart.

Sand Dunes and Their Vegetation. On wide, exposed sandy beaches where onshore win is prevail, large quantities of sand are carried shorewards by the pounding waves, and when dried out the particles are blown landwards, where they pile up into dunes. In this country no dunes are as high and extensive as on the Continent.

The sand carried by the wind is fine and dry, so the plants that colonize this soil need a root system capable of binding and holding together the sand grains. The marram grass, *Ammophila arenaria,* is the dominant species and on some of the smaller dunes the only plant that is immediately obvious.

It is a perennial with branching rhizomes which spread rapidly throughout the soil particles and anchor the plant. As the wind whips sand across the surface, the marram grass acts as a windbreak so that this newly blown sand tends to collect around it, thus building up the dune.

In gale conditions so much sand may be deposited that the plant becomes burried, but its rhizomes soon develop new shoots which push their way to the surface. With a strong offshore wind *blowouts* in the dunes may appear. These are deep hollows which expose the rhizomes of the marram grass.

The first formed area of the dune adjacent to the shore is known as the *fore-dune*, and in some localities the sea couchgrass, *Agropyron junceiforme*, is encountered within reach of the spring tides. Its creaping rhizome binds the sand particles as efficiently as marram grass, but its upward growth is not so extensive and the dunes formed are not as high as when marram grass is the colonizer.

Lyme-grass, *Elymus arenarius,* is another colonizer found in some areas This plant is also tolerant of sea water, whereas marram grass is not and colonizes only sand that is out of reach of spring tides.

Most plants growing on sand dunes are xerophytes (that is adapted to grow in dry conditions) due to the poor retentivity of the soil, the exposure to gale force winds and the high temperature of the surface layers in hot sun.

The grasses have rolled leaves to contend with these conditions and their specialized structure adjusts the rate of transpiration to the rate of water intake.

The plant population of the fore-dunes is scarce because the habitat is so unstable, but a few of the possible binders are the sea holly, *Eryngium maritimum,* sea sandwort, *Honckenya peploides,* sea spurge, *Euphorbia paralias,* sand sedge, *Corex arenaries,* and sea convolvulus, *Calystegia soldanella,*

To withstand the dune conditions sea holly has a thick cuticle coated with wax, and the leaves are spiny to reduce the surface area. It is a perennial which grows about 30 cm high, but tends to creep over the surface.

It is a member of the parsley family with blue and mauve florets borne in dense umbels, surrounded with broad, spiny bracts. It blooms during July and August.

Sea spurge is modified in a different manner. The leaves are succulent, having large, colourless cells capable of storing water towards the centre, with the normal green photosynthetic cells nearer the edges.

As transpiration occurs the large cells become flaccid, but soon regain their turgor when water is in ample supply. This perennial is 20 to 30 cm high and the flower is a yellow-green insignificant inflorescence, blossoming from June onwards

Sea sandwort, another succulent is often associated with sea couch-grass along the high water springs mark as it' is also tolerant of salt water. Here it may participate in the formation of low dunes for it is a prostrate creeping perennial only a few centimetres in height.

Its small, inconspicuous, white flowers appear from May to September. The sea convolvulus, or sea bindweed, is a creeping perennial with stems, up to only 30 cm, in length, which do *not* twine like the common hedgerow convolvulus. The flowers, however, may be up to 4 cm in diameter, the five pink petals being marked with a central white stripe.

These are seen from June to September. The small leaves are succulent, with a waxy surface. Sand sedge is another perennial with an extensive creeping underground stem, which makes it a good stabilizer. These rhizomes often grow in straight lines, shown by the position of the aerial shoots.

The aerial stems, which are three-angled, are up to 30 cm high with stiff leaves rolled for the same purpose as in marram grass. This species is unisexual, bearing male flowers at the tip of the stem and female flowers below. It blooms during June and July.

14

LIFE ON MUDDY SHORES

The muddy inlets and creeks of our coast hold little attraction for the ordinary holiday maker, but there are some interesting creatures which quite happily make their homes in such areas. Mud becomes deposited in sheltered regions where there is little wave action, so the slope of such a shore is very gradual.

If our time of arrival coincides with that of low water we may be sorely disapppointed when we find that we cannot see the sea. However, by the third hour of flow the tide will be racing back up the shore, flooding the boots of any unwary fisherman too engrossed in digging bait to notice the incoming water.

This may readily happen around Southend and the rate of flow has to be seen to be believed. On such a shore the *mud,* as we call it, is really a mixture of sand and mud, but as we progress farther up the estuary we find the sand content decreases as protection from wave action increases.

As would be expected, a variation in fauna accompanies this change, though no hard and fast dividing line can be drawn between inhabitants of muddy sand and mud, but when Iugworms are no longer present the sand content is at a minimum.

Muddy shores located around river mouths are built up when the outward flow of fresh water is halted by the inward flow of sea water. During its journey from source to mouth the river erodes some of the loose soil of its banks and the finest particles, *silt,* are carried in suspension down to the mouth where they become deposited once the outward flow is checked.

In very wide estuaries the shores exposed at low water are so extensive and have such a slight gradient that they are referred to as *mudflats.* In narrower estuaries a special problem arises for the would-be colonizers because here the mixing of fresh and salt water greatly affects the overall salinity.

Each animal is adapted to a particular environment and any change affect its ability to survive. The balance between the body fluids of a marine creature and the surrounding sea water is so fine that when the salinity becomes lowered too much water enters the tissues of the animal; on the other hand, when a freshwater animal is subjected to increased salinity, water is drawn out from its body tissues.

Either is harmful and fauna living here have to control this intake or loss of water—a process called *osmoregulation,* since the water movement is by osmosis. Thus we have two types of muddy shore, one with constant and the other with variable salinity.

CONSTANT SALINITY

A muddy beach appears very barren just as a sandy shore do _s since the majority of inhabitants live below the surface, but it does not look so inviting as a stretch of golden sand. Unless there is a reasonable proportion of sand, walking over mud is most difficult and not to be recommended unless one is well equipped with thigh boots.

Only a few specially adapted species live here because fine mud particles clog the breathing and feeding mechanisms of the majority of animals. Let us consider the inhabitants of a tidal harbour where the substratum is sandy mud.

Here are the telltale casts of lugworms and the protruding tubes of sand-masons which were encountered on sandy shores, and below the surface catworms may be found as they can tolerate the presence of a little mud.

Edible winkles abound near stones and leave distinctive tracks as they crawl over soft muddy surfaces. Attached to odd stones, mooring chains and harbour walls at about mid-tide level we may find a few mussels. These are suspension feeders and if too much sediment is deposited around them they produce longer byssus threads, attaching them at a higher level in order to pull themselves upwards and thus bring their inhalent and exhalent openings above the silt; during this operation the old threads are torn free.

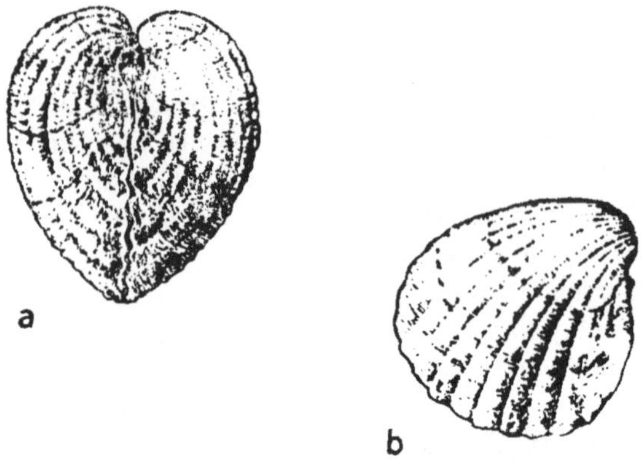

Figure 14.1: Edible cockle, Cardium edule.
(a) side view showing the two valves and hearrt-shaped outline and (b) single valve.

This is one time when the foot of an adult mussel comes into use, for normally the foot is only really active in young mussels when they are moving around searching for a settlement site at the correct level. In estuaries where loose stones are, prolific, mussel populations become extensive and form mussel-beds.

In a few areas these are cultivated, but in Britain fresh mussels are not a popular delicacy. Great care must be taken to cleanse them thoroughly as they readily harbour bacteria and noxious substances from the indrawn water.

This is done by keeping the mussels in clean sea water, or fresh water containing the requisite amount of salt, for several hours ; commercially this is usually for a period of forty-eight hours.

Other rocky shore inhabitants are abundant where there is suitable attachment and cover, and at low water vertical zonation often shows up clearly on harbour walls.

By raking through the surface layers of the middle and lower zones we are sure to dislodge some edible cockles, *Cardium edule,* as they are shallow burrowers. Cockles are suspension feeders with short siphons. However, they have a large foot typical of deep burrowers but, instead of drawing the cockle far below, it is used to roll the shell along the surface.

This is accomplished by a sudden straightening movement of the curved foot, provided its tip is in contact with the sand. In favourable environments the populations are dense, forming cockle-beds. Commercial beds are usually situated in sandymud estuaries such as the Thames; here the largest beds are at Leigh-on-Sea.

Other suspension feeders to be found on the lower shore are the various kinds of carpet shell, *Venerupis,* with oval shells, somewhat amgular along the posterior edges. The empty valves are frequaently found alongside' those of cockles.

The sand gaper, *Mya arenaria,* one of the largest shore bivalves. is to be found here in sandy mud. The siphons, which may extend to an length of 30 cm, are joined by a tough sheath.

These animals are suspension feeders and the fringed openings of the siphons just reach the surface, where a slight hollow in the substratum is the only indication of their presence below. The valves are oval, reaching some 10 cm in length and, as the foot of the adult is relatively small, these gapers can be dug up more easily than many other bivalves, such as razotsbells, as they are incapable of rapid downward burrowing when disturbed.

We may find a few of the pretty thin tellin shells of sandy shores, provided that sand content is high but in more muddy areas its place is taken by the Baltic tellin *Macoma balthica.* This deposit feeder has heavier, dull shell which is not so compressed as the thin tellin.

Occasionally a Baltic tellin may be observed on the surface extending its foot in an effort to drag itself along. It leaves a track about 5 mm wide, which usually loops back to its original position.

Netted dog-whelks may be seen pushing their way through sandy mud in far greater numbers than on clean sand since detritus, which constitutes the bulk of their food, is far more abundant here.

In the lowest regions another whelk *Ocenebra erinacea,* commonly called the sting winkle despite the presence of a siphonal groove, may

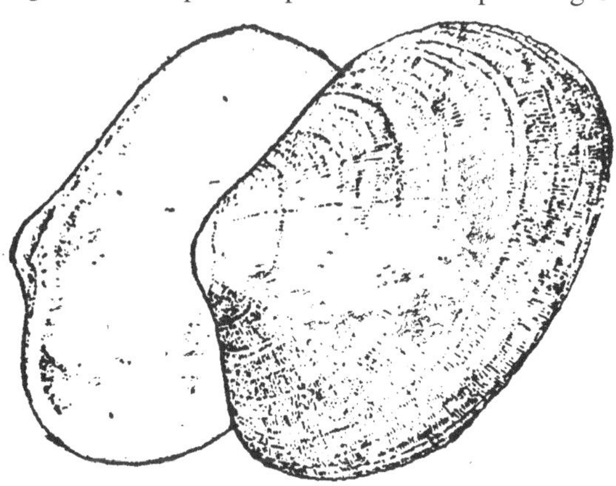

Figure 14.2: Valves of the carpet shell, Venerupis decussata.

be recognized by its thick ridged shell. Like the majority of whelks it is carnivorous and its prey consists of bivalves and barnacles. Sting winkles are partial to oysters and are therefore regarded as pests by oystermen.

All these inhabitants are also found in wide estuaries where the substratum is sandy mud and the water fully saline. Turning now to regions of mud, it is as the sand content decreases that a corresponding decrease in variety of species occurs.

However, this does not necessarily indicate a reduction in the number of inhabitants because these animals adapted to a mud environment form large populations.

Tubes of fine mud, about 5 mm in diameter, protruding some 8 cm above the surface on the lower shore, belong to the beautiful peacock worm, *Sabella penovina.* When covered by the tide this annelid extends its crown of feathery tentacles to sift out suspended food and absorb oxygen from the water.

When disturbed the crown rapidly retracted. Another tubeworm, *Myxicola infundibulum*, is not so conspicuous since the opening of its larger mud tube is flush with the surface. The ragworm, *Nereis diversicolor,* recognized by the red line running from head to tail along the centre of its back, glides over the surface of soft mud, preventing itself from sinking by traversing a wide area as it progresses along its wavy path.

It is very active during high water in its search for food ; however, when the tide recedes it burrows into the mud for protection, but this is only a temporary home. *N. diversicolor* feeds in the normal way of all ragworms but is also capable of straining of suspended particles from sea water when within its burrow.

The larvae of this species, although able to swim, remain in the surface and mud instead of becoming members of the temporary plankton, as is usual with most ragworms. Disturbance of the surface mud near low water mark may reveal a few shrimps, for these crustaceans, although abundant on sandy shores, can tolerate mud and here *N. diversicolor* probably constitutes their main item of diet.

Corophium volutator, a relative of the common sandhopper, burrows in mud and forms large populations Although a burrowing form, this amphipod crawls over the surface and on ebb-tide a few specimens may be found exposed at the water's edge in the wet mud ; as soon as the water drains away they retreat below.

Corophium is also capable of swimming and records show that

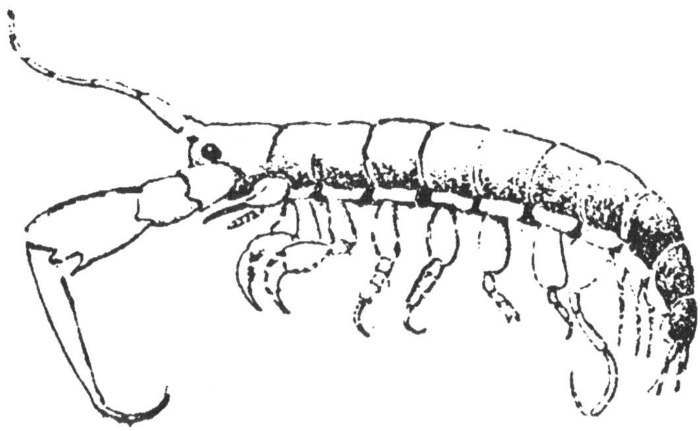

Figure 14.3: Corophium volutator.

whole populations make local movements, probably when there is some adverse change in their environment.

In small shallow pools may be observed long, mobile siphons extending from the mud and encompassing a wide arc in search of organic debris. These belong to peppery furrow shells, *Scrobicularia plana,* bivalve deposit feeders which live in large populations in soft mud.

The oval valves are greatly compressed enabling the animals to burrow deeply, perhaps to a depth of 25 cm in large specimens, and once below they rarely move their positions. The valve *of Scrobicularia* may reach a length of 54 mm but such a specimen would be eighteen years old.

Growth is rapid for the first few years, but after ten years the rate becomes reduced to about 1 mm per year. *Sacrobicularia* is an edible bivalve, but not much favoured in the country. However, in France it is a popular delicacy and locals may frequently be seen up to their knees in mud, delving up to their elbows in mud in search of the bivalve

Baltic tellins are found alongside *Scrobicularia* since they live in mud as well as sandy mud, but they do not burrow so deeply. In some areas these two deposit feeders are present in equal numbers, but in others the population of one may be so dense that few specimens of the other found. Both suck up any suitable organic detritus, but a proportion of their food consists of micro-organisms living amongst the mud particles.

VARIABLE SALINITY

So far the effect of decrease in particle. size on shore inhabitants has been considered, but now this must be discussed in conjunction with variable salinity.

Where rivers meet the sea, intermingling of fresh and salt water occurs, but the extent of this mixing is controlled by many factors such as the shape of the estuary, its geographical situation, strength of the tides, direction of coastal currents, rate of flow of the fresh water, etc.

Combination of all these diverse conditions is far too complex for consideration, here, but from the aspect of plant and animal populations there are two basic types of estuary

1. Estuaries with water of *increasing salinity from* surface to bottom, that is with a vertical salinity gradient. This occurs when the incoming sea water flows beneath the outgoing fresh water and therefore the salt content low on the shores is greater than towards the banks. In these estuaries most of the marine animals inhabit the lower zones, their numbers decreasing towards the upper mud lapped by the freshwater surface layers.
2. Estuaries with water of the *same salinity* from surface to bottom. This occurs when the incoming sea water mixes completely with the outgoing fresh water, so here little variation in salinity occurs over the littoral zone and marine species inhabit the whole region.

The salinity never remains constant at any one point along an estuary, but follows the ebb and flow of the tide so that the salt content is highest at high water and lowest at low water.

Even this varies from day to day as sea water penetrates farther upstream during spring tides than during neap tides.

Climatic conditions also play their part in controlling the salinity. Heavy rainfall increases the volume and force of the river outflow thus producing a reduction in salinity along the length of the estuary and in dry seasons the reverse occurs, the outflow *of* fresh water decreases and the salinity becomes raised.

It is not so much the range of salinity but the *rate of change* of salinity which controls colonization. Provided the lowering of salinity is very gradual, some marine animals can successfully adopt themselves to life in estuaries.

If rocks and stones are scattered in the mud the common shore crab, *Carcinus maenas,* happily migrates into regions of slightly lowered salinity and fishermen sometimes place tins or jars upside down along a stony stretch of estuary in the hope that young shore crabs will use them as protective covering during moulting; when they are soft-backed these crabs are particularly good bait. When berried the females move seawards and do not return upstream until after the eggs have hatched, which indicates that the larvae are not so tolerant of lowered salinities as the adults.

Rough and edible periwinkles, *Littorina saxatilis* and *L. littorea,* survive in estuaries, but *L. saxatilis* is more tolerant of lowered salinities than *L. littorea.*

Some seaweeds can withstand slight reductions in salt content, and of the brown wracks the brackish water species, *Fucus secranoides,* predominates. The green seaweed *Enteromorpha* may be abundant and extends farther upstream than any other species.

Shrimps do not mind lowered salinities provided the water is warm, so they venture up estuaries in the spring but return seawards in the autumn. However, like the shore crab, females carrying eggs move down into fully saline water.

The small prawn, *Palaemonetes varians,* is a brackish water species found in pools and swimming near the surface at high water alongside the river banks, where they can easily be caught in a fine-mesh hand nct. This prawn is almost transparent and only 2-3 cm long.

Several isopods of the genus *Sphaeroma* tolerate reduced salinities and their habit of rolling up into a ball in adverse conditions enables them to survive in cracks in the floor of dried out pools until the tide teturns.

Corophium volutator, the burrowing amphipod already discussed is found well upstream and as the young develop within the brood pouch of the female and emerge as miniature adults there is no hazard of the larvae being carried out to sea by the ebb-tide.

Other amphipods of the genus *Gammarus* live in estuaries, but each species tolerates certain salinities only, so that they are found at different heights up the estuary.

The ragworm, *Nereis diversicolor,* also tolerates lowered salinities and, as mentioned previously, the larvae remain in the surface mud, thus ensuring that they stay in the correct habitat for adult life. If, like the majority of ragworms, the larvae were planktonic, they might drift out to sea never to find their way back into an estuary.

Of the bivalve molluscs, the edible mussel tolerates dilution of sea water and therefore mussel-beds may extend some distance up river. Although mussels can survive in quite low salinities, they do not grow so rapidly nor reach a maximum size under such conditions.

The burrowing bivalves *Scrobicularia* and *Macoma* tolerate considerable reduction in salinity, but *Scrobicularia* penetrates farther upstream than *Macoma*.

The truly brackish-water mollusc is the tiny univalve, *Hydrobia ulvae,* which often forms dense populations. It browses on *Enteromorpha* or any available organic detritus.

Besides crawling over the mud it sometimes burrows just below the surface and occasionally it floats in the upper waters, accomplishing this by secreting a mucous raft for itself. This may well be a dispersal mechanism.

Farther upstream freshwater fauna become dominant and once freshwater species only are present, the limit of the estuary has been reached, since an estuary is that region of a river with water of variable salinity.

Salt-Marshes and Their Vegetation

Salt-marshes bound the landward side of mud-flats wherever the tidal flow is not too strong to prevent colonization by vegetation. This depends on the flow at spring tides, for a seedling may germinate during neap tides only to be uprooted at spring tides.

The formation of a salt-marsh commences when seeds, carried by the water and deposited together with salt, germinate and mud particles become trapped around the base of the growing plants. Small areas of stabilized mud are built up, and mare and more plants take root, until small islands of vegetation dot the shore.

Further sediment collects, increasing the size of these islands until eventually some of them fuse and form a system of creeks and channels along which the incoming tide flows.

Sometimes the islands merge to encircle completely a bare patch of mud, and the incoming water then flows around these hillocks of vegetation, trickling over and filling the central hollow only at spring tides. These isolated depressions are called *salt pans.*

During neap tides the water within these salt pane gradually evaporates, thus increasing the salt content, and sometimes during extremely hot weather they dry out completely leaving a cruet of salt on the surface of the mud.

During heavy and continuous rainfall the water in these pans may be considerably diluted, making the gap even wider between the lowest and highest salinities. These conditions are too unfavourable for germination of seeds and therefore salt pane usually remain devoid of vegetation.

These salt pane are rounded in shape, but elongated pane may be formed when creeks become blocked, either by the vegetation from each side growing across and causing the deposition of mud or by incaving of the sides.

Often the edge of a fully formed salt-marsh gradually becomes so eroded by water movements that *a salting cliff* is formed with bare mud below and salt-marsh vegetation above. In many estuaries indentations in these salting cliffs form excellent mud berths for boats during the winter months, as the water rise only the full height of the cliff and covers the saltings during spring tides.

Now that we have some idea how salt-marshes develop it is obvious that the plant colonizers of such areas must be specialized to withstand regular submergence or partial submergence by see water ; they are *halophytes.*

Glasswort or marsh samphire, *Salicornia stricta, is* a common primary colonizer of bare mud. It is a succulent annual with upright, cylindrical, branched stems, which are notched and bear small scale leaves only; the whole plant is bright green, though with age it may become tinged with red or yellow.

Glasswort may grow to a height of 25 cm and its inconspicuous, petal-less flowers appear during August and September. Although an annual, the dead stems remain upright for some while and silt continues to collect around them.

From a distance mud with a sparse population of glasswort look rather like a desert with miniature cacti. Glasswort colonizes only areas of firm mud since its root system is shallow. Therefore in soft, mobile mud it is replaced by cord-grass, *Spartina* spp. a perennial with deep vertical roots fot anchorage and horizontal rhizomes ramifying throughout the surface layers for stabilization of the substratum.

Cordgrass grows in large tufts, from 30 to 120 cm high and its pale yellow flower spikes appear from July to September. *Spartina* is so efficient in trapping mud and debris that man plants it in certain areas to help reclaim land from the sea. Even when glasswort is in primary colonizer, cord-grass becomes established farther inland in regions of softer mud.

In sandy mud sea poa, *Puccinellia maritima*, is the pioneer, forming thick tufts around which silt soon collects. This perennial may grow to a height of 30 cm, but the plants are often prostrate, forming a turf. It is in flower during July and August.

A variety of halophytes become established above the zone of primary colonizers and the following are some of the commonest species forming the general salt-marsh vegetation.

Common seablite, *Sueda maritina,* usually occurs at low levels just above glasswort, though it may be found farther upshore. It is an annual, often very small, but sometimes reaching a height of 50 cm.

The branched stem is smooth and bears many short, cylindrical pointed green leaves, which become tinged with red during the autumn. The flowers, which appear from July to October, are green, small and *inconspicuous*.

Sea aster, *Aster tripolium*, is a perennial growing to a height of approximately 60 cm and its flowers, which bloom during August and September have yellow discs surrounded by pale mauve ray florets, very similar to the common garden Michaelmas daisy. However, in certain localities such as East Anglia a particular variety occurs in which the mauve florets are absent.

Sea purslane, *Halimione portulacoides,* is often very abundant in well-drained saltings, but tends to be confined to east and south coasts. This is a straggly perennial with stems some 20 to 45 cm long trailing over the ground and bearing shorter erect branches with small, eliptical, greyish leaves.

The small yellow flowers, arranged in short spikes, are unisexual, but both male and female flowers develop on the same plant. They are in bloom from July to October.

During July and August some saltings, particularly those on the east coast, are a blaze of mauve. This is the beautiful sea lavender, *Limonium vulgare, in* full bloom and even though the individual tubular flowers are tiny they are crowded together towards the tip of the leafless flower stalks and *en masse* give a lovely display.

Sea lavender is a perennial growing from 10 to 30 cm high, and its lanceolate leaves are arranged in a rosette. Sea pink, which has already been mentioned, is also a member of the salt-marsh community, but only in the upper levels as it is not very tolerant of high salinities.

It probably survives here because its long roots penetrate below the more saline upper layers. Scurvy-grass, *Cochlearia officinalis*, a perennial varying in size from 10 to 25 cm, with thick, fleshy, long-stalked, heartshaped leaves, inhabits the middle zone of saltings. The fourpetalled white flowers, which may be tinged with mauve, are approximately 8 mm in diameter and bloom from April to July. Sea-spurrey, *Spergularia spp.,* found on the middle levels of saltings, is recognized by its five-petalled, deep pink flowers, 8-16 mm in diameter, in bloom from June to September.

The much branched slender stems tend to trail and the small leaves are fleshy. Sea wormwood, *Artemesia maritima,* becomes established in the uppermost levels of saltings and from a distance appears as a delicate silvery plant, some 30 cm high.

The stems and slender leaflets are covered with a down of fine hairs and the whole plant has a pleasantly aromatic smell. The small, yellow, daisy-type flowers, crowded into short spikes, appear during August and September.

Sea plantain, *Plantago maritima,* found on spray-washed cliffs also inhabits the middle and upper zones of saltings alongside sea lavender and sea pink.

INDEX

A

a M. edulis 22
a Pacific coast 57
a salting cliff 275
A. nodosum 222
A. vulgaris 29
absolutely smooth 253
absorb 167
absorbing 196
abundant 98, 150
abundant compared 191
abyssal 138
accompany 135
accomplished 133
accumulate 173
accuracy 100
achieved 140
Acmaea 9, 23, 24
acorn barnacles 185
acorn-worms 97
Actinia 9
Actinia equina, but 238
adaptations 200
adaptive 135
adenosine triphosphate 166
adequate 175
adequately 168
advantageous 128
advection 102
Aeolidia papillosa, 238
affinities 132
Africa 109, 175
Agarum 20
aggregations 129
aggressively 153
Agropyron junceiforme 264
Alaria esculenta 225
Alaska 4
Alcyoninum digitatum, 246
algae 210, 212
alginate 210
alichondria, 245
alternately 4
Alternatively 8
always 239
amenable 219
Ammodytes tobianus, 259
ammonia 102
Ammophila arenaria, 263
amongst 261
amphipods 123, 148, 153
Amphitrile, 239
Anaerobic 45
anaesthetizes 214
and 256
Anemonia sulcata. 238
anglerfishes 136, 137
angles 3
Angola Basin 139
animal life 218, 253
animals 132
animals survive 186
Anomia ephippium, 246
Antarctic Convergence 166, 175
Antarctic Intermediate 109
antarctic seas 158

Antarctic slope 157
Antarctic Surface Water 107
Antartic Intermediate 110
antartic region 111
Antedon bifida. 246
Anthopleura elegantissima 26
Anthopleura xanthogrammica 9
anticipated 182
Anurida (=Lipura) maritima. 237
Aphrodite aculeato 260
Aplysia punctata, 244
apogee 3
apparatus 214
apparent 187
appreciable 164
appreciably 93
approximately 173
aquatic 1, 163
Arabia 175
Archidoris pseudoargus, 245
Arctic 140
Arenicola 47
Arenicola marina 256
Argentine 94
Aristotle's lantern 214
Arithyllis vulneraria, 234
Armeria maritima, 233
armoured dinoflagellates 169
Arnenicola spp., 47
arrow-worms 119, 120, 132
Artemesia maritima, 277
arthropods 132
Ascophyllum 212, 222
Ascophyllum, 223
Ascophyllum nodoosum 222
Ascophyllum nodosum
204, 210, 221
assimilated 170
Aster tripolium 276
Asterias forbesi 22, 29
Asterias rubens, 240
Asterias rulgaris 22
Asterina gibbosa, 246
Astropecten irregularis, 257
Athanas nitescens 249
Athanas nitescens, 246
Atlanti 94
Atlantic 108
Atlantic Ocean 186, 194
atmosphere 100, 182, 233
atmospheric 7, 193
atoll 141
Attachment 214
attributed 10
Audouinia 239
aurora borealis. Diatoms 163
austero 150
automatic cameras 145
automatic tide gauge 204
autumn 175
auxospore stage 163
Avonmouth 182
awesome 91

B

B glandula, 21
B. balanoides 29, 236
B. balanoides. 29
B. cariosus 21, 29, 32
B. cariosus, 19, 21
B. cariosus is 21
B. cariosus. 21
B. glandula 21, 32
backbones 236
background 176
bacteria 131, 170
bacterioplankton 119
bait 148
Balanns. 215
balanoides 19
Balanus 19, 22
Balanus, 205

Balanus balanoides
19, 22, 29, 30, 214
Balanus balanoides, 185, 236
Balanus cariosus 21, 22, 28
Balanus glandula 19, 21, 32
Balanus glandula, 21, 29
Balanus glandula. 21
Balanus perforatus, 185
Balanus. 29
ballast 169
Barbara 153
barnacle 214, 237
Barnacles 205
barnacles 11, 186, 191
barometric 195, 196
barren 253
barriers 138
basalt 97
basins 4, 176
bathypelagic
118, 121, 125, 136, 137, 139
bathypelagic realm 137
beach 182
beadlet anemone Acrini equina
200
beam 100
beardworms 123
beautiful 160
Beginning 182
behavior 127, 134, 146
beneath 253
Benguela 175
benthic 119, 140
benthic animals 125
benthic environment 141
benthic life 94
Benthic organisms 119
Bifucaria rotunda 226
billfishes 121, 174
binary fission. 189
biogeography 101
biological 131
Biological Factors 18
biological sciences 89
biologist 104
biologists 103
bioluminescence 121, 135, 137
biota 176
bivalves 185
black 219
bladder-like 169
bladders 226
bleaching 219
bleak 218
Blennius pholis 241
Blepharipoda occidentalis 40
block 61
blowouts 264
bluefin tuna 103
bodies of animals 131
Bonapartia 121
Bopyrus, 250
Botryllus schlosseri 214
Botryllus schlosseri, 244
bottom 102, 146
bottom-dwelling 93
boundary 195
boxlike 237
branching 219
Brazil 94
breaking 186
breaking bubbles 112
breaks 115, 175
breathable atmosphere 126
breathe 124
brilliant 163
bristle-worms 97
bristles 133
Bristol 182
Bristol Channel 182
Britain 221
British Isles 178, 186

brittle stars 148
brittle-stars 97
broad spectrum 143
broad taxonomic similarity 176
broadcasts 146
brotulids 150
brownish photosynthetic 163
Bruun 98
Buccimum undatum 261
Bullard 90
buoyant 104
burrowing 139
burrows 140
by Pisaster, 32
byssal threads 11

C

C. stellatus. 236
Calanus 189
Calcareous flagellates 166
calcareous flagellates 169
California 152, 166, 175, 210
Calliacus parasitica, 246
Calliostoma zizyphinium 245
Calothrix confervicola 232
Calyptraea chinensis. 246
Calystegia soldanella, 264
Cambrain 119
Cambrian 89
camera 156
Canaries 94
Cape Verde Basins 94
Capitella. 47
Caprella, 245
carapace 261
carbon dioxide 166
Carcinus maenas 214
Carcinus maenas, 239, 272
Cardium edule, 255, 268
Caribbean 10, 97
Caribbean Sea 111
carnivores 120, 132
carota 234
carragheen 219
Cathamalus 19
Cedross Island 153
cellulose 161, 170
centimetre 103
Central Waters 110
centric 163
centrifugal 2, 3
centrifuging 160
Centtrales 163
cephalopods 99
Ceramium rubrum 230
Cereus pedunculatus, 238, 259
Cetaceans 119
cetaceans periodically 152
Challenger 160
Challenger in 145
Challenger. 99
Challenger's 145
channels 186
characteristic 105, 145, 173
characteristically 195
characteristics 6
chemical 131
chemosynthetic 46
chemosynthetic bacteria 170
Chile 93
chilled 97
chlorophyll 167, 169, 188
chloroplasts 163, 205
chocolate-brown 94
Chondrus 20, 22, 29, 228
Chondrus, 29
Chondrus crispus
22, 30, 219, 228
Chondrus crispus 229
Chondrus crispus 22, 28, 29
Chondrus crispus 20
Chondrus 22, 29

Chorda filum, 226
chordates 99
Chthamalus 19, 21
Chthamalus predominates 205
Chthamalus stellatus
29, 214, 236
cilia 133
Ciona, 245
circles 180
circulated 176
Circumpolar Water 106
cirrate octopods 122
Cladophora, 229
Clams 140
Clara squamata, 9
Clavelina lepadiformis 245
clean 258
climax 30
Cliona celata. 251
clone 26
clusters 221
CM-2 200
cnidarians 119
coastal cities 130
coastline 237
coasts 194
Coccolithophores 160
coccolithophores 160
Coccolithophorids 160
coccolithophorids 160, 161
coccoliths 160
Cochlearia officinalis, a 276
Codium, 227
coldblooded, 183
colleagues 121
Collisella 9, 23, 24
Collisella digitalis 25
Collisella digitalis, 25
Collisella scabra 25
combination 204
combs 133
commensalism. H. lunulata 240
commercially harvested 152
commonest 236
communities 179
community 141, 176
community structure 8
comparable 184, 191
comparatively 139
comparison 219
compensation 168
competition, predation, 19
competitors 131
compiled 181
complex life cycle 210
complicate identification 186
compressed 195
concentrations 127, 166, 169
concerned 187
condensation 112
conditions 182, 192
Congo 139
consequent flooding 186
conservation 98
conservative properties 105
considerable 181
consideration 177
considerations 169
conspicuous 135
constitutes 139
constricted 230
consumer 191
consumers 190
continental 93, 153
continental shelves 176
continental slope 106
continual abrasive 186
continuation 115
continues 220
contradicted 99
controlling 184, 196
convection 175

convection current 168
convergence 166
Conversely 130
cooler 174
copepod crustaceans 119
coral islands 141
Corallina 215, 228
Corallina, 229
Corallina officinalis 228
Corallina 229
Corex arenaries 264
Coriolis acceleration 76
Coriolis Force 106, 112
Cornwall 185
Corophium 270
Corophium volutator 270, 273
correspondence 133
Corystes 258, 260, 261
Corystes cassivelaunus 258
Coupled 1
coupled 194
coverings 158
crabs 97, 148, 184
cradle 89
Crangon crangon (=C. vulgaris) 259
creatures 141, 146, 148, 152, 189, 194
Crepidula 244
Crepidula fornicata, 244
Cretaceous 161
creviced rock 212
crevices 185, 218, 233
Crithmum maritumum, 233
Critical survey 123
critical tide levels 6, 16
cruise 97
Crustaceans 248
crustaceans 99, 120, 148
crustazean 237
Cryptopsaras 122
ctenophores 132
Cucumaria, 241
cucumbers 97
Cyanea 119
Cyanophyta 164
Cyclopterus lumpus, 242
Cyclothone 119, 122
Cyclothone. 119, 120
cylindrical 220
Cystoseira tamariscifolia 226

D

damaged 182
damaged promenades 186
darkness 140, 187, 189
Daucus carota, 234
daylight 167
decomposition 173
decrease 192
decreased 111
deep 225
deep oceanic trenches 157
Deep Pools 225
deep-sea 177
deepocean 156
Deepsea 97
defensive 135
degassing 90
Delessaria 231
Delessaria sanguinea 231
delineate 6
Dendraster 43
Dendraster excentricus 39, 41
Dendrodoa grossularia, 245
densely populated 13
Density 103
depness 196
depressed 212
descend 117
desiccating 4
Desiccation 7

desiccation
6, 11, 12, 196, 219, 253
detritus feeders 12
development 129
diameter 180
Diatom cells 130
diatom-rich 166
Diatomaceous 166
diatoms 166, 169, 212
dichotomous 219
dichotomously 223
Dictyota dichotoma 228
die 124
different 253
digitalis 24
dimensional 131
diminished 3
dimly lighted 125
Dinoflagellata 160
dinoflagellates
160, 161, 163, 167, 170
Diplecogaster (=Lepadogaster) bimaculata, 242
disadvantage 12
discontinuity 192
discoveries 159
dispersal 194
dispersed 140
displayed 187
distance 156
distinct 192
distinctive 160
Distribution 195
distribution
4, 146, 166, 176, 196
distribution undoubtedly 129
disturbance 135
disturbed 190
diurnal tides 4
divalent ions 168
divergences 174
diverse 89, 98, 176
diversity 118, 176
divisions 177
dogfish 261
domain 124
dominant 124
Donax 39, 40
Donax vittatus 255
downpull 204
downward 130
drastically 192
dredges 145
driftline 260
droplet 127
dry 225
dwellers 219
Dynomean (= Sertularia) pumila 243

E

E. intestimalis 20
E. intestinalis 28
E. intestinalis. 23
eastern Pacific 175
ebb 182
Ecbinus 214
Echinocardium 257
Echinocardium cordatum, 257
Echinocardium. 258
Echinus esculentus is 214
echo-sounders 91
ecological 7
ecology 161
Ectocarpus 223
eddies 175
edible periwinkle 185
Elymus arenarius, 264
Emerita 40
Emerita analoga 40
emersion 195
emphausiids 132

en masse 276
enchanced 196
encountered 6, 236
encroach 148
endemic 98
enduring 144
energy 166, 188
energy-rich 167
enormous 191
enough light 118
Ensis 40
Ensis ensis, 255
Ensis siliqua, 254
Enteramorpha intestinal is 20
Enteromorpha
46, 229, 247, 273, 274
Enteromorpha, Ascophyllum 210
Enteromorpha intestinalis, 23
Enteromorpha. 9
environment 8, 156, 233
environmental 8
environmental niches 140
enzyme 104
epibenthic 140
epibenthic animals 125
epifauna 123, 176
epipelagic 122
epiphyte 230
epiphyte ; 222
epiphytic habit 222
epizooic 243
Equatorial 110
equatorial 113, 131
equatorial countercurrent 174
equatorial Pacific 174
equilibrium 103, 112
equipped 168
Erebus 158
Eryngium maritimum, 264
Ethmodiscus rel 169
Ethmodiscux rex 169
Eugula, 245
Eulalia viridis, 244
Eunice harassi 251
euphausiids 119, 136
euphonic 173
euphonic zone 173
Euphorbia paralias, 264
euphotic zone 164
European coasts 204
eurythermal 103
Evaporation 112
evaporation 8, 99
evolutionary 119
excrete 124
exhausting 152
exhibiting 237
expansion 90
experience tides 2
experimental 214
Experiments 167
explanations 135
exploratory 156
explosions 90
exposed 196, 204, 205
exposed rocky coasts 186
exposure 4, 178, 181, 204, 229
exposure varies 182
expressed 4
exquisite 127
extensive 1
extreme 181, 196
Extreme High Water Neaps, 180
Extreme HIM Water Springs,
180
Extreme Law Water Neaps, 180
Extreme Low Water Springs. 180
extremes 10
exudes 225

F

F. serratus 223

F. spiralis 221
F. vesiculosus 221, 222, 223
F. vesiculosus. 222
fact 3
Faginism 139, 156
Falkand Islands 210
familiar 182
farther 182
fauna 182, 186, 236
feature 100
fecal pellets 131
feed 124
females 222
fertilize 163
fetch 186, 204
fewer 191
filter feeders 12
filtering 139
fireflies 137
firm 225
fisheries 143, 157
fishes 97, 119
fishlines 156
fivorous 135
flagellates 130
flagellum 161
flatter shell 204
floating 158, 230
flooded 182
flora 1, 182
flotation 168
flow 78, 182
flows 106
fluctuates 2
fluctuating 196
Fluctuations 192
fluctuations 2
Flustrellidra (=Flustrella) hispida 245
flying-fishes 121
Foeniculum vulgare 235
food chain 190, 191
food economy 141
fore-dune 264
forminifera 123
forms 220
fossils 90
fourth hours 182
fracture 65
fracture zones 55
fragile cell 169
freeze 6
freezing 10
fresh water 223
frond 225
fronds 219
frost 199
Fucaceae 210
fucoid fronds 225
fucoids 210
Fucus 210, 212, 223, 244
Fucus ceranoides 223
Fucus secranoides, 273
Fucus serratus 210
Fucus serratus low 214
Fucus serratus. 229, 243
Fucus spiralis, 220
Fucus spiralis, Fucus vesiculosus 210
Fucus vesiculosus 210
Fucus vesiculosus, 221
fugitive 20, 26
functionally 177
functioning 146
Futaminifera 89

G

G. cineraria, 244
G. strigosa 240
gales 182
gametophyte 205
Gammarus 273

Ganges Canyon 93
gaping 153
gastropods 99, 132
Geiger-Muller 170
Gelathea squamifera, 240
gelatinous threads 169
generalist 103
Geographical 178
geographical 184
geomorphology 2
Geophysical Year 110
German chemist 171
germinate 163
Gibbula cineraria 212
Gibbula lineata, 238
Gibbula umbiltcalis, 244
Gigartina 229
Gigartina stellata 229
Gigartina stellata C. crispus 228
glass-sponges 123
Glaucus 120
glowworms 137
glucose 166
Glycera 41, 48
Glycera convoluta, 257
Gobius paganellus, 242
Gommaric locusta, 239
Goneplax 261
Goneplax rhomboides (= G. angulata) 261
Gonichthys coccoi 120
Gonyaulax polyedra 170
Gracilaria 46
gradual 123, 180
Grand Banks 115
grandest 91
Grantia compress, 244
gravitational 180
gravitational generating 2
grazers 12, 22
Grazing 129
grazing 19
Grazing herbivores 205
Greater depths 147
greatest 180
green algae 46
Green plants 188
greenbrowns 218
greenish 161
grenadier 153
grey sharks 121
grooved 161
grotesque 145
grow 124
growth 167, 186, 192
Gulf Stream 194
gulpers 136
gummifer, 234

H

habitat 178, 188
habitats 178
hagfish 154
Halichondria panicea 244
Halidrys siliquosa, 226
Halimione portulacoides, 276
Halobates spp. 120
halophytes. 233, 275
hanging 221
hardness 185
Harmothoe, 258
Harmothoe lunulata, 240
harvest 156
Hedophyllum 20
Hedophyllum sessile 20
Hemiptera 120
herbivore 188
herbivores 131
herbivorous 120
herbivorous zoo-plankton 125
heteropods 132
heterotrophic 162

Hiatella 251
high cone 238
high tide 3
higher 210
Himanthalia elongata, 225
Hippolyte varians, 249
history 161
holdfast 218, 222
Homarus gammarus (=H. vulgaris) 250
home scar 9
homes 9
Honckenya peploides, 264
hop 237
horizontal 13
horizontally 225
Hormosira banksi 215
Hormosira banksii 210
horny tongue 210
house 133
hunting 236
Hydrobia ulvae, 274
hydrogen 131, 171
hydrogen donor 170
hydrogen sulfide 130
hydrostatic 103
Hymeniacidon. 244
Hyperoplus (=Ammodytes) lanceolatus, 260

I

identification 156
igneous 91
illuminated 187, 193
immediately 128
immense 153
immersed 12
immobile centric diatoms 170
in midwater 168
inconspicuous 246, 276
increasing 173
increasing salinity from 272
indestructible 158
Indian 94, 108
Indian Ocean 110, 175
individuals 155
inescapable 131
inexpensive 157
infauna 176
influence 187
infra-red 117
infralittoral fringe, 15
infralittoral zone 15
ingesting 214
inhabitants 125, 146, 178, 182, 205
inherent 6, 174
innumerable hagfish 153
inorganic 164, 191
inorganic substances 170
intelligence 144
intensity 171, 192, 193
Interaction 134
interactions 124, 144
interconnected 124
interesting 187
Intermediate 109
interrupt 176
interstitial 253
Intertidal 6, 196, 1, 4
intertidal animals 9
intertidal rocks 196
intertidal zone 9
interval 180, 146
introduce 177
invasion 139
inversely 132
Invertebrate 98, 236, 105, 153, 176
Ireland 204
Irish moss 219
irregularly 230

island 204
isotherm 101
isothermal 102
Isuridae 103

J

jellyfishes 123
journeys 218
juveniles 139, 155, 156

K

keystone species 22
kilometers 13
Kuroshio 116

L

L. digitata 224, 225
L. hyperborea, 224
L. littoralis 212, 243
L. littorea 212, 242, 273
L. neritoides 212
L. palliata 212
L. saccharin, 225, 224
L. saxatilis 212, 273, 210, 237
laborious 142
lacken 130
Lacuna, 247
lamellate 163
Laminaria 210
Laminaria digitata 210, 224
Laminaria hyperborea 210
Laminaria saccharin 225, 210
Laminaria setchelli 20
Laminaria 231, 247
Lampadena 122
land habitat 178
land-based 166
Lanice conchilega. 256
lantern fishes 136
lanthina spp. 120
Lapidoplax 258
Lapidoplax digitata 258
large kills 150
large shrimps 148
Larvacea 133
larval stages 120
Lasaea rubra 237
latitudes 3, 127
Laurencia pinnatifida 229
laverbread 232
Leathesia difformis, 229
leeward 176
Lepadogaster lepadogaster (=L. gouani) 242
Lepas anatifera, 262
Leptosynapta inhaerens 258
Lessionopsis Ititoralis 20
lethal limits 7
lichens. 232
Lichina pygmaea, 232
Lichina pygmea. 237
lifeforms 176
light 131
light levels 129
Limmoria lignorum 262
Limonium, binervosum 233
Limonium vulgare, in 276
Limpets 210
limpets 11, 186, 190, 238
Lineus 240
Lithophyllum 228, 238, 247, 251
Lithothamion 247
Lithothamnion 228
Lithothamnion. 228
little ice age 87
littoral 180, 182
littoralis 212
Littorina 14
Littorina litrorea 28
Littorina litrorea, 29
Littorina littorea 10
Littorina littorea, 23, 242
Littorina littorea is 199

Littorina nerioldes 183
Littorina neritiiodes, 237
Littorina neritoides, 13, 210
Littorina saxatilis 273
Littorina unifasciata 10
live 124
local distribution 24
Loligo 99
Lomentaria articulata 230
Lomentaria 230
long periods 182
longicornis 239
Lottia 27
Lottia gigantea 32
Lottic gigantea 27
Lower California 152, 153
lownward 238
luminescent 162
luminous bacteria 137
luminous plankton 137
lunar 180

M

M edulis 29
M. californianus 19, 20, 25
M. californianus, 20, 21
M. californianus. 20
M. edulis 22, 29
M. edulis 29, 29
Macoma 47, 274
Macoma balthica 269
Macoma 274
Macrocystis pyrifera 210
Macropipus (=Portunus) depurator 261
Macropipus (=Portunus) puber, 246
Macropodia 245
macrourids 122
Mactridae 255
magma 90
maintenance 189
Maja (= =Mafia) squinado 246
mako sharks 121
makoshark 103
manganese-nodule 152
manifested 7
mantle 91, 238
mantle spreads 204
manufactured 125
many 61
margin 93
Marine 104
marine 1, 219
marine environment 132
marine organisms 6
marine-biological 143
Marphysa sanguinea.Pollydora 251
marvellously integrated 118
masked 258
masses 176
Master ochraceus 29
mate 124
maturity 220
may 235
Mean High Water Neaps, 180
Mean High Water Springs, 180
Mean Low Water Neaps, 180
Mean Low Water Springs, 180
meaningful importation 156
measuring 170
mechanisms 10, 127, 129
Mediterra-nean 195
Mediterranean 185
medusae 123, 132
Medusae jellyfishes 104
meiobenthic 176
Melanocetus 122
melobenthic 123
members 134
Membranipora membranacea.

244
Meredith Sessions 146
mesopelagic
118, 121, 122, 136, 174
mesopelagic zone 122
metamorphic 91
Meteor 110
Mexico 185
Micro-flagellates 161
micro-flagellates 169
micro-fossils 161
micro-organisms 135
microhabitats 8
microscopic 112, 135, 140
microscopic dimensions 127
microscopic food 141
microscopist 158
mid-ocean ridges 157
midday 6, 181
midlittoral 14
midlittoral zone 195
midnight 181
midoceanic 91
midrib 223
migrating 134
migration 134
migrations 118
Milford 182
mimicry 137
minimum 192
minimum requirements 166
minor role 163
mix tides 5
mixed layer 102
mixed tides 4
mobile 214
mobility 167
moderate 181
Moderate oil pollution 205
modifications 233
moisture 195
molecules 173
mollusks 11
molten 90
molts 131
Mondonta lineata are 212
monopolize 153
Morchellium, Aplidium 245
morphology 13, 161
Motion 153
motion 146
move 124
mucous scum 158
mucus 9, 200
mud, 266
muddy 94, 178
mudflats. 267
muscles 120
mussels 140
Mutilus, 31
Mya arenaria, 269
Myctophum punctatum 120
Mylitus 32
myriad glowing 190
mysterious 132
Mytillus 29
Mytilus 22, 28, 29, 205
Mytilus, 11, 22
Mytilus californianus 19, 21
Mytilus edulis 22, 25, 30, 214
Mytilus edulis, 9, 13, 29, 244
Mytilus 28, 22
Myxicola infundibulum 270
Myxocephalus (= Cottus) scorpius
241

N

N. diversicolor 270
nannoplankton 127
Nassarius 256
Nassarius reticulatus 256
Natica 48, 255

Natica alderi 255
Natlca 43
natural laws 126
navigation 146
neap 180, 196
necessary 187
neighbor 148
neighbouring oceanic waters 175
nekton 119
nektonic 119
nektos 119
nematode 123
Nephthys 257
Nephthys hombergi 257
Nephthys 257
Nephtys 41
Nereis diversicolor 257, 270, 273
Nerencystis 20
Nerita peleronta 10
neritic 91
Nerophis lumbriciformis, 251
Nests 140
neuston 120
neustonic 164
never 228
Newfoundland 94, 115
niche 187
nitrated 173
nourishment 222
Noctiluca 161
Nodolittorina tuberculata. 10
non-conservative 105
non-flowering 218
non-motile 119
normally 182
north 175
North Pacific 111, 166
Northeast Monsoon 174
Northern Hemisphere 76
northern hemisphere 199
Norwegian 108
Norwegian oceanographer 105
notably copepods 120
Nucella lapillus, 237
number 148
numbers 184
numerous 156, 170, 185
nursery 176
nutrient 117, 173, 174, 176, 193
nutrient-rich 127
nutrient-yielding 173
nutrients
129, 130, 131, 170, 173, 191

O

oarweed 225
Obelia genticulata 243
obscure 135
observation 76
observations 158
observed 204
obstruction 186
occasionally 115
occurrence 130
ocean 76, 91, 100, 130
oceanic 166, 176
oceanographers 98, 103
oceanographic 108, 143
Ocenebra erinacea, 269
octopuses 136
L. saxatilis, 242
Scrobicularia 271
Olivella biplicata 10
Olivella columellaris 41
omnivores 120
omnivorous 190
onshore gales 186
onslaught 218
oozes 94
Ophiothrix fragilis 240
opportunistic 20, 25
opportunity 4

opposite 180
optimum 187, 192
Orchestia. 237
ordinarily 146
organic 187
organic cycle 191
organic material 129, 131
organisms 104, 164, 185, 196
organized 177
orientation 125
oscillating 134
oscillations 76, 204
osmoconformers. 12
osmoregulation, 267
ostracod crustaceans 119
outcrop 140
outstanding 166
overcome 186
overhang 199
overlapping 156
oxygen 171
oxygen content. 38
oxygen electrode 170
oxygen stress 143
Oxypode 43
Oyashio 116
oysters 11

P

P. pavonia 227
Pacific 150
Pacific deep water 112
Pacific Gyre 150
Pacific Ocean 113
Pacific Oceans 108
Pacific water 112
Padina 227
Padina pavonia, 226
Pagurus (=Eupagurus) bernhardus 261
Palaemon (=Leander) seratus, 249
Palaemon elegans 214
Palaemonetes varians, 273
Palaernon (=Leander) squilla 248
Palinurus elephas (=P. vulgaris), 250
parallel 113, 166
parcel 90
particle size. 34
particles 162, 253
particular 129, 204
particulate 173
passive, 26
Patella, Acmaea, 9
Patella aspera 215
Patella vulgata 200
Patellavulgata 23
Patina pellucida, 247
patterns 195
Pelagic 119
pelagic 119, 128
pelagic life 176
pelagic plants 119
pelagic realm 127
pelagic tunicates 104, 119, 120
Pelvetia 220, 221
Pelvetia canaliculata 210
Pelvetia canaliculata, 221
pendulous 204
penetration 7
Pennales 163
perigee 3
periodic 2
periodic counterblow 129
periodic exposure 236
periods 100, 219
periwinkles 190
permanent 176, 189
Peru 93, 175
Peru Currents 175
Phaeophyceae 219

Pholas dactylus, 252
Pholis (=Centronotus) gunnellus, 241
phosphates 173
phosphorescent 190
photographed 155
photographic 156
Photographs 94, 145
photographs 145, 146
Photosynthesis 167
photosynthesis 104, 110, 118, 167, 188
photosynthesis, 187
photosynthetic 162, 170, 171
phototaxis 160
Phycodrys 231
Phycodrys rubens 231
phyla 236
Physalia 120
Physalla 120
physical 131
Physical Factors 15
physical factors 2
physical parameters 6
physiology 143, 161
phytoplankton 119, 125, 127, 129, 133, 160, 166, 167, 170, 171, 173, 175, 192
phytoplankton, 189
phytoplankton community 168
phytoplankton production 168
piddocks 185
pigment 205
pigments 120
pillars 97
Pilumnus hirtellus, 246
Pirimela denticulata 239
Pisaster 21, 22, 32
Pisaster ochraceus 32
Pisaster ochraceus 21
Pisaster ochraceus can 22
Pisaster ochraceus is 21
plankton 104, 110, 135, 160, 165, 189
plankton, 119
plankton shells 94
plankton. 189
Planktonic 210
planktonic 117, 132, 165
planktonic animals 120
planktonic communities 133
planktos, 119
plant cells 131
plant-bearing 160
Plantago maritima 277
Plantago maritima, 234
platelets pierced 161
plenty 219
plotting 105
plough 174
Plumaria 230
Plumaria elegans is often 230
Pogonophora 123
poised 168
polar regions 100
polar seas 3
Polinices 43, 48
Pollicipes polymerus 19
Polysiphonia 222
Polysiphonia 222
Pomatoceros 243
Pomatoceros triqueter 214
Pomatoschistus (=Gobius) minutus 260
population 145
populations 150, 178, 181, 218, 236
Porcellana platycheles 239
Porphyra, Fucus 9
Porphyra umbilicalis 231
Porpita 120

Portuguese 120
Portumnus latipes 260
Postelsia 28
Postelsia palmaeformis, 27
Postelsio 28
potential 157
powerfully predaceous 136
prairie wolf 148
precipitation 99
predation. 20
predators 12, 253
predatory assemblages 135
predictability 6
predominant 9
predominantly 123, 126
presented 218
presuming 191
prevailing 196, 204
primary 188, 191
Primary productivity 175
prime factor 178
principal prey 156
problem 178, 200
producing 130
productive 97, 150, 176
productive equatorial 150
Productivity 171, 174
profusion 218
promenades 182
prominent 113, 166
pronounced 111
proportions 173
protoplasm 104, 189
protoplasm, 183
protoplasmic flagella 160
Psammechinus miliaris 240
psychrosphere 101
pteropod molluscs 119
published 181
Puccinellia maritima 275
pursuance 89
Pycnogonum, a 238
pyramid of numbers 191

Q

Quantification 156
quaternary 190
questions 142
quickened 117
quickly 156, 173
quiescent 6
quite motionless 168

R

Radioaria 158
radula 210
rain 125
raining 45
Ramalina 233
ramifications 156
random 152
rat-tall 97
rate of change 272
reaches 182
reappears 175
reasonable 146
receptacles 222, 223
receptacles,, 220
recirculation 131
recognizable 195
recognizably stratified 176
recolonize 184
reconnaissance 146
recovery 146
rectification 134
recycling 173
red 210
red algae 46
red tides 130
red-nosed 260
reddish organisms 118
reduction 214

reflector 137
refractory material 138
reinoculation 133
relationship 191
relatives 166
released 221
Relics 90
reluctance 154
remarkable 11
remarkable adaptations 176
remnants 125
renewal 163
replacement 156
representatives 138
reproduce 124, 221
reproduction
129, 167, 171, 175, 192
reproductive structures 225
reserve 164
reservoir 125
residence 111
respiration 167, 168
respiratory 12, 167
response 187
restrict 196
retard 170
Retracing 97
retreating 184
return 168
returning 125
reverse applying 196
Rhodophyceae 219, 229
Rhodymenia palmata, 231
Richard Shutts 146
ridges 65
rift valley 97
ripples 140
Rivularia atra 232
rock cracks 218
Rock Pool Vegetation 225
rocks 90, 158
rocky 178
rocky shores 4, 205, 218
rootlike 218
rotating flagellates 127
rotation 3
rotten stone 158
rounding islands 175

S

Sabella penovina. 270
sablefish 152
Saccorhiza polyschides, 225
Sacculina. 239
Sacrobicularia 271
Sailla verna 235
Salicornia stricta 275
salinities 8, 101
Salinity 8, 171
salinity 100, 110
salinization 143
salps 132
salt pans 274
same salinity 272
sand 253
sand-banks 186
sand-bars 186
sandy 178
sanitizing 148
Sargasso Sea 115, 129
sauries 121
saxatilis 212
saxicola, 241
scabra 24
scallops 140
Scalpellum scalpellum 243
scarcity 180
scatter randomly 189
scattered 173
scavengers 145, 148
scent 148
Scotia Arcs 97

Scrobicularia 271, 274
Scrobicularia plana 271
Scrobicularia 47
sea 108
sea snails 97
sea urchins 148
sea-cucumbers 123
sea-squirt 245
sea-urchins 97
sea-weeds 218
sealevel 196
seals 119
seamounts 157
searchlights 137
seas 108
seashore 178
seasonal 102, 121, 168, 173
seaweed 210
seaweeds
178, 186, 218, 220, 253
second hour 182
secondary 188
section 156
sedentary 186
self-motion 128
semidiurnal tides. 4
Sepiola atlantica, 259
seres, 30
serpulid polychaete worms 11
setae 169
settles 125
shaded 199
shadow zone 170
shallow bottoms 129
shallow seas 219
shallower 146, 156
Shcherbinin's 174
shell-secreting 238
shelter 205
sheltered 184, 186, 205
shelves 91, 123
shingle 178
shore 226
shore molluscs 199
Shrimps 148
shrinkage 163
shrivelled 219
shrubs 13
Sidnyum 245
signific-ance 158
Silene martima 234
siliceous 163, 168
Silicoflagellara 163
Siliqua 39, 40
siliqua, 255
silt, 266
Silurian 161
Sinking 130
Sinking experiments 169
siphonophores 104
skippers 121
slab 76
slanting 100
slightly compressible 98
slimy 226
slop 204
slopes 199
slows 182
sluggish 111
small 160, 191
small Chthamalus stellatus 19
Smallness 128
smallness 169
smashing 11
snail Thais lapilius, 22
snails 148
snow 147
snowing 3
solidifying 64
Somaliland 175
sonic-sounding 146
sources 128

south 175
South Africa 210
South Devon 218
southeastward 97
southernmost 185
sparse 176
sparse food 140
sparsely inhabited 146
Spartina 275
specialists 103
Species 166
species 164, 170, 176, 194, 237
species belonging 127
Specimens 9
specimens 156
spectacularly 135
spectrum 124, 167
spending 134
Spergularia rupicola 233
Spergularia spp., 277
Sphaecelaria 223
Sphaecelaria 223
Sphaeroma 273
spines 169
Spirorbis 243
Spirorbis borealis 214
Spisula 40, 43
sponges 89, 158
sporophyte 210
spottiness 133
spreading 64
spreads 94
Spring 3
spring 180
spring tides 6
squid 119, 121
squids 136
stable 185
stationary 156
stay 168
steady 99
stellate bracelet 163
stenothermal 103
Stickiness 133
stimulates 199
sting-fish 259
stops 163
strandline 260
strata 91
strawberry 238
Stream 115
striking feature 13
Structure 219
subarctic 166
sublittoral 195
submarine 139
submerged 12, 129, 180, 182, 196, 219, 220
submerged countercurrents 134
submergence 142, 236
submersible 145
subpolar 175
subsequently 8
substantial 144
substantially bypassed 142
substrate movement 35
substrates-rock 8
substratum 186
subtropical 120, 121, 166, 176
subtropical gyres 117
subtropical snails 10
Succession, 30
succession 26
successive 124
successive collapse 148
Sueda maritina, 276
sufficient 4, 167
sufficiently dense 150
suffused 120
suggest 163
sulfur bacteria 46
sulphates 191

sunlight 118, 188
sunlit richer 141
supra 195
supralittoral fringe. 14
surface 111
surface creatures 150
surface eddies 129
surroundings 170, 188
survival 185, 187
survive 253
suspended 195
sustain 7
sustainable 177
swell 180, 204
swimming 189
Sycon 244
symbiosis 232
Symbolophorus veranyi 120
symmetrical 163
sympathetic 139
synthesized 125

T

T. arvense, 234
T. canaliculata 21
T. emarginata 21
T. lamellosa 21
T. lapillus. 29
T. monacha, 245
Taaningichthys. 122
Talitrus saltator. 260
target alteration 137
tearing 11
Tectarius muricata 10
Tegula funebralis also 32
Telia felina 246
Tellina tenuis, 255
temperate 166, 175
temperature 100, 129, 131, 140, 185, 193, 199
temperature tolerance 199
temperatures 184
temporarily 129
temporary plankton 194
Teredo 262
terrestrial 1, 218
territoriality 26
territories 148
Terror 158
Thais 21, 22, 32
Thais (=Nucella) lapillus 214
Thais lamellosa 32
Thais lapillus 29
Thais lapilus, 29
Thais. 21, 32
thallus 219, 220
Tha's 30
thermocline 102, 121, 168, 173, 174
thermocline, 192
thermohaline 112
thermosphere 110
three-quarters 101, 168
thresher-sharks 121
tidal ebb 195
tide 2, 180
tiny molecule 143
Tivela 40, 43
Tivela stultorum 38
tolerate 8, 104
tons 152
topographically diverse 13
topography 176
topshells 190
Torquay breakwater 184
Torrey Canyon 214
Trachinus vipera, 259
transform 65
transparent 118, 163, 168
trapped 131
trawls 145
trees 13, 127

Trichodesmium erythraeum 164
Trichodesmum 164
Tripleurospermum (=Matricaria) maritimum 234
Trivia arctica 245
tropical 10, 120, 121, 166, 176
tropical ocean 164
tropical regions 103
tube worms 140
tuna-fishes 121
turbidity 94
turbulence 130
Turbulent 168
turbulent 214
turbulent-convective 130
turgor 219
turtles 119
twice 180, 196
twilight 168
twilight zone 118
twilight-thermoline-mesopelagic 122
twist 226
typify 124

U

ultimate 152
Ulva 46, 205, 232
Ulva lactuca 205
Ulva lactuca, 229
unarmoured 161
unattached 164
unbranched bootlace weed 226
uncovered 187
undercurrents 117
undercutting 186
understanding 171
undivided 161
undoubtedly 129
unexplored 139
unfavourable conditions 186
unlighted midlayers 125
unpigmented flagellates 132
unpredictable 12
unrestricted 89
unspecialized 157
unstable, 185
unstable shores 186
unsuspecting 153
uppermost 1
upwelling 127, 130, 175

V

Valencienneiius 121
vanishing 118
variation 238
various bacteria 191
varying 178
vegetation 218
vegetative 163
Vegetative reproduction 220
Velella 120
velocities 130
Venerupis 269
Venerupis spp. 248
Venus striatula 255
Verrucaria 204, 210
Verrucaria maura 232
vertical 173
vertical circulation 131
vigorous 145
Vinciguerria 121
virtually 167
volcanic 91
volcanic breath 91
volcanoes 90
volume 110
voraciously 192
Vorrucaria 205

W

water retention 34